BK 940.537   M528S
SHADOW OF PEARL HARBOR : POLITICAL CONTROVERSY
OVER THE SURPRISE ATTA   /MELOSI, MA
1977   10.00   M

3000 463613 40014
St. Louis Community College

D0906374

940.537 M528s   M
MELOSI
  THE SHADOW OF PEARL HARBOR
                      10.00

WITHDRAWN

St. Louis Community
College

Library

5801 Wilson Avenue
St. Louis, Missouri 63110

BRO
DART   PRINTED IN U.S.A.

                              23-263-002

THE SHADOW OF PEARL HARBOR
Political Controversy over
the Surprise Attack, 1941–1946

THE SHADOW OF PEARL HARBOR

Political Controversy over the Surprise Attack, 1941-1946

By

MARTIN V. MELOSI

TEXAS A&M UNIVERSITY PRESS

College Station and London

Copyright © 1977 by Martin V. Melosi

All rights reserved

Library of Congress Cataloging in Publication Data

Melosi, Martin V   1947–
   The shadow of Pearl Harbor.

   Bibliography: p.
   Includes index.
   1. World War, 1939–1945—Causes. 2. World War,
1939–1945—United States. 3. Pearl Harbor, Attack on,
1941. 4. United States—Politics and government—
1933–1945. I. Title.
D742.U5M44   940.53'75   77-23578
ISBN 0-89096-031-3

Manufactured in the United States of America

FIRST EDITION

With love, to Carolyn

Contents

Preface

AMERICANS were shocked. In a clandestine raid on Sunday morning, December 7, 1941, hundreds of Japanese carrier-launched airplanes crippled the bulk of the United States Pacific Fleet berthed at Pearl Harbor, Hawaii. The attack was part of a massive simultaneous assault on American, British, and Dutch strongholds in the Pacific, including the Philippines, Siam, and Malaya. Believing they had little choice but to strike first in the wake of rapidly deteriorating relations with the United States, Japan planned its desperate ploy hoping to gain a quick advantage against its enemies. The next day, December 8, the United States and Japan were officially at war, and soon thereafter Americans became fully engaged against the Rome-Berlin-Tokyo Axis.

Americans were unprepared for a Pearl Harbor. Preoccupied with war news from Europe, they had paid little attention to the Sino-Japanese War and were unaware that the mounting tensions in the Pacific might lead to armed conflict between the United States and Japan. With news of the attack on Oahu, almost everyone rallied to defend their country against the sudden foe. As news commentator Marquis W. Childs noted: "No American who lived through that Sunday will ever forget it. It seared deeply into the national consciousness, shearing away illusions that had been fostered for generations. And with the first shock came a sort of panic. This struck our deepest pride. It tore at the myth of our invulnerability. Striking at the precious legend of our might, it seemed to leave us suddenly naked and defenseless. . . ."[1]

[1] Childs, *I Write from Washington*, p. 241.

Accustomed to success and victory as a way of life, Americans found the Pearl Harbor disaster almost impossible to accept. Defeat was bitter—with more than three thousand casualties, five battleships and three cruisers destroyed or disabled, and almost every airplane in flames—especially at the hands of a small island nation in the Orient. Hawaii, furthermore, was not merely an exotic oasis but also a sentry post traditionally considered within the "natural frontiers" of the United States. To attack it, and succeed, was tantamount to an assault on the mainland.

As the greatest naval defeat ever suffered by the United States, and as the immediate act which precipitated an official declaration of war against Japan and eventually Germany, the Pearl Harbor incident became a great watershed in twentieth-century American history and the subject of an extensive postwar historical debate. That debate focused upon the reasons for United States entry into World War II, with particular emphasis upon the breakdown in Japanese-American relations. Historians and commentators, more familiar with American than with Japanese sources, gave their attention to the foreign policy of Franklin D. Roosevelt and his administration, seeking to determine the extent to which the United States contributed to the coming of war. For those who were convinced that Roosevelt's policies were eminently sound, the conclusion was elementary: an aggressive, expansionistic Japanese Empire forced the conflict upon the American government, which was merely trying to protect the nation's legitimate interests in Asia and the Pacific. For those who were skeptical or critical of the Roosevelt foreign policy, it was easier to imagine that an insensitive, rigid, and bellicose administration forced Japan to strike out against the United States in self-defense. Often the severest critics charged that the Democratic president sought a "back door" to enter the war and intentionally goaded the Japanese into attacking the Pacific Fleet, conveniently exposed at Pearl Harbor.[2]

[2] For information about the postwar historical debate, see Wayne S. Cole, "American Entry into World War II: A Historiographical Appraisal," *Mississippi Valley Historical Review* 48 (March, 1957): 595–617; Louis Morton, "Pearl Harbor in Perspective: A Bibliographic Survey," *U.S. Naval Institute Proceedings* 81 (April, 1955): 461–468; Louis Morton, "1937–1941," in *American–East Asian Relations: A Survey*, ed. Ernest R. May and James C. Thompson, pp. 260–290; Robert H. Ferrell, "Pearl Harbor and the Revisionists," *The Historian* 17 (Spring, 1955): 215–233; Louis M. Sears, "Historical

Not until the 1960's did some historians modify these polar positions, most notably in *Pearl Harbor as History: Japanese-American Relations, 1931–1941*, edited by Dorothy Borg and Shumpei Okamoto. The end product of a binational historical conference held at Lake Kawaguchi, Japan, in the summer of 1969, *Pearl Harbor as History* represented an attempt to examine the prewar policies of the United States and Japan from both sides of the ocean. As the authors stated in the introduction, ". . . the Kawaguchi papers and the conference discussions served to demonstrate that the period of Pearl Harbor, like other important periods that gradually receded into the past, had come to be dealt with as history."[3]

Yet the strides made in understanding the motives and policies of Japan and the United States before December 7 did not resolve all of the questions which the Pearl Harbor affair raised. At the core of the analysis of Roosevelt's foreign policy was a specific and emotional controversy over responsibility for the disaster, which formed the basis for the postwar historical debate. Immediately after the attack, people wondered if the surprise raid would have been thwarted by better American defense preparations, if Washington officials had foreseen a possible attack and had done all they could to alert the Pacific outpost, and if the local Hawaiian commanders had faltered in their duty to protect the fleet. These were questions raised by a people extremely confused by the rush of events in December. And in seeking to find a simple explanation for why the United States should succumb in battle to a foe long considered inferior, they identified the breakdown in vigilance with individuals or groups charged with defending the country.

The controversy over responsibility, which extended from December 7, 1941, until the end of the public congressional investigation in mid-1946, is more significant as a key episode of domestic political confrontation than as a prologue to a postwar historical debate. Largely ignored by students of World War II, the question of Pearl Harbor responsibility became a partisan political issue with na-

Revisionism Following the Two World Wars," in *Issues and Conflicts: Studies in Twentieth Century American Diplomacy*, ed. George L. Anderson, pp. 127–146; John McKechney, "The Pearl Harbor Controversy: A Debate among Historians," *Monumenta Nipponica* 18 (1963): 45–88.

[3] Dorothy Borg and Shumpei Okamoto, eds., *Pearl Harbor as History: Japanese-American Relations, 1931–1941*, pp. ix–xv.

tional repercussions during wartime. It perpetuated the isolationist-internationalist debate of the 1930's and early 1940's. It pitted a Democratic executive and his supporters against congressional Republicans. And it was used to challenge the New Deal administration's domination of foreign policy making.

In an atmosphere of uncertainty, insecurity, and suspicion which followed the Pearl Harbor attack, critics of the Roosevelt administration quickly demanded the public disclosure of all information available about the causes of the disaster. Fearing a volatile political debate which such public disclosures might inspire—possibly resulting in the discrediting of FDR's war preparedness program and his forthcoming conduct of the war—the Democratic administration tried to shelve the question of responsibility for the duration of the conflict, silence its critics, and keep national attention fixed on the war effort. To what extent Roosevelt and his high officials succeeded (or failed) in minimizing the domestic impact of Pearl Harbor and in keeping blame away from themselves is the focus of this book.

A study of the heated political controversy over Pearl Harbor from 1941 through 1946 should uncover some significant perspectives of wartime political behavior and clarify why the surprise attack on Hawaii has persisted as a topic of interest to the present day.

Acknowledgments

A project of this kind could not have been completed without the advice, aid, and encouragement of numerous individuals. The staffs of several libraries, especially the Franklin D. Roosevelt Presidential Library; the Library of Congress Manuscript Division; the Princeton University Library; the Hoover Institution on War, Revolution, and Peace; the University of Texas Library; and the Naval Historical Division of the Department of the Navy, were generous with their time. Special thanks must go to the fine staff of the Division of Rare Books and Special Collections of the University of Wyoming Library, particularly Dr. Gene Gressley and his assistants David Crosson and Esther Kelley. William Cunliffe, Sandy Smith, and Edward Reese of the Military Archives Division of the National Archives provided splendid assistance and directed me to many useful documents; Dr. James O'Neill, Assistant Archivist of the National Archives, helped me obtain some important documents; Robert Blum, formerly of the Senate Foreign Relations Committee staff, directed me to some good sources; and the Office of the Judge Advocate General of the Navy uncovered a vital group of papers relating to the navy's role in the various Pearl Harbor investigations.

I also wished to thank several individuals and depositories for permission to quote from material in the following collections: Henry L. Stimson Papers (microfilm), Sterling Memorial Library, Yale University; Frank McNaughton Papers, Harry S Truman Presidential Library and Mr. Frank McNaughton; reminiscences of H. Kent Hewitt, Trustees of Columbia University in the City of New York; Husband E. Kimmel Collection, University of Wyoming Library and Captain Thomas K. Kimmel.

Interviews and advice from the following people clearly enhanced my understanding of the Pearl Harbor incident and its aftermath: Judges Gerhard Gesell and Homer Ferguson, Drs. Gordon Prange and Forrest Pogue, Commander Charles Hiles, and Mr. Percy Greaves, Jr. And of course a major debt goes to those who read all or part of my manuscript and gave useful criticism: Drs. Michael Belknap, Gordon Bennett, William Braisted, Larry Hill, Clarence Lasby, and Richard Pells.

Dr. Robert Divine not only lent his well-known expertise and critical eye to this work, but also had the uncanny ability to know what I wanted to say and how to draw it from me. Four other individuals indirectly aided me in this project: Dr. Jules Karlin, who taught me the fundamentals of research; Dr. Lewis Gould, who was enthusiastic about the project from the onset; Dr. Wayne Morgan, who taught me how to write "positively"; and Dr. Roger Beaumont, who gave me valuable advice about publishing my study.

Funding for the project was made possible by the timely support of the International Studies Association of the University of Pittsburgh, the Eleanor Roosevelt Institute, and the University of Texas at Austin.

Finally, I want to thank my wife Carolyn not only for her superb editing of the manuscript, but also for tolerating the eccentricities of a budding historian.

MARTIN V. MELOSI

THE SHADOW OF PEARL HARBOR
Political Controversy over the
Surprise Attack, 1941–1946

1

Shock Waves in December

THE Pearl Harbor disaster inspired conflicting impulses in most Americans. Eagerness for revenge was entwined with a sense of insecurity brought on by a fear of further Japanese reprisals. Walter Lippmann reflected the mood, suggesting that Americans had to become "an awakened people" whose very existence as a nation hung in the balance of the impending conflict.[1]

Appalled by the insidious surprise attack, passionate hatred of "those little yellow bastards" spread rapidly throughout the country. At a movie theater in Dallas, patrons received news of the disaster with momentary silence, then a steelworker in the audience yelled: "We'll stamp their front teeth in." From Tin Pan Alley blatantly anti-Japanese songs began to flood the broadcasting networks. By 6:00 A.M., December 8, Max Lerner had already written "The Sun Will Soon Be Setting on the Land of the Rising Sun." Mills Music Incorporated quickly published the garish tune "You're a Sap, Mister Jap." Public opinion surveys taken soon after December 7 clearly revealed the hostile feelings toward Japan. Respondents to one poll selected "treacherous," "sly," and "cruel" as words which best described the Japanese people. In another poll, the majority of those surveyed advocated the immediate bombing of Japanese cities.[2]

[1] *Washington Post*, December 9, 1941, p. 19.
[2] *Time* 38 (December 15, 1941): 17; Newsweek 18 (December 22, 1941): 65–66; Hadley Cantril and Mildred Strunk, eds., *Public Opinion, 1935–1946*, pp. 501, 1067, 1941; Ernest D. Rose, "How the United States Heard about Pearl Harbor," *Journal of Broadcasting* 5 (Fall, 1961): 285–298; Correspondents of *Time, Life*, and *Fortune, December 7: The First Thirty Hours*; Geoffrey Perrett, *Days of Sadness, Years of Triumph: The American People, 1939–1945*, pp. 203–206.

Below the surface of this wrath the Hawaiian assault had shaken credence in American invulnerability and had raised doubts about the legendary national invincibility. Many citizens feared further air attacks, conceivably on the North American coastline. Rumors and scares were rampant on the Pacific slope, but even on the Atlantic seaboard local authorities prepared for possible air raids. Overreacting to the emotion of the moment, Rear Adm. Clark H. Woodward, in one of his news commentaries, suggested that the Japanese or their allies would probably make sporadic "hit and run" attacks against the United States to terrorize the population and to break morale. He warned that it was not unreasonable to expect "an unannounced air raid on some coastal town or industrial center at most any time—now that we have enemies across both oceans."[3]

The association of Japan with Nazi Germany and Fascist Italy also caused great uneasiness. The overriding American impression was that the alliance of Germany, Italy, and Japan, formulated in September, 1940, as the Tripartite Pact, represented a partnership for world conquest. Donald Nelson, executive director of the Supply, Priorities, and Allocations Board, insisted that although the attack had been accomplished by the Japanese, in reality it was directed primarily from Berlin. The *Chicago Tribune* even spread a rumor circulating on Capitol Hill that German pilots carried out "the damaging blitzkrieg" on Pearl Harbor and that some of the airplanes bore swastikas.[4]

American entry into World War II provided an outlet for hatred of Japan. Bombs could repay bombs; inflicting casualties on the Japanese could revenge American casualties. But military solutions could not completely alleviate the sense of insecurity and uncertainty which the December 7 disaster engendered. Chauvinistic Americans found it inconceivable that diminutive Japan could emas-

[3] News commentary for INS, December 19, 1941, Box 4, Clark H. Woodward Papers, Library of Congress, Washington, D.C. See also Perrett, *Days of Sadness*, pp. 205–206; Richard R. Lingeman, *Don't You Know There's a War On? The American Home Front, 1941–1945*, pp. 25–62; *Newsweek* 18 (December 22, 1941): 22–23, 25; *New York Times*, December 8, 1941, p. 3; Cantril and Strunk, *Public Opinion*, pp. 1067–1068; *The Gallup Poll: Public Opinion, 1935–1971*, I, 311.

[4] *New York Times*, December 8, 1941, p. 4; *Chicago Tribune*, December 9, 1941, p. 4; *Newsweek* 18 (December 15, 1941): 26, 84; Roper-Fortune Poll 31, December, 1941, Roper Public Opinion Research Center, Williams

culate the United States' prized fortress of the Pacific without the intervention of factors other than meticulous strategy and effective tactics. In an entirely egocentric fashion, nearly all Americans concluded that the only way the United States could suffer such a complete defeat was if the nation either had inadequately prepared for a possible surprise attack or had momentarily dropped its defenses. Based on this assumption, government leaders sought to uncover the reasons for the breakdown in vigilance by determining what part Japanese espionage and intrigue played in the success of the air raid and to what extent Americans were responsible for the inadequate defenses. By consensus, Americans accepted as accurate the alleged contributions of Japanese clandestine operations to the success of the attack, which reinforced their belief that Japan was ultimately to blame for the disaster. But in trying to determine responsibility for the inadequate defenses, no consensus was reached, opinion was polarized, and the question of American culpability became the backbone of a controversy which continued long after the end of the war.

The roots of the inquiry into the role of espionage, sabotage, and fifth-column activity as contributory factors to the Pearl Harbor fiasco are deeply imbedded in the animus against Japanese aliens and Japanese-Americans living in Hawaii and on the mainland. Hostility toward Orientals has a lengthy history in the United States, going back at least to the turn of the century for the Japanese. White Americans living in areas with large Japanese populations, especially along the Pacific coast and in Hawaii, regarded them as social pariahs and economic threats. Pearl Harbor heightened the distrust of local Japanese, immutably associating them with their foreign counterparts who executed the attack. To many Americans "a Jap was a Jap." Zealous authorities in Norfolk, Virginia, did not even wait to hear from FBI agents before jailing every Japanese they could find. In Nashville, the Tennessee Department of Conservation requisitioned six million licenses to hunt Japanese. The purchasing department rejected the request, noting, "Open season on 'Japs'—no license required."[5]

College, Williamstown, Mass.; *Public Opinion Quarterly* 6 (1942): 151–152, 311; Cantril and Strunk, *Public Opinion*, pp. 1097, 1173, 1175.

[5] *Time* 38 (December 22, 1941): 13; Roger Daniels, *Concentration*

The ultimate act of prejudice against the Japanese, arising out of an unrealistic fear that they threatened the American war effort from within, was the decision in February, 1942, to place all Japanese-Americans and aliens residing on the West Coast in relocation camps. Anxieties over further military and naval defeats in the Pacific; pressure from local and state officials in the West; elimination of the vocal opposition to relocation; acquiescence by the Department of Justice, Congress, and the military hierarchy; plus the blessings of the president made the decision possible.[6]

The official justification for the encampment policy was "military necessity." In his final report on evacuation, Lt. Gen. John L. De Witt, commander of the Western Defense Command and the Fourth Army, asserted that the Pacific Coast Japanese were concentrated "near many highly sensitive installations essential to the war effort" and that hundreds of organizations were in existence which "actively engaged in advancing Japanese war aims."[7]

The official justification for relocation clouded the more explicit reasons hidden between the lines of De Witt's report—the latent distrust of the Japanese, awakened by the Pearl Harbor attack and enhanced by an overreaction to alleged espionage and sabotage activity on American soil. The general concluded that the presence of "a large, unassimilated, tightly knit racial group, bound to an enemy nation by strong ties of race, culture, custom and religion," along the allegedly vulnerable coastline, constituted "a menace which had to be dealt with."[8]

However, 64 percent of the slightly more than one hundred thousand persons constituting the supposed threat were American born. They already had been barred from the most sensitive military installations, and they had not instigated any traitorous acts

Camps USA: Japanese Americans and World War II, pp. 26–38; Morton Grodzins, *Americans Betrayed: Politics and the Japanese Evacuation*, pp. 202–204, 261–263, 383; Edward H. Spicer et al., *Impounded People: Japanese-Americans in the Relocation Centers*, pp. 25ff., 54–55.

[6] Daniels, *Concentration Camps USA*, pp. 33–38, 42–73; Grodzins, *Americans Betrayed*, pp. 202–203, 361–362, 383; Perrett, *Days of Sadness*, pp. 216–217.

[7] De Witt to George C. Marshall, June 5, 1943, memorandum in U.S. Department of the Army, Western Defense Command and Fourth Army, *Final Report: Japanese Evacuation from the West Coast, 1942*, pp. vii–viii.

[8] Ibid.

against the United States. The Japanese community's only crime was the misfortune of being small in size, easily recognizable, and highly concentrated in a number of specific geographic pockets. Curiously, the United States government did not subject German- and Italian-Americans or the large Japanese population in Hawaii to the same fate as that of the Pacific Coast Japanese. Military necessity as a rationalization appears pale in the face of such inconsistencies.[9]

As long as the Japanese-American/Japanese alien question remained unresolved in the last weeks of December and early 1942, the threat from sabotage and espionage seemed gravest, and speculation about how it influenced the Japanese victory at Pearl Harbor retained vitality. Immediately after the attack, the FBI, under a blanket presidential warrant, began arresting enemy nationals, of which Japanese were a large group. The press gave considerable publicity to this initial roundup.[10] When Secretary of the Navy Frank Knox returned from his December fact-finding tour of Hawaii, the issue of covert Japanese activities gained national prominence. After delivering a prepared statement about his inquiry, Knox told the press contingent that one reason for the successful aerial assault was "cooperation from the Hawaiian Islands themselves," which resulted in substantial information being passed on to Tokyo. "The most effective fifth-column work in this war," he added, "was done in Hawaii, with the exception of Norway." Without substantiating these claims, Knox officially legitimized the rumors circulating throughout the country about undercover activities.[11]

The President's Commission on Pearl Harbor, headed by Associate Supreme Court Justice Owen J. Roberts, indirectly sustained Knox's accusations in its report in January, 1942. Roosevelt had charged the Roberts commission with determining if any derelictions of duty or errors of judgment on the part of army and navy personnel contributed to the success of the air raid. Questions about covert Japanese operations were not directly in its province, and it generally ignored them. The subsequent commission report, how-

[9] U.S. Department of the Interior, War Relocation Authority, *WRA: A Story of Human Conservation*, pp. 196–198.

[10] Grodzins, *Americans Betrayed*, pp. 232–233.

[11] *New York Times*, December 16, 1941, pp. 1, 7.

ever, indicated that prior to December 7 Japanese spies, some posing as Japanese consular agents and others with no open relationship with the Japanese foreign service, collected and transmitted information to Tokyo concerning ship movements, air reconnaissance, and so on. The report did not mention sabotage or any significant fifth-column activity, but strongly implied that Washington had severely restricted FBI surveillance of potential saboteurs and espionage agents that likely had been working in Honolulu. The Roberts commission did not reiterate Knox's charges, but neither did it contradict them.[12]

By the time the president's board released its report in January, many Americans, despite little or no documentation, willingly accepted the claim that Japanese undercover projects contributed to the disaster at Pearl Harbor and continued to operated subsequently. After all, were not the Japanese cunning? treacherous? deceitful? Had not the attack been too easily accomplished? What happened in Hawaii surely might occur in California! Under the stress of war, Americans found solace in the most sinister, dramatic, and simplistic explanations for defeat instead of attempting to unravel the complexities of the disaster.

In Congress, Rep. Martin Dies (Democrat, Texas) had already sought to make political capital out of the espionage issue. The outspoken chairman of the House Committee on Un-American Activities (HUAC) gathered fifty-two witnesses in August, 1941, who were apparently willing to testify that Japanese spying was taking place on the Pacific Coast. Dies dismissed them in September when the Department of Justice disallowed the proposed public hearings. Supported by the president and the secretary of state, the attorney general based his decision on the desire to avoid public displays which might embarrass Japan and possibly lead to a break in relations.[13]

After the United States entered the war, Dies tried to tie his

---

[12] "Report of the Roberts Commission, January 23, 1942," in U.S. Congress, *Pearl Harbor Attack: Hearings before the Joint Committee on the Pearl Harbor Attack*, 79th Cong., 1st sess., pt. 39, pp. 12–13, 20–21.

[13] Francis Biddle to Thomas H. Eliot, February 20, 1942; Biddle to Dies, August 13, 1941; Dies to Biddle, August 27, 1941; Matthew F. McGuire to Dies, September 8, 1941, in U.S. Congress, *Congressional Record*, 77th Cong., 2d sess., 1942, 88, pp. A880–881; *New York Times*, December 11, 1941, p. 24.

charges of Pacific Coast espionage to the Pearl Harbor issue. He released a summary of his "evidence," and, in a House debate on January 28, charged that the Roosevelt administration suppressed his report before the war. He added, "A fear of displeasing foreign powers and a maudlin attitude toward fifth columnists was largely responsible for the unparalleled tragedy of Pearl Harbor. . . ."[14]

These accusations caused a stir in Congress. The House Rules Committee debate over extension of HUAC provided a forum for discussing them, and East Harlem congressman and ultraliberal Vito Marcantonio provided the major challenge. In a radio address on February 19, Marcantonio, a vehement opponent of HUAC's questionable practices, claimed that Congressman Dies failed to expose or "to exterminate" the Japanese agents involved in the espionage by not making the intelligence data available to the executive branch. "[I]nstead of giving the information . . . ," he stated, "[Dies] gave the Attorney General mere evasion commonly known as the good old fashioned run-around." Marcantonio then charged HUAC with "the grossest dereliction of duty in the history of our country."[15]

In the end, the Rules Committee decided to extend the well-entrenched HUAC, but the debate over the spy activity persisted. Finally, in late February Dies produced his report. Despite expectations, it proved to be speculative at best.[16] But Dies's allegations, although never substantiated, reinforced the worst fears in Americans and helped produce a consensus on the contribution of sabotage and espionage to the Pearl Harbor disaster. Even Marcantonio, who adamantly criticized HUAC's prewar activities, did not question the existence and vitality of covert Japanese operations.

Other congressional groups helped to perpetuate the rumors of extensive pre–Pearl Harbor undercover operations. In February and March, 1942, a congressional committee headed by Congressman

---

[14] Congress, *Congressional Record*, 77th Cong., 2d sess., 1942, 88, pp. 407–410, 800–801.

[15] Radio transcript, February 17, 1942, Official File 320, Franklin D. Roosevelt Papers, Franklin D. Roosevelt Presidential Library, Hyde Park, N.Y. See also U.S. Congress, House, *Hearings before the Committee on Rules*, 77th Cong., 2d sess., 1942; August Raymond Ogden, *The Dies Committee*, pp. 249–255.

[16] U.S. Congress, House, Special Committee on Un-American Activities, *Report on Japanese Activities, 1942*, 77th Cong., 2d sess., 1942. See also Ogden, *Dies Committee*, pp. 255ff.

John H. Tolan (Democratic, California) began conducting hearings on "national defense migration," but devoted most of its time to the issue of West Coast Japanese. Throughout the hearings, Tolan and others referred to covert activities in Hawaii as point of fact.[17] Tolan soon discovered, through assurances from the FBI and Secretary of War Henry L. Stimson, that the Japanese had committed no sabotage before or after Pearl Harbor. By that time, the myth of extensive Japanese espionage and sabotage was too well entrenched to reverse the opinions of most Americans.[18]

The consensus reached on Japanese responsibility, overt and covert, for Pearl Harbor did not account for the lack of defense preparations in Hawaii. Although the Japanese surprised the base, why did the army and navy put up such weak resistance? Could this attack have been repulsed or prevented entirely? Unwilling to concede that the Japanese may have outsmarted their foes, many Americans sought the parties who were to blame for the lack of preparedness and the breakdown in vigilance. Before the search was over, the question of American culpability would assume the proportions of a major controversy.

The debate over responsibility grew on fertile ground. National unity was more hope than reality in December, 1941. Pearl Harbor had momentarily turned Americans' attention away from their differences, but it could not allay internal divisions such as those produced by the isolationist-interventionist debate over entry into the war. Political philosophies, goals, and postwar aims were still at variance. Partisanship would continue as long as Democrats and Republicans vied for power and as long as supporters and detractors of the Roosevelt administration sought ways of soliciting political advantage.[19]

[17] U.S. Congress, House, Select Committee Investigating National Defense Migration, *Hearings*, 77th Cong., 2d sess., 1942. See also Bradford Smith, *Americans from Japan*, pp. 264–273; Daniels, *Concentration Camps USA*, pp. 74–82.

[18] James Rowe, Jr., to Tolan, April 20, 1942; Stimson to Tolan, March 3, 1942, in U.S. Congress, House, Select Committee Investigating National Defense Migration, *Fourth Interim Report*, 77th Cong., 2d sess., 1942. See also Grodzins, *Americans Betrayed*, pp. 130–133; Smith, *Americans from Japan*, pp. 265ff.

[19] The Roosevelt administration was very aware of these societal rifts. Office of Emergency Management, Intelligence Report 1, December 15, 1941, and

The war united interventionists and isolationists out of conven-
ience, not out of conviction; patriotism and a hatred of Japan briefly
supplanted their rivalry. But both sides remained wary of their old
foes. To the interventionists the Japanese attack was disturbing, but
the United States' entry into the war, which they had long advocated, was not. As Russell Briney of the Louisville chapter of the
Council on Foreign Relations stated: "[I]t is plain that Pearl Harbor changed no one's thinking very much. Pearl Harbor was a
shock, a terrible shock, but it brought a sense of relief and release."
The interventionists quickly supported the war effort and generally
accepted the official explanations about the causes of the Hawaii
disaster.[20]

For most isolationists, with their ideology publicly discredited,
support for American involvement in World War II became inevitable. Pearl Harbor had erased any hope of remaining aloof. But
the disaster did not destroy "the coherence of the isolationist position absolutely" as historian Manfred Jonas argued.[21] Indeed, it provided isolationists and other administration critics with an issue to
continue the attack against the Roosevelt foreign policy. The December 7 raid, they would assert, did not arise out of any isolationist policy but because the Democratic administration was not
vigilant. In a society disrupted by a sudden thrust into war, the
abeyance of political antagonisms only momentarily concealed the
festering Pearl Harbor controversy.[22]

The lack of details about the attack stimulated the initial speculation about the quality of American defenses before the war. In
his *New York Times* column, Arthur Krock conjectured that the

Office of War Information, Survey of Intelligence Material 23, May 13, 1942,
President's Secretary File, Roosevelt Papers; Robert E. Sherwood, *Roosevelt
and Hopkins: An Intimate History*, p. 437.

[20] Percy W. Bidwell, ed., *Our Foreign Policy in War and Peace: Some
Regional Views*, pp. 5, 8, 11, 16–20; Mark C. Chadwin, *The Hawks of World
War II*, pp. 266–269.

[21] Jonas, *Isolationism in America, 1935–1941*, pp. 273–287.

[22] *Chicago Tribune*, December 8, 1941, p. 1; Jerome E. Edwards, *The
Foreign Policy of Col. McCormick's Tribune, 1929–1941*, pp. 1–3, 181–183,
207–211; *Washington Post*, December 9, 1941, p. 19; December 10, 1941, p.
17; *Newsweek* 18 (December 15, 1941): 21; *New York Times*, December 9,
1941, p. 44; Laurence S. Wittner, *Rebels against War: The American Peace
Movement, 1941–1960*, pp. 34–39; *Time* 38 (December 22, 1941): 67–68.

surprise nature of the air raid, combined with deficiencies in personnel and military equipment, especially 90 mm antiaircraft guns, led to the Japanese victory.[23] Ernest Lindley of the *Washington Post* acknowledged the inability of military experts to foresee the potency of the Japanese air force, but ultimately blamed the defeat upon "apathy and anti-war sentiment at home."[24] Barnet Nover, also of the *Washington Post*, raised what would be a persistent feature of the Pearl Harbor debate—the question of responsibility of the Hawaiian Command. "To be sure," he wrote, "those whose duty it is to defend Hawaii appear to have been caught with their guards almost completely down."[25]

Newspaper speculation about the air attack might have been of fleeting significance had not congressional members begun to raise the same points as early as the war declaration debates. Landslide votes in favor of declarations against the Axis and legislation for large military appropriations attest to the virtually unanimous support for the war effort. But the demonstration of solidarity did not preclude the raising of queries about responsibility for Pearl Harbor. In both houses of Congress the brief debate over the war resolutions produced grandiloquent speeches denouncing Japan and its Axis cohorts and ignited righteous indignation over the sneak attack.[26] Some senators and congressmen were unwilling to plot a course for war without simultaneously determining how and why the war began. The motivations for these queries were complex. Many legislators simply wanted to know why more than three thousand casualties resulted and why the core of the Pacific Fleet lay in rubble; others saw an opportunity to make political capital. But almost everyone, outraged by the inability of the United States to repulse the attack, sought to place the blame on the "responsible parties."

In the House of Representatives, Republicans and Democrats alike registered their concern. Bewildered by the events of the previous day, Roy O. Woodruff (Republican, Michigan) could hardly

[23] *New York Times*, December 10, 1941, p. 5.
[24] *Washington Post*, December 10, 1941, p. 17.
[25] Ibid.
[26] Congress, *Congressional Record*, 77th Cong., 1st sess., 1941, 87, pp. 9521 ff. See also Roland Young, *Congressional Politics in the Second World War*, pp. 8, 11–13.

believe what had happened to what he called "the pride of the armed forces." "There will have to be," he stated indignantly, "an explanation—sooner or later—and it had better be good." A few days later, the longtime Progressive Republican and Roosevelt advocate had calmed down, announcing his satisfaction with the efforts of the administration to investigate the disaster.[27] But one of Woodruff's Michigan colleagues, John D. Dingell (Democrat, Michigan) had a much more critical attitude. An avid New Dealer who actively participated in the enactment of several important recovery and reform bills, Dingell gained substantial congressional and press attention by demanding the immediate courts-martial of several high military and naval officers associated with the Hawaiian Command, including Adm. Husband E. Kimmel, commander in chief of the Pacific Fleet, and Maj. Gen. Walter C. Short, commander of the Hawaiian Department. He charged that the army and navy at Pearl Harbor were caught off guard, "if they were not sound asleep in the same bed."[28] Almost immediately, James E. Van Zandt (Republican, Pennsylvania), the former national commander of the Veterans of Foreign Wars who was on active duty with the navy, protested Dingell's charges and vociferously defended Kimmel and Short. He called on Dingell to curb his remarks until the administration filed an official report on the incident. Other congressmen supported Van Zandt's opinion to wait and see, and, for the moment at least, any direct action was postponed.[29]

The Senate debated the question of responsibility more hotly than did the House. On December 8, the *New York Times* reported that Sen. Tom Connally (Democrat, Texas), chairman of the Foreign Relations Committee, supposedly gave Secretary Knox "uncharted hell" for Pearl Harbor. He neither confirmed nor denied the story, but did query where American airplanes and patrols had been during the attack. Connally's indignation with the Navy Department and Knox stopped with innuendo, however. The Democratic stalwart was well aware of the political dangers of a public inquiry at this early stage in the war.[30]

[27] Congress, *Congressional Record*, 77th Cong., 1st sess., 1941, 87, pp. 9522, 9992.

[28] Ibid., p. A5507.

[29] Ibid., pp. A5504, 9564ff.

[30] *New York Times*, December 9, 1941, p. 4.

Sen. Charles W. Tobey (Republican, New Hampshire), a former isolationist, caused the real furor in the Senate. On December 9, before the president's anticipated address to the nation scheduled for that evening, Tobey asked David I. Walsh (Democrat, Massachusetts), chairman of the Naval Affairs Committee, if the chief executive intended to give a detailed account of the damage suffered in the Pacific. Walsh, who had previously announced that the navy was in no position to release such information, reiterated that "it would be proper for us all to wait and learn just what the President thinks it proper to say under the circumstances and to follow his leadership." But Tobey insisted that Congress and the American people should be fully informed, and, in a less than subtle jab at Knox, he insinuated that the secretary had overestimated the readiness of the navy in a message to the president shortly before the Hawaiian debacle. "[T]he pride of the American people in their Navy and their confidence in some officials," he goaded, "has been terribly hurt in the past 24 hours." Proadministration forces in the Senate, namely Walsh, Connally, and majority leader Alben W. Barkley (Democrat, Kentucky), now insisted that, in Walsh's words, "Talk and rumors ought to cease," and the senator from New Hampshire should wait to hear what the president would say that night.[31]

So they waited. But on December 11 the debate reopened, this time with more recriminations and heated exchanges. In an attempt to demonstrate nonpartisanship, Tobey announced that the Republican conference passed a resolution pledging support for the administration's war policy. "There is no schism under the Capitol dome," Tobey added, "and none in the Nation today." He then proceeded to contradict that statement. Reminding the Democrats of their pleas to forego criticism until after the president's speech, Tobey declared that he had "listened in vain for a definite statement as to the losses which were suffered in the debacle at Pearl Harbor." Sen. Millard E. Tydings (Democrat, Maryland) immediately rose to the administration's defense, arguing that such information should not be put in the enemy's grasp. After all, he noted, "as this struggle

[31] Congress, *Congressional Record*, 77th Cong., 1st sess., 1941, 87, pp. 9542–9544.

proceeds we must all realize that sometimes it is better Americanism not to withhold the truth when it can be told, but to withhold it when it aids our enemies more than it serves our own people." (The Senate gallery responded to Tydings's remarks with a burst of applause.) Tobey addressed himself to Tydings's rebuttal, then turned his attack on Knox once again. At this point Scott W. Lucas (Democrat, Illinois), an ardent administration supporter, challenged Tobey's sources of information about the supposed Navy Department derelictions and inefficiency. "I do not believe that the Senator from New Hampshire knows what he is talking about," Lucas said flatly. "Insofar as negligence is concerned, look at your own record from the standpoint of national defense," he admonished. Walsh, in an attempt to quell the storm, appealed to his colleagues to have confidence in the decisions of the president in this matter, for he was "not merely President Franklin D. Roosevelt; not a President of the Democratic Party; not a New Deal President, but a war President. . . ."[32] By this time the opposing factions in the Senate had already obliterated the pretense of congressional unity and nonpartisanship.

Both House and Senate debates over responsibility for Pearl Harbor opened the floodgates to a potentially volatile controversy. Dingell had raised the issue of dereliction of the Hawaiian Command, which would gain great momentum, especially in proadministration circles. Tobey's salvos against the Democrats, especially the Department of the Navy and Secretary Knox, posed an immediate political threat to the administration. Accusations were getting uncomfortably close to the White House, and administration supporters in Congress who realized that fact attempted to defend the integrity of the president and reaffirm that he would uncover and make public the truth about the attack—in time.

The debate which rankled congressmen and senators, when superimposed over a society not totally committed to "unity," was likely to proliferate and become more pointed. An investigation of

<hr />

[32] Ibid., pp. 9656–9662. See also Tobey to S. Carl, December 20, 1941, Charles W. Tobey Papers, Dartmouth College Library, Hanover, N.H.; *New York Times*, December 12, 1941, pp. 10–11; *Chicago Tribune*, December 12, 1941, p. 11.

the circumstances surrounding the Pearl Harbor disaster, no matter how it might detract from the war effort, was imperative lest the rumor mill persist. If the Roosevelt administration refused to initiate it, chances were likely that Congress might conduct an inquiry of its own.

2

A Policy of Evasion

ON December 7, 1941, Washington reverberated with shock waves emanating from Hawaii. At a special meeting of Treasury Department officials that evening, the stunning nature of the surprise attack was the central topic of conversation:

Morgenthau: It is just unexplainable. And they caught us as unprepared as the others—just the same.

Foley: Must be worse than anybody realizes.

Morgenthau: Much, much worse. I just can't say—much worse than anybody realizes. . . .

Mrs. Morgenthau: Was it a terrible shock to the President?

Morgenthau: Must be—must be.

Bell: Merle mentioned when he flew back ten days ago what a wonderful target those ships would make at Pearl Harbor.

Cochran: Those ships were all tied up and they were a perfect target.

Morgenthau: That's what Stimson kept saying. He kept mumbling that all the planes were in one place.

Cochran: Yes—in back of that little peninsula.

Morgenthau: They haven't learned anything here. They have the whole Fleet in one place—the whole Fleet was in this little Pearl Harbor base. The whole Fleet was there. . . .

Morgenthau: They never can explain this. They never will be able to explain it. . . .[1]

On that day, high administration officials had little time to

[1] Special meeting of the Treasury Group, December 7, 1941, Diary of Henry Morgenthau, Jr., Book 470, Henry Morgenthau, Jr., Collection, Franklin D. Roosevelt Presidential Library, Hyde Park, N.Y. Morgenthau was secretary of the treasury; the other individuals in attendance, save Mrs. Elinor Morgenthau, were high officials in the department. Edward Foley was general counsel, Daniel Bell was undersecretary, and Merle Cochran was a special adviser on monetary matters.

speculate about anything other than preparing the country for war. The president and his closest adviser, Harry Hopkins, were having lunch when Secretary Knox informed them of the air raid in progress at Pearl Harbor. Roosevelt accepted the news as accurate and told Hopkins that the attack was just the kind of unexpected act of which Japan was capable. He then quickly called Secretary of State Cordell Hull, informed him of the report, and instructed him to receive the Japanese envoys, Kichisaburo Nomura and Saburo Kurusu, who had an appointment with the secretary that afternoon. Hull was not to mention that he had received news of the attack, but to listen to them and then "bow them out." Soon afterwards, Chief of Naval Operations Harold R. Stark called Roosevelt and confirmed the attack. At that point the president ordered Stark to execute the agreed orders in the event of hostilities in the Pacific. The rest of the afternoon and evening of December 7 proceeded at the same hectic pace: a press release was prepared, high-level meetings were scheduled, a declaration of war was drafted. The details were endless, and the whirlpool of events spilled over into Monday without pause.[2]

Regardless of the solemn task of preparing for war, the Roosevelt administration found no respite from questions concerning the breakdown of defenses in Hawaii. The surprise nature of the air raid, the nation-wide curiosity, and the incessant rumors prompted the administration to gather the facts as soon as possible. Within a few days congressional and press queries about domestic responsibility for the disaster would increase the chances for a sensitive political melee.

In President Roosevelt's war message of December 8 he explained the Pearl Harbor incident in terms not soon forgotten: "Yesterday, December 7, 1941—a date which will live in infamy— the United States of America was suddenly and deliberately attacked by naval and air forces of the Empire of Japan."[3] Yet the pious phrases leading to war were little solace for a nation anxious

[2] Harry Hopkins, Personal Memo of the Events of December 7 . . . , microfilm of personal letters, roll 19, Harry Hopkins Papers, Franklin D. Roosevelt Presidential Library, Hyde Park, N.Y.; press conferences, December 7 and 8, 1941, Box 41, Stephen T. Early Papers, Franklin D. Roosevelt Presidential Library, Hyde Park, N.Y.

[3] War declaration, December 8, 1941, in *The Public Papers and Addresses of Franklin D. Roosevelt*, comp. Samuel I. Rosenman, X, 514.

to learn more about the incredible attack. From the onset the administration wanted to keep the issue out of public attention until they found a propitious moment. Early on the morning of December 8, Archibald MacLeish, director of the Office of Facts and Figures (OFF), hurried to the Cabinet Room to discuss the attack with the president's closest advisers. He was noticeably upset, and he adamantly urged that Roosevelt publicly reveal in detail the damage suffered at the Pacific base. Other important officials held similar views, but Robert E. Sherwood and Samuel I. Rosenman, who were particularly close to the chief executive, clearly opposed the action. They argued that detailed disclosures might inform Japan how damaging its blow had been. FDR accepted Sherwood's and Rosenman's assessment, and after consulting with the chief of staff and others he decided that while he would not minimize the gravity of the attack, neither would he provide specific information possibly useful to the enemy.[4]

At his press conference on December 9, Roosevelt closely adhered to this decision, declaring that further details about the attack were not yet forthcoming. Frank L. Kluckhohn raised the issue about domestic responsibility for the disaster, but FDR likewise shirked that question and continued to be evasive throughout the afternoon session.[5]

The OFF also maintained the official silence. MacLeish came under heavy criticism from the press for not elaborating on the first reports from Hawaii, although he had little choice but to obey the president's directives. Pearl Harbor continued to nag the OFF in other ways as well. While the surprise attack gave the United States an obvious reason for declaring war, the nature of the incident made it difficult to attribute American entry to any cause other than self-defense. Officials of the OFF, and later of the Office of War Information (OWI), feared that if Americans continued to view the war only as a response to the air raid instead of an effort to destroy fascism, wartime and postwar cooperation with the Allies would suffer. Pearl Harbor as well would limit the range of issues which the information agencies could exploit for propaganda purposes.[6]

[4] Rosenman, *Working with Roosevelt*, p. 309.
[5] Press conference 790, December 9, 1941, in *Complete Presidential Press Conferences of Franklin D. Roosevelt*, XVIII, 348ff.
[6] Sydney S. Weinberg, "What to Tell America: The Writers' Quarrel in

Controlling the speculation about the disaster was a constant irritant made more difficult by the lack of sufficient firsthand information. Secretary Knox took the initial step to discover what he could by planning a trip to the Pacific base to survey the scene of the disaster.[7] Disturbed by the rumors rampant throughout the country and fearful of the prospect of "a nasty congressional investigation," he quickly informed the president of his decision on December 8: "With your permission, I'm leaving in the morning." FDR asked him where he was going. "Pearl Harbor," he replied, "with your permission." Roosevelt then asked him what he thought he could accomplish by such a mission. "I can find out a great deal more there than here."[8]

On the next morning the navy secretary departed. While traveling to Hawaii he studied a large body of information received in Washington regarding conditions at Pearl Harbor. Since this was an investigative visit, once he arrived in Hawaii on December 11 he remained detached from the local naval command except to interrogate them and conduct his business. Knox spent only thirty-two hours in Oahu interviewing various personnel and examining the

---

the Office of War Information," *Journal of American History* 55 (June, 1968): 76–78; Sydney S. Weinberg, "Wartime Propaganda in a Democracy: America's Twentieth-Century Information Agencies" (Ph.D. diss., Columbia University, 1969), pp. 197–198, 249; remarks by Philleo Nash to Mrs. Sharp, January 9, 1952, Official File 5015, Franklin D. Roosevelt Papers, Franklin D. Roosevelt Presidential Library, Hyde Park, N.Y.

7 Since the army had responsibility for protecting the fleet at berth and the island base, Chief of Staff George C. Marshall sent Col. Charles W. Bundy, chief of the plans group of the War Plans Division, and Maj. Gen. Herbert A. Dargue of the Air Corps to investigate the army side of the attack. However, the plane carrying the two officers crashed en route, and there was no attempt to replace them with other investigators. The War Department at this stage would have to rely upon Knox's evaluation. See press conference, December 18, 1941, microfilm reel 135, Henry L. Stimson Papers, Manuscripts and Archives, Sterling Memorial Library, Yale University, New Haven, Conn.; Forrest C. Pogue, *George C. Marshall: Ordeal and Hope, 1939–1942*, pp. 234–235.

8 Press conference 947, April 28, 1944, *Complete Presidential Press Conferences*, XXIII, 137–138; Knox to Paul Scott Mowrer, December 18, 1941, Box 1, Frank Knox Papers, Library of Congress, Washington, D.C.; Frank E. Beatty, "The Background of the Secret Report," *National Review* 18 (December 13, 1966): 1262.

wreckage. Immediately on the flight home he began to write his report.[9]

There was considerable speculation about what Knox's report would include and strict security to insure that the president was the first to hear whatever news the secretary had to disclose.[10] On reaching San Diego on December 13, Knox made no public statement. In fact, for an hour preceding the announcement of his arrival, Navy Department officials ordered all local radio stations off the air, presumably to prevent news of his airplane's landing from leaking out.[11]

Even before Knox's scheduled return to Washington on December 14, Roosevelt began to assess the battle losses in the Pacific. He called a navy conference to draw up plans for repairing the damaged ships and building new ones. Gossip circulated about possible coordination of the military and naval commands in the mid-Pacific under the leadership of Adm. William D. Leahy, the former chief of naval operations,[12] but the president avoided direct discussion of the disaster while Knox was on his fact-finding tour. At his press conference on December 12, reporters persisted in questioning him about the attack. James Wright indicated that some of the White House press corps were still "nervous" about being scooped on the facts about Pearl Harbor. Attempting to allay his uneasiness, Roosevelt told Wright that Knox had just arrived in Hawaii the night before and then warned that individuals who planned to "tell all, and publish all" had better wait until Knox submitted his report. But Wright continued:

> Just as a specific case—yesterday, on the floor of the Senate, there were a lot of things said there that seemed to be transgressing entirely our own understanding of what. . . .
> The President: (Interposing) I think you are absolutely correct.
> Wright: (Continuing) But you cannot ignore what a Senator says on the floor of the Senate. [Referring to Tobey's charges.]

[9] Beatty, "Background of the Secret Report," pp. 1262–1264; Knox to Mrs. Knox, December 14, 1941, Box 3, Knox Papers; press conference 947, April 28, 1944, *Complete Presidential Press Conferences*, XXIII, 137–138.

[10] Knox to FDR, December 13, 1941, telegram, Box 78, President's Secretary File, Roosevelt Papers.

[11] *New York Times*, December 14, 1941, p. 23.

[12] Ibid., p. 22.

The President: No, but you can characterize it in one of those well known news paragraphs—you know—which are not entirely factual. (Laughter). . . . The Senator who made these statements didn't know one damn thing about it. He repeated somebody's gossip. He made it as a statement of fact, which he had no right to do whatsoever. And that has to be off the record. (Laughter)[13]

Again, Roosevelt had kept the hounds at bay.

The return of Secretary Knox to Washington on December 15 carried with it the hope that he could squelch the most outlandish rumors about the disaster. Despite his promise to see the president immediately upon his return, he first visited Stimson. He told the secretary of war that the losses of personnel were dreadful, but that the ship damage was less than anticipated. On the central question of responsibility, Knox believed that everyone had been "asleep," and both cabinet officials accepted the premise that there had been "remissness" in the army and navy. They desired to avoid any interdepartmental feud and agreed to keep the question of culpability on "a basis of no recrimination but inflexible responsibility and punishment."[14] At this meeting they began to formulate a hard line for dealing with responsibility at the lower echelons of command, which would characterize the Roosevelt administration's policy throughout the war.

This was not a surprising move for Stimson, given his long service in government, which had helped to inspire his aggressive nationalism. Although he had entered public life as a Theodore Roosevelt "trust buster" at the turn of the century, the former Wall Street lawyer had a stronger commitment to the conservatism of Elihu Root and William Howard Taft. In a long and varied public career Stimson had been in important policy-making positions, including secretary of war under President Taft, governor general of the Philippines in the late 1920's, and most notably secretary of state in the Herbert Hoover administration. Although a loyal Republican for many years, Stimson acted as liaison between Hoover and FDR during the interregnum of 1932–1933 and developed a good relationship with the president-elect. When Roosevelt sought

13 Press conference 791, December 12, 1941, *Complete Presidential Press Conferences*, XVIII, 364ff.

14 Diary of Henry L. Stimson, December 15, 1941, XXXVI, 108, microfilm, Stimson Papers.

to broaden the base of his support in 1940 and bring into the administration more experienced men to bolster the national defense program, he turned to the seventy-three-year-old veteran public servant, who was given the responsibility of preparing the army for possible action. Stimson, as one of the most adamant proponents of American intervention in World War II, was relieved that the United States finally had a provocative act upon which to base its entry into the war. He was indignant with the manner of the attack and its consequences in loss of life and property, but he was fully convinced that he and the War Department had done everything they could to forestall it. If there was to be any assessment of blame beyond blaming the Japanese, it would have to be at the scene of the disaster. As he wrote in his diary on December 7: "It has been staggering to see our people there, who have been warned long ago and were standing on the alert, should have been so caught by surprise."[15] Yet in his December 11 press conference he gave no hint of these feelings and made no mention of "inflexible responsibility."[16] Stimson was unprepared to initiate a debate over culpability at this time, but he would soon contradict his public demonstration of impartiality when he relieved from duty the army commanders at Hawaii.

Secretary of the Navy Knox, although not as dogmatic as Stimson, shared the war secretary's strong sense of nationalism and belief in the need for a powerful military establishment. The chunky, red-haired bureaucrat had made his national reputation as a successful newspaper publisher, especially in association with the *Chicago Daily News* and the Hearst empire. His ventures into Republican politics had been failures, especially as the GOP's vice-presidential candidate in the disastrous 1936 campaign. His loyalty to FDR's administration took some time to cultivate, given his past political affiliation and his outspoken criticism of the New Deal between 1933 and 1936. After the 1936 election, Knox at least gave his

[15] Ibid., December 7, 1941, XXXVI, 82–83; Stimson to General Muirhead, December 15, 1941, reel 105, Stimson Papers; *New York Times*, October 21, 1950, pp. 1, 6; Henry L. Stimson and McGeorge Bundy, *On Active Service in Peace and War*, p. 391; Richard N. Current, *Secretary Stimson: A Study in Statecraft*, pp. 169–170.

[16] *New York Times*, December 12, 1941, p. 11; Diary of Henry L. Stimson, December 11, 1941, XXXVI, 97, microfilm, Stimson Papers.

public support to the Democratic administration, and, like Stimson, he was brought into the government in 1940 to undercut Republican opposition and add strength to the burgeoning preparedness program. A strong advocate of a two-ocean navy, Knox also actively supported compulsory military training, selective service, and massive aid to Great Britain in its fight against Germany. Since Knox was a central architect of the administration's defense program preceding American involvement in the war, like the war secretary he too believed that responsibility for Pearl Harbor must reside at the bottom of the chain of command, not the top. He found it "simply incredible" that the army and navy had made no preparations for an air attack. However, he confided to Adm. Claude C. Bloch, commander of the Fourteenth Naval District, that the Pearl Harbor inquiry was his most difficult task as secretary of the navy, but that it had been carried out with the best interests of the navy in mind, "hard though it was on certain individuals." Knox may have been more reluctant than Stimson to accuse the local commanders of derelictions, but the results were the same, since he recommended the removal of the navy commander at Hawaii.[17]

The report Knox presented to Roosevelt clearly indicated a lack of readiness on the part of the Hawaiian Command, although it did not dwell upon individual responsibility except by innuendo. Since his visit to Hawaii was brief, not meant to be a full-scale investigation, his report was necessarily general and sketchy. Knox affirmed that the air attack was a complete surprise to both the army and the navy and that the initial success was due primarily to lack of "a state of readiness" against such as assault. Because of the strength of the fleet stationed at Pearl Harbor, neither local commander, Admiral Kimmel or General Short, considered air attack likely. Knox noted that the Navy Department had sent Kimmel a general war warning on November 27, but Short stated that he had not received a December 6 warning from the War Department until after the attack started. The secretary attached no judgment to the issue

---

[17] Knox to Bloch, January 19, 1942, Box 2, Claude C. Bloch Papers, Library of Congress, Washington, D.C.; Knox to Mowrer, December 18, 1941; Knox to Theodore Roosevelt, Jr., December 18, 1941; Knox to J. C. Coates, January 7, 1942, Box 1, Knox Papers; *New York Times*, April 29, 1944, pp. 1, 8. See also George H. Lobdell, "A Biography of Frank Knox" (Ph.D. diss., Indiana University, 1954).

of the warnings, but suggested that both the army and the navy commanders had prepared carefully—unfortunately for the wrong kind of attack. Short, fearing sabotage, went to sabotage alert and, as a preventive measure against tampering, bunched planes on the airfields, which made bombing them very simple. Kimmel, on the other hand, believed the principal danger to the fleet to be submarine attack and took the necessary precautions.[18]

Beyond the lack of preparedness for air attack, Knox cited other contributing factors to the defeat, some of which were beyond the control of the local commanders. As stated earlier, he believed that Japanese fifth columnists played a large role in the successful execution of the attack. He also noted inadequate numbers of fighter planes and antiaircraft artillery, which Washington provided. Yet the secretary did not stress these qualifying factors emphatically enough to supplant the overriding impression that the Hawaiian Command was ill prepared for an air attack.[19]

After Roosevelt reviewed Knox's findings, he called a meeting for the following morning with Hull, Stimson, Knox, and other high officials. He directed the war and navy secretaries to hold separate press conferences, at which time they were to admit equal responsibility of the services for failing to prepare for the raid. The president then handed Knox a list of points, presumably gleaned from the secretary's report, which he wanted announced at the news conference. These notes contained all the information the administration was willing to make public at the time. Heading the list was a statement that the Japanese had failed in their attempt to knock the United States out of the war before it began. On the issue of inadequate defenses there would be no attempt to conceal the fact that the military and naval forces were not on the alert against air attack, but it would be noted that after the initial surprise the defense was heroic. And most significantly, it was revealed that the president would convene a formal inquiry with further action dependent on the facts gathered.[20]

[18] "Report of the Secretary of the Navy. . . ," in U.S. Congress, *Pearl Harbor Attack: Hearings before the Joint Committee on the Pearl Harbor Attack*, 79th Cong., 1st sess., pt. 24, pp. 1749–1756.

[19] Ibid.

[20] Memorandum by FDR, undated, President's Secretary File, Roosevelt Papers; Frank E. Beatty, "Another Version of What Started War with Japan,"

Knox's public announcement on December 15 was essentially a verbatim rendering of the president's instructions and for the moment, at least, seemed to allay the worst fears about the attack.[21] Both the press and radio gave substantial coverage to the report, and many of the stories emphasized that losses were less than anticipated. Ernest Lindley of the *Washington Post* called the report a "model of clarity and propriety."[22] A *New York Times* editorial, pleased that the administration disclosed some information about the incident, stated: ". . . it was almost possible to hear the immense sigh of relief that arose yesterday when news of [Knox's] statement reached the American public."[23] And the *Nation* applauded the Knox report as "fairly extensive and unvarnished," given that the full story of Pearl Harbor was likely to remain untold until after the war.[24] In an intelligence report which assessed reactions to the disclosure, the OFF asserted that columnists, radio commentators, and editorial writers of all persuasions received the report "with warm approval," and they optimistically noted that it would have a positive effect upon restoring public confidence in the navy and the government's war information policy.[25]

A poll taken on December 24 in part substantiated the OFF's claims. Asked which of the following statements came closest to describing "the way the news of the attack on Pearl Harbor was handled," those surveyed responded:

There was absolutely no excuse for holding back the Pearl
Harbor news for a whole week. 7%

I can see why the government may have wanted to hold
back the news, but on the whole I think it did more
harm than good to hold it back. 6

It would have been nice to know immediately what
happened, but it is probably best that the news was
held back to keep from helping the enemy. 53

_____
U.S. News 36 (May 28, 1954): 50; Beatty, "Background of the Secret Report," p. 1264.

21 *New York Times*, December 16, 1941, pp. 1, 7.

22 *Washington Post*, December 17, 1941, p. 17.

23 *New York Times*, December 16, 1941, p. 26.

24 *Nation* 153 (December 20, 1941): 626.

25 Office of Emergency Management, Intelligence Report 2, December 22, 1941, Box 159, President's Secretary File, Roosevelt Papers.

We had no right at all to expect the story of our
losses at Pearl Harbor any sooner than we got it—
in most countries we wouldn't get the real news at all.   .   .   . 28

Don't know.   .   .   .   .   6[26]

It is not surprising that Americans received the news of the
report so favorably. Almost everyone, including government officials,
had only a superficial knowledge about the disaster in that first
week of war. Knox had placed the losses in more or less concrete
terms, which were better than many had hoped. The question of
responsibility was still rather nebulous, but the president's promised
investigation was meant to resolve that issue. The Knox report,
therefore, did not provide much additional fuel for the controversy,
which remained largely speculative and general. Of course, critics
of the administration continued to raise doubts. For example, the
Chicago Tribune took a few subtle jabs at the Washington officials,
and the *New Republic* loudly hinted that beyond blaming the authorities at Pearl Harbor, responsibility for the attack ultimately
belonged to national government leaders, "who, until the last min-
ute, followed a policy of appeasement that made adequate war
preparations much more difficult."[27] In order for these accusations
to mature into a full-scale debate, more concrete issues about Pearl
Harbor would have to arise.

With the decision to relieve Kimmel and Short of command,
fissures and cracks began to disrupt the relative calm which release
of the Knox findings had produced. Blame for the disaster was
finally being personalized at the lowest echelons of command. Admiral Kimmel and General Short were to be singled out as the
primary culprits. This was an unfortunate occurrence, since both
men were at the zenith of their careers. The tall, broad-shouldered
navy commander from Kentucky, the son of a Confederate Army
officer, had climbed quickly through the ranks since his graduation
from Annapolis. His career spanned such varying assignments as
participation in the 1914 Veracruz campaign, service as a commander in European waters during World War I, and a tour of duty

[26] Hadley Cantril and Mildred Strunk, eds., *Public Opinion, 1935–1946*,
p. 1144.
[27] *Chicago Tribune*, December 17, 1941, p. 8; *New Republic* 105 (December 22, 1941): 843.

as budget officer for the Navy Department. In 1915 he caught the eye of Assistant Secretary of the Navy Franklin Roosevelt and served briefly as his aide. Roosevelt later selected him over forty other officers for a major sea command. After Kimmel's promotion to rear admiral in 1937, his career success seemed to be assured. At fifty-nine he became one of the youngest fleet commanders of his time when he accepted the post of commander of the U.S. Fleet in February, 1941. In that position many fellow officers lauded Kimmel as an expert in gunnery, planning, and administration.[28]

Kimmel's counterpart in the army Hawaiian Command, Gen. Walter Short, had not gained the distinction which Kimmel had acquired, but he had risen through the army ranks to a respectable series of assignments. The Illinois native had received a bachelor's degree from the University of Illinois instead of going through West Point. After receiving his commission in 1902, he first served at the Presidio in San Francisco and then drew assignments in the Philippines and Alaska. In 1916 he participated in the punitive expedition against Mexico and served at various posts in France during World War I. After the war he gained some vital experience as a member of the War Department General Staff and then with the Far Eastern section of the Military Intelligence Division. He eventually achieved the rank of major general and was named commander of the Hawaiian Department in February, 1941.[29]

Secretary of War Stimson took the first steps to diffuse the issue of responsibility for Pearl Harbor. He not only attempted to minimize the army's involvement in the Pearl Harbor affair, but also decided in advance of the Knox report to relieve the army commanders in Hawaii, despite his public declaration that replacements were made on the basis of the Knox report. Although Roosevelt insisted that the secretaries issue statements of culpability in order to avoid a disruptive interdepartmental squabble, Stimson delayed his press conference until the navy had taken the brunt of the criticism. In his statement the war secretary announced that Gen. Delos C. Emmons had replaced General Short as commander of the Hawaiian Department and that Brig. Gen. C. L. Tinker had replaced Maj. Gen. F. L. Martin as commander of the Army Air

[28] New York Times, May 15, 1968, pp. 1, 24.
[29] Ibid., September 4, 1949, p. 40.

Corps in Hawaii. Only then did Stimson mention army unpreparedness for the attack. Knox, in his statement, had not announced any
reassignments, stating contrarily that none would be made until
after the proposed executive investigation. But Knox abandoned that
position and, like Stimson, replaced the chief navy officers in
Hawaii.[30]

Stimson's actions helped bring a change in command to Hawaii
before the designated time, but he had in no way worked at cross-
purposes with administration policy. In a December 16 letter to the
president recommending members for the forthcoming investigation, Stimson ended with a confidential statement telling of his decision to send Emmons and Tinker to Hawaii to relieve Short and
Martin. In penciled remarks at the bottom of the letter he noted:
"My opinion is that the housecleaning which I discuss in the last
paragraph should be synchronized with a similar housecleaning in
the Naval Command, and all announced at the same time."[31]

The replacement of Short and Martin may have been a fait ac-
compli for Knox and Roosevelt, but no coercion on the part of the
secretary of war is evident. In the case of Knox, he came to the conclusion that the local commanders were responsible for the success
of the attack at about the same time that Stimson did. He did not
emphasize this strong feeling in his report, but his attitude was
clear in his private conversations. On his return from Hawaii, he
talked with Adm. Chester W. Nimitz, soon to be commander in chief
of the Pacific Fleet, and explained how Kimmel and his staff were
understandably shaken by the attack, "So shaken that their recent
estimate of the situation completely revised the strategy of the Pacific war." Knox insisted that a new commander had to be sent to
Hawaii, "One who could dispel the gloom and sense of fear that
permeated Pearl Harbor and inspired a bold offensive." The secre-

[30] Paul S. Burtness and Warren U. Ober, "Secretary Stimson and the First
Pearl Harbor Investigation," *Australian Journal of Politics and History* 14
(April, 1968): 24–29. See also Current, *Secretary Stimson*, pp. 169–170; *New
York Times*, December 18, 1941, pp. 1–2; *Newsweek* 18 (December 27, 1941):
21–22.

[31] Stimson to FDR, December 16, 1941, Box 101, President's Secretary
File, Roosevelt Papers. See also diary of Henry L. Stimson, December 17,
1941, XXXVI, 113, microfilm, Stimson Papers; Congress, *Pearl Harbor Attack*,
pt. 3, pp. 1528ff.

tary, at that moment, asked Nimitz to go to Hawaii to replace Kimmel.[32]

The president had time to countermand Stimson's orders to replace Short and Martin, but he did not. The public announcement of Emmons's and Tinker's arrival in Hawaii came after Stimson's letter to Roosevelt. Either the secretary of war's decision was of little immediate interest to Roosevelt, or he affirmed the action taken. With both his secretary of war and secretary of the navy in concurrence on basic policy, he was unlikely to protest.

In the face of war, the relief of Kimmel and Short and the unification of command in Hawaii, announced on December 17, was not an unusual decision on the surface.[33] At the primary line of defense, those charged with protecting the Pacific Fleet and the naval base at Pearl Harbor were most likely to be the first individuals singled out as responsible for lack of adequate preparations. But by replacing the local commanders, who as yet were not found guilty of any derelictions, the administration was assigning blame for the disaster at the lowest official level possible and leaving the way open for criticism which might extend the blame beyond the Hawaiian Command. The forthcoming presidential investigation would either quell the emerging controversy or ignite it.

[32] Nimitz replaced Kimmel as commander in chief of the Pacific Fleet; Adm. Ernest J. King became commander in chief of the U.S. Fleet. Both commands previously had been codified under Kimmel. See John Toland, *But Not in Shame: The Six Months after Pearl Harbor*, p. 89; Knox to Rawleigh Warner, December 23, 1941, Box 1, Knox Papers.

[33] *New York Times*, December 18, 1941, p. 4; December 19, 1941, p. 24; *Chicago Tribune*, December 18, 1941, p. 16; Marshall to Emmons, December 20, 1941, Box 1, Delos C. Emmons Papers, Hoover Institution on War, Revolution, and Peace, Stanford, Calif.; Louis Morton, *Strategy and Command: The First Two Years*, pp. 143–145.

3

Hasty Investigation

ON Tuesday evening, December 16, Press Secretary Stephen T. Early announced that President Roosevelt had named a board of inquiry, headed by Associate Supreme Court Justice Owen J. Roberts, to investigate the sneak attack upon Hawaii.[1] The purpose of the Roberts commission was to acquire the facts about the disaster, but it was also to defuse the Pearl Harbor issue before it interfered with the war effort and—quite significantly—before it raised a public furor that could degenerate into a full-scale political controversy. Yet the immediate result of the inquiry was not to curtail debate but to enhance it. By citing the Hawaiian commanders, Admiral Kimmel and General Short, with dereliction of duty, the Roberts commission's report would mark the beginning rather than the end of the squabble over Pearl Harbor culpability which would persist throughout the war and eventually spill over into the postwar years.

The timing of the inquiry is significant. Coming at the moment when American appetites had been whetted by the Knox report, the potentialities of a congressional investigation were very real. Considering the momentum of events and Roosevelt's political sensitivity, an executive inquiry was inevitable. And as soon as Knox returned from his fact-finding jaunt, the president declared his intention to act.[2] His announcement about the formation of a commission came the next day, and he signed the official order on December 18.

In appointing members for the board, Roosevelt and the key

---

[1] Press conference, December 16, 1941, Box 41, Stephen T. Early Papers, Franklin D. Roosevelt Presidential Library, Hyde Park, N.Y.

[2] Press conference 947, April 28, 1944, in *Complete Presidential Press Conferences of Franklin D. Roosevelt*, XXIII, 138.

administration officials sought individuals with good public reputations whose eventual report would be accepted confidently. After
outlining his general requirements, the president left the selection
process to the secretaries of war and the navy. On the afternoon of
December 15, Knox called Stimson and told him that FDR had decided to designate a commission consisting of two army officers, two
navy officers, and a civilian chairman. The navy secretary said he
would recommend Adm. William H. Standley, former chief of naval
operations, and Adm. Joseph M. Reeves, former commander in chief
of the U.S. Fleet. For the chairman's position, he suggested federal
judge Philip C. Sullivan from Chicago.[3]

Immediately after the conversation with Knox, Stimson began
to consider his own appointments. Deliberating over a number of
possible candidates, he settled on Maj. Gen. Frank R. McCoy, who
had served on the Lytton commission, which had investigated the
Japanese takeover of Manchuria. McCoy had had long service in
the Philippines and was president of the Foreign Policy Association. For the other army position Stimson eventually decided upon
Brig. Gen. Joseph T. McNarney, who was on active duty with the
Army Air Corps. In a telephone conversation with Marshall, Stimson concluded that an airman should serve on the board "in view of
the fact that the problem was really one of air and the problem of
delinquency connected with it was also connected with air." Marshall then suggested McNarney, and Stimson concurred. For the
civilian appointment, the secretary surmised that Judge Sullivan did
not have "guns enough" in the way of reputation to hold such a position of prominence. He believed Justice Owen J. Roberts was a
superior choice, not only because of his position on the Supreme
Court, but also because he had been one of two government prose-
cutors of the famous Teapot Dome case and had investigated the
Black Tom incident.[4]

Once the secretaries made their choices, Stimson wrote the
president. In recommending Roberts, he stated that the justice had

[3] Diary of Henry L. Stimson, December 15, 1941, XXXVI, 109–110,
microfilm, Henry L. Stimson Papers, Manuscripts and Archives, Sterling Memorial Library, Yale University, New Haven, Conn.; press conference, December 16, 1941, Box 41, Early Papers; *New York Times*, December 17, 1941, 9.

[4] Diary of Henry L. Stimson, December 15–16, 1941, XXXVI, 109–111,
microfilm, Stimson Papers.

a reputation "for getting down to the bottom of a factual situation" and thus could command the confidence of the country in this vital undertaking. Roosevelt knew McCoy personally, and Stimson reminded the president that the major general possessed a "breadth of view, superlative character, and wide similar experience" with investigations like Pearl Harbor. He also suggested that since no retired Air Corps officer was fit for the assignment, McNarney was "the best air man we have for that purpose."[5]

The men selected for the commission met the administration's needs very well. They were all individuals of solid reputations, their backgrounds were varied, and, except possibly for McNarney, who was the only one in the group still on active duty, they were detached from direct involvement in the Pearl Harbor affair. A résumé of opinion assembled by William L. Langer, director of research for the Coordinator of Information—British Empire Group, echoed this favorable impression of the members. Of 236 articles dated December 16 through 28 dealing with the Roberts commission, 107 referred specifically to the appointments and 104 were unconditionally favorable.[6] This overwhelming press response reinforced what the administration already believed about the selections and seemed to presage a receptive treatment of the commission's eventual findings.

After the war, however, critics of the Roosevelt administration suggested that the members, with the possible exception of McCoy and Standley, were predisposed to censure the Hawaiian commanders and that the Roberts commission was a "kangaroo court" where Kimmel and Short could not have gotten a fair hearing.[7] This appraisal is too severe, but as the administration's hand-picked group,

[5] Stimson to FDR, December 16, 1941, Box 101, President's Secretary File, Franklin D. Roosevelt Papers, Franklin D. Roosevelt Presidential Library, Hyde Park, N.Y.

[6] "Résumé of Public Opinion about the Commission to Investigate the Attack at Pearl Harbor," in U.S. Congress, *Pearl Harbor Attack: Hearings before the Joint Committee on the Pearl Harbor Attack*, 79th Cong., 1st sess., pt. 24, pp. 1287–1304.

[7] Charles A. Beard, *President Roosevelt and the Coming of the War, 1941: A Study in Appearances and Realities*, p. 278; George Morgenstern, *Pearl Harbor: The Story of the Secret War*, pp. 41–42; interview with Admiral Standley, May 1, 1962, Harry Elmer Barnes Collection, Division of Rare Books and Special Collections, University of Wyoming Library, Laramie.

the board members were likely to carry out their instructions literally and also to try to avoid perpetuating a debate over the issue of Pearl Harbor responsibility. There were some internal rifts in the commission. As Admiral Standley suggested in his memoirs, the board was split between forces clearly antagonistic to the local commanders and those who were more dispassionate. Roberts was not enamored with the Hawaiian commanders, and Reeves, in particular, clearly lacked confidence in Kimmel and Short. Although Standley essentially agreed with the majority of the commission members that the local commanders must accept blame for the disaster, he could not adhere to the premise that they were solely responsible as the eventual report implied. From the first meeting of the group he felt the tone of the inquiry was decidedly against the local commanders and was likely to make them scapegoats.[8]

There was no absolute guarantee how the individuals on the board would react, given the volume of material they would examine and the impressions they would receive from the witnesses. More significantly, the predilection of the commission members was secondary to the narrow construction of the president's charge in determining the outcome of the investigation. The purpose of the inquiry as stated in the charge was simply to determine whether any derelictions of duty or errors of judgment on the part of army and navy personnel contributed to the Hawaii disaster.[9] This meant that the investigation would deal almost exclusively with the Hawaiian Command, its defense responsibilities, and the immediate reasons for the success of the attack. The executive-initiated inquiry would not be self-evaluating at the highest levels; Washington officials were clearly removed from the province of the commission's scrutiny. Any other course was unthinkable for the Roosevelt administration, convinced as they were of the soundness of their prewar policies and actions.

The prejudgment of the local commanders by the war and navy

[8] William H. Standley and Arthur A. Ageton, *Admiral Ambassador to Russia*, pp. 80 ff., 86–90. See also Standley to Delia Kimmel, February 10, 1943, Box 3; Kimmel to Charles Rugg, August 17, 1945, Box 5, Husband E. Kimmel Collection, Division of Rare Books and Special Collections, University of Wyoming Library, Laramie.

[9] Executive order, December 18, 1941, in Congress, *Pearl Harbor Attack*, pt. 24, p. 1306.

secretaries compounded the limited scope of the commission's charge. By relieving Kimmel and Short of duty on the opening day of the Roberts commission proceedings, the secretaries enhanced the seeming imperative to study the Pearl Harbor affair from the narrow local perspective. The board members were being guided, wittingly or unwittingly, toward only one possible conclusion.

Knox's and Stimson's close association with the board persisted throughout the investigation; they were never too distant from the members' activities. In fact, the first meeting of the board took place in Stimson's office with Knox present. The secretary of the navy explained in detail what he had seen in Hawaii, and Stimson urged the members not to limit themselves to questions of individual "delinquency and responsibility" but to examine the whole question of the defense of the island to determine whether the system in effect was adequate, if Pearl Harbor could be defended against air attack in the future, and in general "to get a line on the whole problem of our western fortress."[10]

The secretary of war also kept tabs on the inquiry through casual meetings with individual board members. Several times he discussed the investigation over dinner with his personal friend, Frank McCoy, and lunched with General McNarney. He even dined with Chairman Roberts on January 20 at the home of Supreme Court Justice Felix Frankfurter, where they talked until midnight about the views the chairman had formed on the general situation in Hawaii "as distinguished from his decision which is not yet ready for announcement." They talked as well about the defense of the islands and about their concern over "the great potential danger" coming from the large Japanese population in Hawaii.[11]

There is little justification to read any sinister or clandestine motives into the encounters between the board members and the army and navy secretaries. The close relationship was unavoidable given that the high officials were investigating their subordinates. Knox and Stimson, however, had no reason to obstruct the inquiry. The narrow construction of the executive charge itself precluded a

[10] Diary of Henry L. Stimson, December 17, 1941, XXXVI, 114, microfilm, Stimson Papers; Congress, *Pearl Harbor Attack*, pt. 7, p. 3283; memorandum, December 17, 1941, microfilm reel 127, Stimson Papers.

[11] Diary of Henry L. Stimson, January 20, 1942, XXXVII, 51, microfilm, Stimson Papers.

wide-ranging exploration of the Pearl Harbor issue, especially the role of Washington. Their constant attentiveness to the commission, of course, insured that any deviations from the prescribed plan would not go unnoticed.

The actual proceedings of the Roberts commission demonstrated the restrictive nature of the inquiry. The members held three sets of meetings—in Washington from December 18 through 20, in Hawaii from December 22 through January 9, and finally in Washington again until January 23. Most of the individuals interrogated either were directly involved in the defense of Pearl Harbor or were civilian eyewitnesses. Approximately 41 percent of those called were army personnel, 29 percent were navy personnel, and 30 percent were civilians. In all, the board questioned 127 witnesses. However, it did not examine under oath the high command, namely Marshall and Stark or their staffs, but merely asked them to provide background material for the members to study. No Washington figure of stature testified in any capacity other than informational.[12]

In preparing for the inquiry, the army and navy provided the members with war plans, maps, orders, and, according to Roberts, "every document that could have bearing on the situation at Pearl Harbor." After the board reviewed these documents, the officers who presented them were asked to explain their significance. As a result of these early conferences, the commission formulated its plan for taking testimony, interrogated its witnesses, and then studied copies of documents on file in Hawaii which had originated in Washington.[13]

The documentation which the commission examined was incomplete. Especially glaring was the omission of the "Magic" intercepts. "Magic" was a generic cover name given to the entire American cryptanalysis operation of cracking ultrasecret Japanese diplomatic codes and ciphers. The ability of American leaders to read the intercepted messages between the Japanese government and its ambassadors and ministers and the reports of Japanese military attachés and secret agents gave the United States a potentially

[12] Statistics were gleaned from witness lists in Congress, *Pearl Harbor Attack*, pt. 22, pp. iv–xvi.

[13] Ibid., pt. 7, pp. 3261–3262. For the administrative details of the investigation, see minutes of the Roberts commission, Pearl Harbor File, Box 12, Record Group 125, National Archives, Washington, D.C.

great advantage. Although the diplomatic messages decoded before December 7 did not produce any direct evidence that Pearl Harbor was to be the target of an attack, their existence brought into question just how much Washington knew in advance and how much it sent on to its local commanders.[14] In an interview with Admiral Kimmel's attorney, Charles Rugg, Roberts suggested that the board did not receive the Magic intercepts except for a message of December 7, 1941. He added that the Navy Department either told the commission directly or implied that it provided whatever information was available.[15] In testimony before the congressional investigation on Pearl Harbor which convened after the war, Roberts repeated approximately the same story he had told Rugg. In response to a question about the board's closed sessions, he indicated that secrecy was being maintained to protect the existence of the broken codes. "[A]nd indeed the Navy was rather chary about even telling us about the thing," he added, "for fear there might be some leak from our commission." During further questioning by Michigan Senator Homer Ferguson, Roberts stated that the commission examined all broken codes except Magic and did not even receive synopses of Magic messages. The War and Navy departments told the members generally what was included in them, although the board never received the original messages nor requested them. When Ferguson asked him how some of the findings could have been attained without taking the Magic intercepts into consideration, Roberts became indignant and felt the senator was badgering him and criticizing the commission's performance. He reiterated that what most concerned him was whether the commanders had been advised of the "criticalness of this situation," not what the intercepts might contain. He believed they could not add anything to what he sought.[16] Ultimately, the information in the decoded messages may not have altered the board's findings, but the members relinquished the opportunity to determine the value of Magic as evidence.

Given the narrow charge to the board, the close association

[14] For a more thorough examination of the code issue, see Roberta Wohlstetter, *Pearl Harbor: Warning and Decision*; Ladislas Farago, *The Broken Seal: "Operation Magic" and the Secret Road to Pearl Harbor*.

[15] Rugg to Kimmel, November 16, 1944, memorandum, Box 35, Kimmel Collection.

[16] Congress, *Pearl Harbor Attack*, pt. 7, pp. 3262, 3278–3280, 3284–3285.

with the secretaries of war and the navy, and the restrictions in witnesses interrogated and documentation examined, it was not surprising that the Roberts commission censured the Hawaiian commanders. The report credited the secretary of state with keeping the War and Navy departments "in close touch with the international situation and fully advising them respecting the course and probable termination of negotiations with Japan." In turn, the secretaries of war and the navy kept the lines of communication open between themselves and other high officials and also warned the local commanders of their defense responsibilities. Beyond this point, the commission believed the lines of communication broke down. Granting that the commanders fulfilled their obligations in part by preparing plans which "if adapted to and used for the existing emergency, would have been adequate," they charged Admiral Kimmel and General Short with not conferring adequately with respect to the warnings from Washington and not employing existing plans to provide an adequate state of readiness to meet the emergency.[17] This conclusion was the major departure from the Knox report, which had indicated that the Hawaiian base was properly on the alert against sabotage and submarine attack but not air assault. The Roberts commission viewed the issue from the opposite perspective: since the attack was by air, Kimmel's and Short's preparations were inadequate to meet it. This shift in emphasis put responsibility for the disaster squarely on their shoulders.

The commission outlined other conclusions which seemed to modify their strong indictment of the local commanders and also produced some inconsistencies. For example, the report cited deficiencies in personnel, weapons, equipment, and facilities at Pearl Harbor which made it difficult to maintain defenses on a war footing for any extended period. Yet the following proviso was inserted: "These deficiencies should not have affected the decision of the responsible commanders as to the state of readiness to be prescribed." In this case, Kimmel and Short were expected to do what they could to forestall the attack with what equipment and personnel was on hand, despite the deficiencies. The board further concluded that the failure of the commanders to confer and cooperate with respect

[17] "Report of the Roberts Commission, January 23, 1942," in ibid., pt. 39, pp. 1–21.

to the warnings from Washington resulted largely from "a sense of security due to the opinion prevalent in diplomatic, military, and naval circles, and in the public press, that any immediate attack by Japan would be in the Far East." Thus, the board expected the commanders to prepare for the eventuality of air attack, even though the climate of opinion throughout the country belied that possibility.[18]

The report noted contributory factors to the defeat which were clearly beyond the control of Kimmel and Short. Most of these dealt with faulty communications between Washington and Hawaii, including the failure of the War Department to observe that Short believed he had fulfilled the requirements of the warnings, the emphasis in the war warnings on Japanese aggression in the Far East and on antisabotage measures, and the nonreceipt of a December 7 message notifying Hawaii of impending attack. Another factor addressed itself to Japanese culpability, especially "[d]isregard of international law and custom relating to declaration of war by the Japanese and the adherence by the United States to such laws and customs."[19]

The additional conclusions were an intriguing assortment. The report minimized the Japanese role in the success of the attack to virtual exclusion, relegating it to a "contributory factor." The various qualifications also placed the extent of the local commanders' guilt in some doubt. The report blamed Kimmel and Short for not heeding the warning messages, but the nonreceipt of the December 7 message was listed as a contributory factor to the defeat. The commanders were in the precarious position of having responsibility for protecting the base and, despite the circumstances, were to be held completely accountable for the disaster. The criteria for indicting the local commanders, however, were not extended beyond Hawaii.

Roberts submitted the completed report to the War and Navy departments for review to determine if it divulged any military secrets.[20] Finding it essentially free of sensitive disclosures, the com-

[18] Ibid.
[19] Ibid.
[20] Richard N. Current, *Secretary Stimson: A Study in Statecraft*, pp. 171–172.

misson chairman delivered the document to the Oval Office on January 24. While he and the president met, Stephen Early told the White House press corps about the meeting, adding that he hoped the report "does fix the responsibility in such language that it may be released almost textually to you."[21] In their two-hour session, Roosevelt read the report in full while Roberts waited and answered whatever questions the president asked. After finishing, Roosevelt asked, "Is there any reason why this report should not be given to the public in its entirety?" The justice assured him there was not. At that point FDR tossed the document across his desk and ordered one of his secretaries, "Give that in full to the papers for their Sunday editions."[22]

The administration hoped that the Roberts report would quell the critics, arrest the rumors, and end the debate over responsibility before it began. Those most intimately associated with the investigation and concerned about its results were optimistic that the press, the Congress, and the public would receive the report favorably. This was especially true for Secretary Stimson, who spent Sunday morning poring over newspaper accounts of the disclosure. He noted in his diary: ". . . It is an admirable report, candid and fair, and thorough in its study of the facts. It points out with merciless thoroughness the faults in the defense of Hawaii on December 7th. . . ." But he lamented that the report could not go into what he perceived as the real underlying problem: Both services had not fully learned the lessons of the development of air power in respect to the defense of a navy and a naval base; the nation had grown to rely on the impregnability of Pearl Harbor.[23]

Aside from Stimson, others in the administration expressed enthusiasm about the impression the report had already made on the country. The OFF's February 2 intelligence report stated: "The Roberts' Report is praised in press and radio for candor; general complacency is blamed for the Pearl Harbor disaster. Alleged withholding of a portion of the Pearl Harbor story has been generally accepted in the press as motivated by conditions of security." An-

21 Press conference, January 24, 1942, Box 41, Early Papers.

22 Roberts to Samuel I. Rosenman, May 20, 1949, in *The Public Papers and Addresses of Franklin D. Roosevelt*, comp. Samuel I. Rosenman, X, 565.

23 Diary of Henry L. Stimson, January 25, 1942, XXXVII, 64, microfilm, Stimson Papers.

other statement read: "The Roberts report *given sensational treatment in press and radio.* Many newspapers printed the report in full; the majority quoted extensively. Headlines stressed guilt of Kimmel and Short."[24]

Although the OFF may have dramatized the response to the commission's findings, there was a considerable amount of favorable reaction in the press and on radio to encourage the administration. *Time* believed the judgment against the commanders was harsh but measured, assuring that Americans were not hunting for scapegoats.[25] Raymond Swing, in a radio broadcast of January 26, stated that he did not believe Washington was completely free of responsibility, but he accepted the verdict of the Roberts commission against Kimmel and Short.[26] Even the anti-Roosevelt *Chicago Tribune* carried a story about the report staying close to administration guidelines.[27]

Some reactions, while agreeing with the findings of the commission, were more indignant. An editorial in *America* declared that the United States had "a grossly incompetent admiral and an equally incompetent general on guard at that post of first military importance." It concluded that a court-martial might determine why unfit officers were kept in the service and might also help weed out all incompetents in the military who were appointed for favoritism instead of capability.[28] And newsman Raymond Clapper noted on January 27: "As I read the Roberts report on Pearl Harbor, I kept thinking that would be a hell of a way to run a newspaper. I don't know anything about military affairs. But I have been around newspaper offices all my life. A newspaper office is organized to be ready for the unexpected. But I never saw a newsroom that was as slack and sloppy as the Roberts report shows the Army and Navy at Hawaii to have been."[29]

[24] Office of Emergency Management, Intelligence Report 8, February 2, 1942, Box 159, President's Secretary File, Roosevelt Papers.

[25] *Time* 39 (February 2, 1942): 16–17.

[26] Radio broadcast, January 26, 1942, Box 16, Raymond Swing Papers, Library of Congress, Washington, D.C.

[27] *Chicago Tribune*, January 25, 1942, pp. 1, 14.

[28] *America* 66 (February 7, 1942): 490.

[29] Clapper, *Watching the World*, ed. Mrs. Raymond Clapper, pp. 288–290.

The hope that the commission's report would subdue all rumors and concretely affix blame for the disaster was a pipe dream. There was enough speculation in the press and on radio about responsibilities beyond the Hawaiian Command to provide a potentially serious challenge to the Roosevelt administration's stand on the Pearl Harbor affair expressed in the Roberts report. An editorial in the *New York Times* accepted the primary guilt of Kimmel and Short, suggesting, "No long-distance check-up from Washington, five thousand miles away, even if it had been more thorough than the report actually showed it to be, could have compensated for negligence and incompetence on the spot." But beyond the immediate accountability there remained "a longer even if less definite chain of responsibility," the most important links being the local commanders, their superiors in Washington, Congress, and the commander in chief himself—all of whom assumed necessary precautions were taken. The editorial concluded that the principle which the parties involved in the case of Pearl Harbor should have adopted was Herbert Spencer's advice: "Do not suppose things are going right till it is proved they are going wrong, but rather suppose they are going wrong till it is proved they are going right."[30]

Some criticisms were more explicit and more directly emphasized faults of the high command and other Washington officials. After reviewing the Roberts report, Oswald Garrison Villard suggested that a "searching inquiry" would be in order to determine if there was any "whitewashing" of superior officers in Washington.[31] An editorial in the *Chicago Tribune* declared, "It will be well to have a further investigation to disclose whether officers and officials senior to the investigators were as untouched by responsibility for the catastrophe as might first appear."[32] *Commonweal* inquired why the War and Navy departments had not issued a formal order placing all Pacific bases on alert at the moment they realized the Japanese negotiations were about to collapse.[33]

Not even the president and his advisers were spared from ac-

[30] *New York Times*, January 28, 1942, p. 18.
[31] Villard, "The Pearl Harbor Report," *Current History* 2 (March, 1942): 11–13.
[32] *Chicago Tribune*, January 26, 1942, p. 10.
[33] *Commonweal* 35 (February 6, 1942): 379.

cusations and queries. David Lawrence of *U.S. News*, an ardent critic of the Roosevelt administration, led the attack. He believed responsibility should not merely rest with the local commanders but should include the officials in Washington as well. He charged that the president was responsible for the failure to coordinate the defense operations, and the chief staff officers were accountable for not verifying whether the local Hawaiian commanders took necessary precautions against surprise attack. Lawrence accused Roosevelt and "his colleagues in the New Deal" of not applying business methods and efficiency to their duties in Washington. He also reproached Congress for neglecting the United States' Pacific defenses and not rectifying the inefficient organization of the War and Navy departments. The *U.S. News* columnist hoped that Kimmel and Short would not be made scapegoats for "the negligence in Washington." And in another editorial he more directly assailed Roosevelt and accused the administration of squelching a congressional inquiry of the disaster. Lawrence rationalized that the airing of the issue during wartime might help prevent future Pearl Harbors by discovering if the same kind of incompetence persisted and if the same attitude toward defense strategy prevailed. His concern, however, was restricted to the policies and practices of civilian officials in the administration with whom he had clashed for many years.[34]

Beyond the more personal accusations of and assaults on Washington officials, the most amazing proliferation of blame for Pearl Harbor was the notion that the American people in general were responsible. Donald W. Mitchell of *Nation* suggested that the disaster was the outcome of faults ". . . which experts have long observed in our army and navy: stupidity and lack of vision in the higher ranks and stubborn non-cooperation between the services. General Short and Admiral Kimmel were products of a system whose faults are now being mercilessly exposed by war." From this indictment he made the mental leap that a great portion of blame belonged to the American people, who were responsible for not taking sufficient interest in a properly functioning armed service.[35] A *New Republic* editorial asserted that the chief lesson of Pearl Har-

[34] *U.S. News* 12 (February 6, 1942): 24–25; (February 13, 1942): 28–29.

[35] Mitchell, "Scapegoats and Facts," *Nation* 154 (February 7, 1942): 155.

bor did not apply simply to the army and navy, but to all Americans. To cast Kimmel and Short as scapegoats, it stated, was unfair, since most army and navy officers shared in the "Maginot-mindedness" of the commanders. The real sin of Pearl Harbor was "the sin of complacence, over-confidence, inertia, the reluctance to abandon our soft and easy way of life."[36]

The Roberts report, far from closing the door to further speculation, opened it wider. Whereas the administration restricted the investigation to the local circumstances of the disaster and immediate responsibility, numerous stories in the press raised questions about long-range policies and turned criticism toward Washington. The Knox report had been sufficiently general not to inspire such a flurry of conjecture and suspicion. But by singling out the local commanders for derelictions and restricting the breadth of the inquiry, the president's commission only highlighted the issues of unpreparedness, the breakdown in interdepartmental communications, faulty intelligence, and so on, without examining them thoroughly. The lingering assumption gaining prominence was: If the local commanders could have been so unprepared for surprise attack, what about their superiors? Had not the attack taken us all by surprise?

As such, the press speculations about responsibilty for Pearl Harbor were inadequate to constitute a threat to the administration. The stories of Washington culpability could incite readers but could not directly affect policy. The Roberts commission's findings would stand unless substantively challenged. Yet when the issues raised in the press and on radio were also raised in Congress, the possibility of reopening the case through legislation became a reality. Faced with the prospect of an extended public debate which could turn national attention away from the war effort and possibly produce high-level recriminations, the Roosevelt administration was not able to relegate the Pearl Harbor incident to history. It would have to quell the suspicions raised by the Roberts report and deal with the local commanders forthrightly.

[36] *New Republic* 106 (February 2, 1942): 134–135.

4

Cover-up!

THE Roosevelt administration's inquiry failed to end the wartime debate over Pearl Harbor responsibility. The rumblings over the Roberts report, initiated in the press, threatened to create a major political crisis. Only through some quick maneuvering by Democratic stalwarts, the pressure of problems imposed by the war effort, and the decision to retire the former chiefs of the Hawaiian Command did the controversy momentarily subside.

Despite its immediate satisfaction, the Roosevelt administration quickly sensed the hostility toward the Roberts report. Some of the president's advisers, like Robert E. Sherwood, seemed confident that the recent critical assaults would be short-lived. He insisted that there was "a minimum of crying over the milk spilled at Pearl Harbor" and believed that most Americans felt the blame was so widely distributed that there was little reason to waste time on recriminations.[1]

Other high officials did not dismiss the issue so easily. They realized that if the president lost the initiative in controlling the Pearl Harbor question, political havoc could result. Before the commission submitted its report, Roosevelt's friend and confidant, Supreme Court Justice Felix Frankfurter, had advised him to meet with Justice Roberts in private and get him "to tell you things that have no proper place in their report—particularly on matters of personnel pertaining not to the past but to what lies ahead." The justice was always "quite impenitent" about the part he played in arranging for Roberts to meet Roosevelt personally to discuss the

[1] Robert E. Sherwood, *Roosevelt and Hopkins: An Intimate History*, pp. 471 ff.

report. He feared a search for scapegoats would divert the country's attention from the war. While Frankfurter respected the right of Congress to investigate the Hawaiian incident, he was fearful that the president's authority would be compromised by "a meddlesome Congressional Committee as Lincoln's had been in the Civil War."[2]

Frankfurter's concern was partially alleviated when Roosevelt publicly disclosed the commission's report, although he told Roberts: "Naturally it stirs many reflections from what I think I can fairly read between the lines. . . ." He added that there was "an inert and unimaginative mentality in command at Pearl Harbor" which he believed still existed on the General Staff and in the Office of Naval Operations.[3]

Of all the high-level advisers, Harry Hopkins was the most unnerved by the growing controversy which had begun to spread throughout Congress. He realized that the initial optimism over the impact of the Roberts report was premature, and he brooded over the negative reactions that were surfacing. Convinced that the criticism of the report coupled with the bleak news from the war fronts in North Africa and on the Malay peninsula would cripple public morale and produce a resurgence of isolationist sentiment, he privately lashed out at those senators he considered the major culprits "who opposed every move to prepare for war." In a confidential memorandum, he bitterly criticized some of the most prominent administration critics. He charged that Senator David I. Walsh (Democrat, Massachusetts), chairman of the Naval Affairs Committee, "hates the British more than he cares about his own country." He called isolationist Senator Wayland Brooks (Republican, Illinois) "a Nazi-minded person" and accused Philip La Follette, former governor of Wisconsin, of being "undoubtedly a Nazi, having been exposed to Hitler in 1938 or 1939. . . ." And he stated that Senator Robert M. La Follette, Jr. (Progressive, Wisconsin), "fine person as he is, is a pacifist. . . ."[4] With all this opposition, Hopkins thought FDR would have to go through many of the same trials as Abraham

[2] Max Freedman, ed., *Roosevelt and Frankfurter*, pp. 644–645.

[3] Frankfurter to Roberts, January 25, 1942, Box 96, Felix Frankfurter Papers, Library of Congress, Washington, D.C.

[4] Memorandum by Hopkins, January 26, 1942, Box 298, Harry Hopkins Papers (Sherwood Collection), Franklin D. Roosevelt Presidential Library, Hyde Park, N.Y.; Sherwood, *Roosevelt and Hopkins*, pp. 491 ff.

Lincoln, not only with Congress but with generals and admirals "whose records look awfully good but who well may turn out to be the McClellans of this war." Unlike Lincoln, he asserted, Roosevelt would replace these "old men" much faster.[5]

The congressional reaction to the Roberts report seemed to bear out Hopkins's concern. Predictably, there was a partisan division. Administration stalwarts like Senate Majority Leader Alben W. Barkley (Democrat, Kentucky), House Military Affairs Committee Chairman Andrew J. May (Democrat, Kentucky), and House Foreign Affairs Committee Chairman Sol Bloom (Democrat, New York) quickly announced their satisfaction with the report. May called it "judicious and impartial," stating that Short and Kimmel "went to sleep at the switch." To reinforce the findings, he decided to put his committee into action if a court-martial was not convened or if the president himself did not dismiss the commanders. "I would like to know," he stated, "what can be done to prevent another Pearl Harbor. The Roberts report was good as far as it went, but it leaves more blanks than it fills in. The system seems wrong, Congress could set up a unity of command." Of course, many of the administration regulars, unwilling to diverge from the president in any fashion, ruled out the possibility of any further investigations. Carl Vinson (Democrat, Georgia), chairman of the House Naval Affairs Committee, declared that a new inquiry or a court-martial was not feasible at this time because high-ranking officers would have to be detached from war duty to testify and serve on investigatory boards.[6]

Administration critics, dissatisfied with the report and skeptical of its thoroughness, challenged the partisans. Especially desirous of carrying the conclusions of the report to their logical end, Representative Dewey J. Short (Republican, Missouri) sought support for court-martial proceedings against the local commanders. But he also suggested that guilt extended beyond the Hawaiian Command: "It's high time we were getting rid of these incompetents. We've got a lot of gold-braiders around here who haven't had an idea in 20

[5] Memorandum by Hopkins, January 26, 1942, Box 298, Hopkins Papers.
[6] *Chicago Tribune*, January 25, 1942, p. 15; *Washington Post*, January 26, 1942, pp. 1–2; *New York Times*, January 27, 1942, p. 4; U.S. Congress, *Congressional Record*, 77th Cong., 2d sess., 1942, 88, pp. 952, A253–255.

years. They should be court-martialed." Senator Robert La Follette, Jr., followed similar lines: "I don't think you can overlook the fact that some of the responsibiilty for this thing was right here in Washington."[7]

Senator Wayland Brooks, an implacable antagonist of the administration, set the standard for recrimination against Washington officials. In a devastating assault, he demanded an immediate investigation of the role of Secretaries Knox and Stimson in the Pearl Harbor affair, posing several insinuating questions: Why had the secretaries inadequately supplied Hawaii in the face of inevitable war with Japan? Who was responsible for the concentration of the fleet in Pearl Harbor, making it vulnerable to air attack? What "private enterprise" diverted Knox's and Stimson's attention from their duty to develop national defenses? What diligence did the Navy and War departments employ to determine how well the local commanders were prepared for possible attack? What "favors" had been extended in granting commissions, advancements, and assignments in our navy and army by the heads of those departments?[8]

Senator Brooks's serious charges and other criticisms of the administration heightened the demand for a further inquiry into the disaster. The Roberts report itself merely raised many crucial issues without resolving them. Furthermore, the exclusion of Congress from participating in the first official investigation of Pearl Harbor only antagonized administration opponents to a greater extent. Senator Walsh had already announced that his Naval Affairs Committee was likely to investigate the circumstances surrounding the attack more fully, implying an examination of the role of Washington officials. On January 25 he announced that his committee would begin an analysis of the Roberts report for what guidance it might give in preparing future legislation and to determine if further scrutiny of high naval authorities was necessary.[9] Congressman Melvin Maas (Republican, Minnesota), ranking Republican on the House Naval Affairs Committee and strong advocate of a big navy,

---

[7] *Chicago Tribune*, January 25, 1942, p. 15; *Washington Post*, January 26, 1942, pp. 1–2; *New York Times*, January 27, 1942, p. 4; Congress, *Congressional Record*, 77th Cong., 2d sess., 1942, 88, pp. 952, A253–255.

[8] *Chicago Tribune*, January 26, 1942, pp. 1, 4.

[9] *New York Times*, January 27, 1942, pp. 1, 4.

agreed with Walsh that a new investigation was imperative. Disturbed that Kimmel and Short had been unfairly singled out in the report, he declared that "the tragedy [of Pearl Harbor] is the tragedy of the system not of the individual."[10]

Hamilton Fish (Republican, New York), the ranking Republican on the House Foreign Affairs Committee, found the recent debate over the Roberts report a propitious time to speak out against administration personnel. Fish, a well-known isolationist and an arch-enemy of the president, represented Roosevelt's own Dutchess County. There was a standing order at the White House that Fish was never to be invited under any circumstances. With an equally strong grudge against the Democratic administration, he denounced the Roberts report as "vague" and demanded a further investigation to "let the chips fall where they may." He especially branded Secretary Knox as a prime culprit. "In any other country," he stated, "the head of the navy would have been removed for the disaster to our navy on Dec. 7...."[11]

By January 27 the individual criticisms of the report proliferated into a more widespread assault on the administration. The key House committees debated whether they should consider further investigation. Congressman May, backing off from his initial interest in court-martial proceedings, decided that the Military Affairs Committee would mark time for the present. "I will wait the President's action on the Roberts report before putting the question to the committee," he said, "But if he doesn't do something we will." The most threatening noises came from the Naval Affairs Committee, where the possibility of a new inquiry was gaining momentum under the leadership of Congressman Maas. The subject of a "thorough study" came during a closed session of the committee on the morning of January 27. The intention of the Republican members was to reexamine the circumstances of the disaster, placing special emphasis on the extent of administration involvement.[12]

The threat of a congressional investigation also arose during

[10] *Chicago Tribune*, January 27, 1942, p. 1; *New York Times*, January 27, 1942, p. 4.
[11] *Chicago Tribune*, January 27, 1942, p. 1; *New York Times*, January 27, 1942, p. 4.
[12] *New York Times*, January 28, 1942, p. 5.

the House floor debate over a major naval appropriations bill. Assistant Minority Leader John W. Ditter (Republican, Pennsylvania) suggested a possible joint House-Senate investigation of Pearl Harbor. In a bold statement, Clare E. Hoffman (Republican, Michigan) placed the blame at the feet of the president: "So long as we have a Commander in Chief who claims credit for all the good things he should not shirk his responsibility and try to pass it on to someone down the line."[13]

Two days after these upheavals, the Democratic regulars mounted a counterattack. In the House Naval Affairs Committee meeting on January 29, they defeated Maas's motion for an investigation by a vote of fourteen to six; in an executive session of the committee, they returned a negative vote on a motion to table a request for the production of the Roberts commission's testimony and documentary evidence. This outcome precluded other congressional committees from initiating further investigations at the time. Maas and his cohorts were clearly disappointed. The Minnesota congressman lamented: "I think it is regrettable that the committee voted as it did. The Roberts report settled nothing fundamental. It fixed the local blame, but not the real cause of the Pearl Harbor disaster. . . ."[14]

For the present, the administration forces had prevented a threatening inquiry. Roosevelt, concerned about the potentially disruptive nature of such an investigation, had kept informed of the debate. On January 29 House Majority Leader John W. McCormack (Democrat, Massachusetts) alerted the president that Congressman James W. Mott (Republican, Oregon), the second-ranking minority member on the Naval Affairs Committee, was attempting to keep the issue alive by requesting that the stenographic report and documents of the Roberts commission be brought before the committee. McCormack believed that action was a "preliminary step of a drive for a Congressional Investigation," and he got Chairman Vinson to table Mott's request. He added that Democrats also stifled a move for an investigation in the Senate. Roosevelt's response to Mott's action was stern: "If you think it would be a good

[13] Ibid.
[14] Ibid., January 30, 1942, p. 4; *Chicago Tribune*, January 30, 1942, p. 1, 5.

thing to have me send for Mott and give him a fatherly talk about how a war has to be run, I will do so." Nothing came of the president's threat because of Vinson's and McCormack's quick maneuvering.[15]

Having averted a politically sensitive investigation, the most important Pearl Harbor issue remaining for the administration was what to do with Kimmel and Short. Since the Roberts report had charged the commanders with dereliction of duty, and since the administration publicly supported that conclusion, some official action was imperative. There appeared to be three realistic choices: reassign the commanders, initiate court-martial proceedings against them, or order their retirement. Reassignment was out of the question, for it was inconsistent with the findings of the commission. The viable choices were court-martial—advocated by a number of congressional leaders—or retirement. In the month following the release of the Roberts report, the administration decided upon what they hoped would be the solution to a knotty problem.

On January 26 General Marshall and Secretary Stimson discussed what to do with respect to General Short.[16] In a letter to Marshall, Short had stated his preference to remain on active duty, but he hesitantly enclosed a retirement application "so that you may use it should you consider it desirable to submit it at any time in the future."[17] Stimson was reluctant to act too hastily lest he and the chief of staff give the impression that they were releasing the commanders without punishment because they felt guilty themselves. But after their meeting Marshall wrote Stimson expressing

[15] McCormack to FDR, January 29, 1942; FDR to McCormack, February 3, 1942; McCormack to Edwin M. Watson, February 6, 1942, Box 13, Official File 400, Franklin D. Roosevelt Papers, Franklin D. Roosevelt Presidential Library, Hyde Park, N.Y.

[16] According to Stimson, the president had virtually left the decision in their hands. See diary of Henry L. Stimson, January 26, 1942, XXXVII, 67, Henry L. Stimson Papers, Manuscripts and Archives, Sterling Memorial Library, Yale University, New Haven, Conn.; Stimson to Cramer, undated memorandum in U.S. Congress, *Pearl Harbor Attack: Hearings before the Joint Committee on the Pearl Harbor Attack*, 79th Cong., 1st sess., pt. 18, p. 3203.

[17] Short to Marshall, January 25, 1942, Box 3, Husband E. Kimmel Collection, Division of Rare Books and Special Collections, University of Wyoming Library, Laramie; Short's testimony in Congress, *Pearl Harbor Attack*, pt. 7, pp. 3133ff.

his opinion that Short should be retired immediately and that it should be done "quietly without any publicity at the moment."[18]

The political ramifications of a court-martial versus retirement seemed to be considerable enough to avoid rushing into a quick decision. Stimson took particular note of the legal advice of the army's Judge Advocate General Myron C. Cramer. In a memorandum to Marshall, Cramer stated that Short was legally subject to a general court-martial or the president could summarily discharge him. Cramer, however, made a convincing case against court-martial, surmising that the results of such a trial would be too unpredictable. If Short were to be acquitted or sentenced to anything less than dismissal, the army and the War Department would be accused of whitewashing the Hawaiian commander. On the other hand, if the court ordered dismissal, critics would charge the administration with persecuting him. Cramer added that such a trial might disrupt the war effort by disclosing secret information and sapping officers from the ranks to serve as witnesses or board members. Faced with a choice between equally onerous alternatives, the JAG recommended a compromise solution—accept Short's retirement in coordination with similar action by the navy with respect to Kimmel.[19]

After a war plans session at the White House on January 28, Stimson met in private with Roosevelt and, among other things, discussed the question of Kimmel and Short. The president informed the secretary that Kimmel had applied for retirement; Stimson said that Short had done the same and added his objections to an immediate court-martial. Roosevelt then outlined a plan of action: The War and Navy departments were to wait for a week and then announce that both former commanders had applied for retirement and that the matter was under study. A week later the departments were to accept the retirement applications with the proviso that the

[18] Diary of Henry L. Stimson, January 26, 1942, XXXVII, 67, microfilm, Stimson Papers; Marshall to Stimson, January 26, 1942, in Congress, *Pearl Harbor Attack*, pt. 7, p. 3139.

[19] Cramer to Marshall, January 27, 1942, memorandum, Army Pearl Harbor Board Files, Box 57, Record Group 107, National Archives, Washington, D.C. (exhibit in Congress, *Pearl Harbor Attack*, pt. 18, pp. 3205–3207); diary of Henry L. Stimson, January 26, 1942, XXXVII, 67, microfilm, Stimson Papers.

action did not bar future courts-martial. Stimson's objections to an immediate trial were to be used as justification for the retirement plan.[20]

Stimson put the plan into operation. He wrote Secretary Knox about suggestions for dealing with Kimmel and Short and enclosed a proposed statement with a saving clause which disclaimed the retirement as "a condonation of any offense" and proclaimed that it would not prejudice any action on behalf of the government.[21] Concurrently, Knox and the Navy Department were examining the retirement question. Not only did the secretary seek the opinion of the navy's judge advocate general, but—largely at the request of the president—he also obtained the advice of the attorney general. The results of his study coincided closely with the opinion of the War Department.[22]

The War and Navy departments had spent considerable time on the retirement question, including much quibbling over wording of the proposed statement. They worked deliberately to avoid an incident that would subject their departments to public criticism. Finally, with the letters composed, they made plans to formally accept the retirement requests of the Hawaiian commanders. Acceptance of Short's request was handed to him on February 18, and Kimmel's followed soon thereafter.[23]

Kimmel had been as reluctant as Short to submit his application. He had done so only after being notified that the general had

[20] Stimson and Roosevelt, January 28, 1942, notes of meeting, Pearl Harbor File, Record Group 125, National Archives, Washington, D.C.

[21] Cramer to Stimson, January 31, 1942, memorandum, Army Pearl Harbor Board Files, Box 57, Record Group 107, National Archives (exhibit in Congress, *Pearl Harbor Attack*, pt. 18, pp. 3208–3210); Stimson to Knox, February 14, 1942, Records of the Secretary of the Navy, Record Group 80, National Archives, Washington, D.C. (exhibit in Congress, *Pearl Harbor Attack*, pt. 19, p. 3907).

[22] Acting assistant solicitor general to assistant judge advocate general, February 14, 1942, memorandum; assistant judge advocate general to assistant solicitor general, February 14, 1942, and attached proposed letter to Kimmel, February 14, 1942, Pearl Harbor File, Box 23, Record Group 125, National Archives.

[23] Diary of Henry L. Stimson, February 18, 1942, XXXVII, 140, microfilm, Stimson Papers; memorandum by J. H. Hilldring, February 17, 1942, in Congress, *Pearl Harbor Attack*, pt. 19, pp. 3800–3801.

submitted a request, inferring this was a suggestion for him to do likewise.[24] The exchange between the Navy Department and Kimmel, however, had clearly disillusioned him. While prepared to accept the consequences of his actions, although not believing himself guilty of derelictions, Kimmel was unwilling to be publicly sacrificed. As he told Admiral Stark, "You must appreciate that the beating I have taken leaves very little that can be added to my burden."[25] Short, likewise, was upset about the adverse publicity he would receive, but it was Kimmel who would vociferously defend himself against the charges of the Roberts commission and the implications of his retirement throughout the war and after. For the moment, they both waited silently for the administration to make public its policy.

Although everything was ready for the disclosure of the retirement applications, the plan was almost subverted when the president suddenly reversed his directive to the service departments. Before the retirement notices were publicized, Roosevelt called Stimson and Knox to the White House for a conference. "He wished us," Stimson said, "to keep the matter 'in cold storage' until he could see us." The president's action caught the secretaries completely off guard. Stimson was particularly concerned that the delay might "leak out in garbled form from sources near the defendants. . . ." He hoped the president realized that fact.[26] At the White House meeting, held on February 25, Roosevelt said that the public temper required courts-martial for the Hawaiian commanders. He preferred to have Kimmel and Short themselves request the trials, in which case they could be delayed until a time "commensurate with the public interest." The president did not want to castigate the of-

[24] Kimmel to Stark, February 22, 1942, Box 3, Kimmel Collection (exhibit in Congress, *Pearl Harbor Attack*, pt. 17, pp. 2729–2730). See also Kimmel to Knox, January 26, 1942; Knox to Kimmel, January 28, 1942, Pearl Harbor File, Box 23, Record Group 125, National Archives (exhibits in Congress, *Pearl Harbor Attack*, pt. 17, p. 2732).

[25] Kimmel to Stark, February 22, 1942, Box 3, Kimmel Collection; Kimmel to Knox, January 26, 1942, Pearl Harbor File, Box 23, Record Group 125, National Archives. See also Congress, *Pearl Harbor Attack*, pt. 17, pp. 2728ff., for further correspondence between Kimmel and Short on the retirement issue.

[26] Diary of Henry L. Stimson, February 20, 1942, XXXVII, 144, microfilm, Stimson Papers.

ficers too severely, but merely issue a light reprimand sufficient to placate public opinion.

The secretaries realized that Roosevelt had completely changed his mind about the fate of the commanders, but they were obliged to follow the orders. Stimson first notified a stunned General Marshall about the changes. Then, as a way of avoiding some serious repercussions, he decided to inform Short and Kimmel before the retirement notification was made public.[27] The revised plan faltered when the army judge advocate general indicated that the commanders themselves could not as a matter of right ask for courts-martial; such trials must originate from sworn charges and specifications. After discussing the matter with Cramer, Marshall, and others, the two secretaries arranged a compromise with the president which coupled the original retirement announcement with a statement declaring that they would prepare charges of dereliction of duty. The trial would be held only when the "interest and safety" of the United States permitted. With the decision reached, they made a simultaneous announcement on February 28.[28]

The publicizing of Kimmel's and Short's retirements ended, momentarily at least, two months of debate over the question of responsibility and the Roberts report. Much to the relief of the administration, Pearl Harbor appeared to be publicly defused "for the duration." The respite from controversy was much shorter than they envisioned. The decision to take a middle course between dismissing the charges against the local commanders and ordering court-martial proceedings did not produce the desired results. Instead of muting the debate, the supposed compromise focused attention upon the plight of the Hawaiian commanders. By retiring them in disgrace, with the threat of future punishment hanging over their heads, the administration created scapegoats on whose fate critics would find cause to reopen the controversy. In the last three years of the war the alleged derelictions of Kimmel and Short would become the focal point for the continuing Pearl Harbor debate.

[27] Ibid., February 25, 1942, XXXVII, 158.
[28] Cramer to Marshall, February 26, 1942, Army Pearl Harbor Board Files, Box 35, Record Group 107, National Archives (exhibit in Congress, *Pearl Harbor Attack*, pt. 19, pp. 3809–3810). See also news releases, February 28, 1942, in Congress, *Pearl Harbor Attack*, pt. 19, pp. 3811–3815.

5

New Battle Lines

AFTER Secretaries Knox and Stimson announced the retirement of Admiral Kimmel and General Short on February 28, the remainder of 1942 brought forth no dramatic revelations to rekindle the debate over Pearl Harbor responsibility. The first anniversary of the attack passed with little of the intensity which had characterized the January and February debates. Of course, innumerable nationwide ceremonial services eulogized the casualties of the disaster in what would become an annual ritual,[1] but even when the Office of War Information released a thorough damage report that month, only the most perfunctory comments appeared in the press.[2]

Thoughts of Pearl Harbor were still remote in the late summer of 1943, but by autumn Democrats and Republicans were embroiled in the controversy again. The congressional election of 1942 was the harbinger of the dispute, despite the fact that the Hawaii disaster was not a burning issue. Only in cases where the administration was interested in purging the most vocal of the prewar isolationists who continued to speak out on war responsibility, such as Hamilton Fish,

[1] See various letters in Box 13, Official File 400; Official File 335; and Box 8, President's Personal File 1820, Franklin D. Roosevelt Papers, Franklin D. Roosevelt Presidential Library, Hyde Park, N.Y. See also Sydney S. Weinberg, "Wartime Propaganda in a Democracy: America's Twentieth-Century Information Agencies" (Ph.D. diss., Columbia University, 1969), p. 268; U.S. Congress, *Congressional Record*, 77th Cong., 2d sess., 1942, 88, pp. 9050–9051, 9347–9348, A4368–4369, A4439; Samuel I. Rosenman, *Working with Roosevelt*, p. 313; *New York Times*, December 7, 1942, pp. 1, 8.

[2] Press conference 865, December 4, 1942, in *Complete Presidential Press Conferences of Franklin D. Roosevelt*, XX, 278–279; *New York Times*, December 3, 1942, p. 24; December 6, 1942, pp. 1, 10; *Life* 13 (December 14, 1942): 31.

Wayland Brooks, and Clare Hoffman, did it emerge even tangential-ly.[3] The overall impact of the election, however, helped to insure the reemergence of the issue. The election produced large gains for the Republicans, who acquired forty-four additional seats in the House of Representatives and nine in the Senate. The GOP now had thirty-seven senators—enough to block a two-thirds vote—and in the House the Democratic majority dropped to as low as two. A steep decline in voter turn-out due to wartime migration, which caused the loss of vital draft-age voters and the working classes for the Democrats, and the surprisingly stable Republican vote meant that the election was a victory for the conservatives. Some of the most prominent liberals and New Deal supporters in Congress were defeated, while some of the most conservative and vehement isola-tionist Republicans and a healthy number of southern Democrats were victorious. The 1942 election aided in strengthening a coalition between Republicans and southern Democrats begun in the late 1930's, and it came close to giving control of Congress to Roosevelt's opponents. In this environment the reintroduction of the Pearl Har-bor debate in Congress could mean a serious challenge to the ad-ministration's hold over the war responsibility question and could develop into a potentially significant issue in the 1944 presidential election.[4]

December 7, 1943, marked the second anniversary of the "day of infamy" and also the date on which expired the time limit of the statute of limitations for prosecuting the Hawaiian commanders.

[3] *Newsweek* 20 (August 24, 1942): 76; (November 16, 1942): 43–46; Roland Young, *Congressional Politics in the Second World War*, pp. 169ff.; Congress, *Congressional Record*, 77th Cong., 2d sess., 1942, 88, pp. 6787, A1465; Independent Committee of the 26th District (New York), May, 1942, letter/flyer, President's Personal File 7820; Pauley to FDR, December 14, 1942, memorandum, and "Explanation and Comments on Election," Box 8, President's Personal File 1820, Roosevelt Papers; "List of Reasons for Demo-cratic Defeat, 1942," Box 1156, Democratic National Committee Papers, Franklin D. Roosevelt Presidential Library, Hyde Park, N.Y.

[4] Richard Polenberg, *War and Society: The United States, 1941–1945*, pp. 187–193; memorandum by Hadley Cantril, December 14, 1942, President's Personal File 1820, Roosevelt Papers; Young, *Congressional Politics*, pp. 22ff.; *Newsweek* 20 (August 17, 1942): 35; H. Bradford Westerfield, *Foreign Policy and Party Politics: Pearl Harbor to Korea*, pp. 136ff.; Donald R. McCoy, "Re-publican Opposition during Wartime, 1941–1945," *Mid-America* 49 (July, 1967): 180.

With respect to the broad implications of the Pearl Harbor affair, this legal point would have been insignificant had not Kimmel and Short been charged with dereliction of duty, relieved from command, retired, and publicly discredited. Their fate had become the object of considerable public curiosity, since the debate over responsibility radiated from their case. The president and his advisers realized this fact and did not want quarreling over the commanders' guilt or innocence to interfere with the war effort. The War and Navy departments hoped to prevent recrimination from spreading beyond the local level, cognizant that any severe criticism of Kimmel and Short could be extended to Washington. In Congress the case of the commanders gave administration detractors effective political ammunition. They could manipulate the alleged treatment of the scapegoats by leveling countercharges against high officials, insisting upon an immediate public trial as a means of disclosing embarrassing or controversial information about the role of the administration in the Pearl Harbor affair. Because of the spectrum of interests in the case, the plight of the commanders became a political football between opposing factions.

A few months before the statute of limitations expired, officials in both the War and Navy departments discussed what steps were necessary to keep the possibility of future courts-martial alive. Desirous of presenting a united front, General Marshall ordered Judge Advocate General Cramer to ask the Navy Department what action it was considering. At this time the high navy officials began to construct their policy. Both Rear Adm. Randall Jacobs, chief of the Bureau of Naval Personnel, and Adm. Ernest J. King, commander in chief of the U.S. Fleet, believed that the president should make the final decision. Jacobs also insisted that it was not in the national interest to permit the case to come to trial at that time.[5] Based on the departmental advice and his awareness of the explosive nature of such courts-martial, Secretary Knox decided on a plan of action; he advised Admiral Kimmel not to plead the statute of limitations in bar of trial if orders for such a trial were not issued before De-

[5] L. E. Bratton to Jacobs, August 4, 1943; Jacobs to Knox, August 17, 1943, memorandum, Pearl Harbor File, Box 23, Record Group 125, National Archives, Washington, D.C. (exhibit in U.S. Congress, *Pearl Harbor Attack: Hearings before the Joint Committee on the Pearl Harbor Attack*, 79th Cong., 1st sess., pt. 19, pp. 3955–3957).

cember 7. Although "the public interest and safety would now permit proceeding with your trial," Knox stated candidly, "I further believe that so long as the war continues it will be manifestly impracticable to have a number of important witnesses appear before the court on account of their war duties." In return for Kimmel's guarantee, Knox promised to grant a trial at "the earliest practicable date subsequent to the expiration of the two year period."[6] Kimmel had little choice but to accept the proposition despite his all-consuming desire to obtain an immediate open court-martial. Knox's terms at least increased the chance of an eventual trial.[7]

Taking an example from Knox's action, the War Department decided upon a similar plan for dealing with General Short. Cramer generally supported the idea of coordinating army policy with the navy's. He suggested that in the event Short did not execute a waiver, a "trusted intermediary" could be dispatched to him and if necessary "display Admiral Kimmel's waiver." He also urged the war secretary to avoid "undesirable alternatives" to this policy such as requesting legislation to extend the statute of limitations or ordering an immediate investigation. A final alternative was to drop the matter entirely, but this action would require presidential sanction. Stimson concurred with Cramer's recommendation and ordered him to follow the navy's example and prepare a waiver.[8]

By the end of September, with the waivers in hand, the case of Kimmel and Short seemed safely postponed until after the war. Noting the increased congressional and press interest in the matter, however, the War and Navy departments decided to make some kind of public statement about their action.[9] On October 2 they re-

---

[6] Knox to Kimmel, received August 27, 1943, Pearl Harbor File, Box 23, Record Group 125, National Archives (exhibit in Congress, *Pearl Harbor Attack*, pt. 19, p. 3953). See also John Wheeler to Knox, September 30, 1943; Knox to Wheeler, November 15, 1943; Mansfield to Knox, November 20, 1943; Knox to Mansfield, November 22, 1943, Records of the Secretary of the Navy, Box 39, Record Group 80, National Archives, Washington, D.C.

[7] Kimmel to Knox, September 7, 1943; waiver, September 7, 1943, Army Pearl Harbor Board Files, Record Group 107, National Archives, Washington, D.C. (exhibit in Congress, *Pearl Harbor Attack*, pt. 19, pp. 3950–3951).

[8] Cramer to Stimson, September 10, 1943; Stimson to Cramer, September 10, 1943; Stimson to Short, September 18, 1943; waiver, September 20, 1943, Army Pearl Harbor Board Files, Box 57, Record Group 107, National Archives (exhibits in Congress, *Pearl Harbor Attack*, pt. 19, pp. 3819, 3823–3825).

[9] Cramer to Stimson, September 27, 1943, memorandum, Army Pearl

leased an abbreviated joint announcement declaring that the courts-martial of the Hawaiian commanders had been deferred until "an appropriate time."[10]

As the deadline of the statute of limitations rapidly approached, congressional interest in the Pearl Harbor issue revived. A fundamental question of authority arose: Did Congress have a responsibility to intervene in this case? The consensus was definitely yes, but the manner of the involvement was still unclear. Should Congress ignore the termination of the statute and accept the waivers as sufficient? Should they demand an immediate trial? Or should they write legislation that would extend the commanders' liability? Given the variety of loyalties, partisanships, and political motivations and the pressures of the war effort, the last choice was the only compromise likely to appease Democrats and Republicans.

On December 1 Congressman Dewey Short introduced House Joint Resolution 199, which would extend the statute of limitations. Short had consistently advocated court-martial of the commanders in order to publicly air the Pearl Harbor issue more fully: "It is a bit strange that these high-ranking officers are not free to tell fully their side of the story. Is someone else being protected by their silence?" Doubting that the signed waivers had sufficient legal standing, he proposed extending the statute of limitations for a year after the signing of peace with Japan. The resolution passed the House over light opposition and was sent to the Senate.[11]

House Joint Resolution 199 came to the Senate on December 7, allowing little time to debate its merits. But as soon as Majority Leader Barkley brought the resolution onto the floor for consideration, Bennett Champ Clark (Democrat, Missouri), outspoken critic of the administration, assailed it: ". . . I am opposed to congressional action to connive at the postponement of the trial of Kimmel and Short so that the delay may be availed of for the purpose of protecting others." Barkley tried to articulate the administration's position

---

Harbor Board Files, Box 57, Record Group 107, National Archives (exhibit in Congress, *Pearl Harbor Attack*, pt. 19, pp. 3828–3829).

[10] *New York Times*, October 3, 1943, p. 44.

[11] Congress, *Congressional Record*, 78th Cong., 1st sess., 1943, 89, pp. 10189, 10314, 10320–10321. See also *New York Times*, December 7, 1943, p. 18.

that any consideration of Pearl Harbor should be postponed until after the war, but Clark pounced upon these statements with a diatribe against Stimson and Knox. He accused them of perpetuating "disgraceful dereliction of duty" by not bringing the Hawaiian commanders to trial, and he decried as "hokum" the idea that the United States was unprepared for the Pearl Harbor attack. He then attempted to reduce the time limit on the statute in order to force an immediate trial. In the face of such contention, a compromise was mandatory. In its final form the Senate version of the resolution extended the statute only six months.[12]

When Congress passed the bill on to the president, it was quickly referred to the War, Navy, and Justice departments for their recommendations. Attorney General Francis Biddle had no objection to the resolution, although he felt it was not likely to have the effect its sponsors desired and was, at best, innocuous.[13] The War and Navy departments scrutinized it much more intensely, since they were apprehensive that Congress would undermine their prerogatives in the case. In the end they tolerated the passage of the legislation but had serious reservations about its effectiveness in extending the period of limitation. Stimson also believed that the resolution contained many "obvious ambiguities" which, if resolved, would be contrived in favor of the accused, and he was unwilling to let Short escape punishment. "In case [Short] should change his mind," the secretary asserted, "and plead [the statute], if the court held the plea still valid, we could still punish him for conduct unbecoming a gentleman and dismiss him from the Army on that score."[14] With general acquiescence to the resolution, Roosevelt

[12] Congress, *Congressional Record*, 78th Cong., 1st sess., 1943, 89, pp. 10347–10350. See also Barkley to Stimson, December 7, 1943, transcript of telephone conversation, microfilm reel 127, Henry L. Stimson Papers, Manuscripts and Archives, Sterling Memorial Library, Yale University, New Haven, Conn.; Allen Drury, *A Senate Journal, 1943–1945*, pp. 17–18.

[13] Biddle to Harold D. Smith, December 13, 1943, Box 74, Official File 5708, Roosevelt Papers; Biddle to Smith, December 9, 1943, Army Pearl Harbor Board Files, Record Group 107, National Archives (exhibit in Congress, *Pearl Harbor Attack*, pt. 19, pp. 3923–3934).

[14] Diary of Henry L. Stimson, December 10, 1943, XLV, 109–110, microfilm, Stimson Papers; Cramer to Walsh, December 9, 1943, transcript of telephone conversation; Cramer to Legislative and Liaison Division, War Department General Staff, December 10, 1943, Army Pearl Harbor Board Files, Box 26, Record Group 107, National Archives; Stimson to Harold Smith, December

signed it December 20, almost two weeks after the statute had run out. This episode was a stop-gap measure at best, since the only certainty which the extension promised was another political battle in six months.[15]

Although the officials of the War and Navy departments were clearly unwilling to begin court-martial proceedings during the war, the Navy Department in early 1944 decided to initiate a secret investigation of Pearl Harbor—the first since the Roberts commission. Increased interest in Admiral Kimmel's case, generated first by the presidential inquiry, then by the debate on the statute of limitations, and finally by the demand of the admiral and his supporters for a day in court, precipitated the investigation. Also, the Navy Department realized that unless it acted quickly, much important testimony crucial to an eventual court-martial could be forever lost because of the death or haziness of memory of the principal officers familiar with the Pearl Harbor case.

Selected to head the new inquiry was Adm. Thomas C. Hart, former commander of the U.S. Asiatic Fleet, who was presently serving on the Navy General Board and carrying out public relations assignments. Secretary Knox set up Hart as a one-man agency empowered to administer oaths, select and subpoena witnesses, and take testimony in the field. He was instructed to interfere with the war effort as little as possible.[16]

The order for the investigation provided that Admiral Kimmel could participate to protect his interests. He would have the right to be present during the interrogations, to have counsel, to testify, and to introduce and examine witnesses. In advance of the formal acknowledgment Hart wrote a personal note to the retired admiral telling him of the coming inquiry and explaining his rights in it. But Kimmel believed that the offer included too many stipulations that

10, 1943 (exhibit in Congress, *Pearl Harbor Attack*, pt. 19, pp. 3925–3926); Knox to Harold Smith, December 11, 1943, Official File 5708, Box 74, Roosevelt Papers.

[15] Wayne Coy to M. C. Latta, December 18, 1943; Rosenman to FDR, December 20, 1943, memorandum, statement by the president, December 20, 1943, Official File 5708, Box 74, Roosevelt Papers.

[16] Reminiscences of Thomas C. Hart, Oral History Project, Columbia University (*New York Times* microfiche), pp. 205ff.; "Precept . . . , February 12, 1944," in Congress, *Pearl Harbor Attack*, pt. 26, pp. 3–4.

would "place his fate completely at the mercy of the Secretary." Thus, he declined to participate.[17] Sometime later he learned that Knox was disappointed that he refused to take part in the proceedings, since they were supposedly instituted at the admiral's request as an excellent opportunity to preserve testimony. Adm. Thomas Gatch, the navy judge advocate general, also thought Kimmel had been "badly advised," since he believed the inquiry was established to clear the Hawaiian commander. However, after having gone through the trauma of the Roberts investigation and the retirement episode, and after being frustrated in his persistent attempts for an immediate public trial, Kimmel was utterly skeptical that the Navy Department would treat him fairly.[18]

Given Kimmel's feelings, Hart decided not to call him or his [Hart's] close friend, former Chief of Naval Operations Harold R. Stark, who was not immediately threatened by court-martial, to testify. Instead, in mid-February, 1944, he proceeded with the interrogations, which took him all over the world. During Hart's approximately six months of inquiry he recorded the testimony of forty high naval officials—mostly admirals.[19] Although he was not required to submit a report along with the evidence gathered, he drew some significant conclusions from his task which were not recorded in the official record of his inquiry submitted on June 15. Hart confided to Admiral Stark that even while the inquiry was kept within narrow limits, it threw some suspicion on the Navy Department's role in the Hawaiian debacle.[20]

The Hart inquiry was not made public until after the war, and

[17] Hart to Kimmel, February 15, 1944, Box 3, Husband E. Kimmel Collection, Division of Rare Books and Special Collections, University of Wyoming Library, Laramie; Husband E. Kimmel, *Admiral Kimmel's Story*, pp. 158–159; Reminiscences of Thomas C. Hart, Oral History Project, Columbia University, pp. 206–208; Hart to Kimmel, February 17, 1944; Kimmel to Hart, February 19, 1944, in Congress, *Pearl Harbor Attack*, pt. 26, pp. 473–474.

[18] Kimmel to Rugg, April 8, 1944; Kimmel to Short, March 8, 1944, Box 3; conference of David I. Walsh, Edward B. Hanify, Charles B. Rugg, May 27, 1944, memorandum, Box 35, Kimmel Collection.

[19] Hart inquiry proceedings in Congress, *Pearl Harbor Attack*, pt. 26. See also Reminiscences of Thomas C. Hart, Oral History Project, Columbia University, p. 208.

[20] Hart to Stark, May 20, 1944; Hart to Stark, June 28, 1944; Stark to Hart, June 2, 1944, Thomas C. Hart Papers, Naval History Division, Department of the Navy, Washington, D.C.

therefore its significance could only be guessed at outside of high administration circles. Aside from fulfilling the requirements of his report, however, Hart provided evidence which cast unfavorable light upon the Navy Department's role in the Pearl Harbor disaster and detracted from the conclusions of the Roberts report. The Hart inquiry was an early indication that the secretaries of war and the navy would find it increasingly difficult to keep Pearl Harbor guilt from proliferating.

It was the circumstances surrounding a further extension of the statute of limitations in the summer of 1944 which most dramatically put the Roosevelt administration on the defensive and forced two new wartime investigations. Because they occurred in an election year, these developments had added significance.

The pressure for a public trial of the Hawaiian commanders weighed heavily on the War and Navy departments. Judge Advocate General Gatch shuddered when Secretary Knox, in his April 11 press conference, announced that he would seek the attorney general's legal opinion on the question of Kimmel's court-martial because he was "confused." Fearing that the navy might lose the initiative in the Kimmel case, Gatch quickly drafted a press release which he believed would "do much toward settling this matter—for the duration of the war at least." This release relied upon the prestige of Fleet Admiral King to reinforce the department's standard rebuttal to demands for an immediate trial. It declared that Secretary Knox had received a memorandum from Admiral King reasserting that navy officers serving on the battlefronts could not be withdrawn in order to participate in court-martial proceedings in connection with Pearl Harbor. For added emphasis the release noted that Knox reaffirmed the validity of Kimmel's waiver with "no necessity to construe any acts of Congress on this subject," and it reemphasized that Hart was in the field carrying out his inquiry. "I would certainly feel derelict in my duty," Knox concluded, "if I took from the Fleet and the fighting fronts for court martial proceedings the officers whom Admiral King has placed in those positions."[21]

Kimmel found no solace in these remarks. As he told his son

[21] Gatch to King, April 13, 1944, memorandum, Box 39, Record Group 80; press release, April 14, 1944, Pearl Harbor Files, Record Group 125, National Archives.

Manning: "I presume you have noted the recent maneuvers in Washington by Mr. Knox and his contradictory statements issued in regard to the court martial. From this mass of confusion I think it is becoming quite clear that the Administration has absolutely no intention of bringing General Short and me to trial."[22]

The War Department, taking note of Knox's recent anxieties, was careful not to raise any issues which might put its stated policy in question. It also continued to maintain a posture consistent with that of the Navy Department, although it had no immediate plans for a new inquiry.[23] The inaction of both departments, however, left them vulnerable to criticism.

As the deadline for the 1943 extension of the statute of limitations approached in the spring of 1944, Congress took the initiative in the Pearl Harbor controversy. In April Missouri's Congressman Dewey Short once again publicly demanded courts-martial for the commanders and advocated a further extension of the statute to insure a guarantee for a trial more binding than the departmental waivers.[24] Hamilton Fish, as well, continued his political pressure on the Roosevelt administration and began yet another furor over Washington's culpability. During a routine debate over a naval bill on May 19, he lambasted the Democrats and demanded a public court-martial to "let the people know who was responsible" for the disaster. He insisted that a court-martial would reveal that Adm. J. O. Richardson had protested against berthing the Pacific Fleet in Hawaii "where it could be attacked"— insinuating a serious lapse in high-level policy making.[25]

In the Senate, similar flare-ups occurred in May. Homer Ferguson (Republican, Michigan) set in motion the debate when he introduced a bill to extend the statute beyond the June deadline.

[22] Kimmel to Manning M. Kimmel, April 27, 1944, Box 3, Kimmel Collection. See also Kimmel to Harry E. Yarnell, May 18, 1944; Rugg to R. A. Lavender, April 24, 1944; Rugg to Sinclair Weeks, March 31, 1944; Kimmel to Rugg, April 5, 1944, Box 3, Kimmel Collection.
[23] Cramer to Nelson, May 17, 1944, memorandum; Stimson to Mansfield, May 18, 1944, Army Pearl Harbor Board Files, Box 35, Record Group 107, National Archives (exhibits in Congress, *Pearl Harbor Attack*, pt. 19, p. 3914). See also William J. Hughes to Cramer, Army Pearl Harbor Board Files, Box 26, Record Group 107, National Archives.
[24] *Newsweek* 23 (April 24, 1944): 36–37.
[25] *New York Times*, May 20, 1944, p. 6; May 13, 1944, p. 7.

Arguing that the War, Navy, and Justice departments had yet to prosecute responsible parties, he felt it was fitting to extend the statute again. For Ferguson—as it was for many others—this extension was not merely meant to sidetrack the issue until after the war, but also to force an immediate trial before the fall election.[26]

Given the precedent for partisan hassling over Pearl Harbor responsibility and the added impact of the upcoming presidential election, the debate over the proposed extension in June, 1944, provided an opportunity for Republicans—and some anti–New Deal Democrats—to implicate the White House. What made the debate vastly more significant and potentially more dangerous for the administration than the 1943 incident was that both House and Senate extension resolutions included demands for immediate courts-martial as a means of making public the whole story of the disaster with the hope of embarrassing Roosevelt and extending guilt beyond the local level. Democratic supporters of the president had an ominous task to diffuse the interest in an immediate trial without making it seem that the administration was neglecting the Hawaiian commanders' rights.

The June debate in the Senate over Ferguson's resolution was tame by comparison with the House turmoil. The impact of the legislation would have been extremely threatening to the White House had not the Democrats on the Senate Judiciary Committee eliminated the most objectionable sections. The three-month extension recommended by Ferguson was increased to one year; a provision requiring immediate courts-martial was stricken completely. A spokesman for the committee, Carl A. Hatch (Democrat, New Mexico), defended the revisions, stating that the majority of the members decided to extend the time limit to "conform" with a similar resolution pending in the House, and they struck the section dealing with the filing of charges without attempting to cover up or prevent prosecution. It was clear, nonetheless, than the Democratic members, influenced by army and navy representatives present at the hearings, had taken the sting out of Ferguson's proposal and virtually emasculated its intent.[27]

[26] Congress, *Congressional Record*, 78th Cong., 2d sess., 1944, 90, p. 4960; *New York Times*, May 30, 1944, p. 7; May 31, 1944, p. 8.
[27] Congress, *Congressional Record*, 78th Cong., 2d sess., 1944, 90, pp.

The debate on the Short resolution in the House on June 5 proved to be more emotion-charged, largely because the Republicans were able to mount a serious and energetic offensive. J. Bayard Clark (Democrat, North Carolina), a member of the House Rules Committee, evoked loud boos and cries of "Shame! Shame!" from Republican members when he spoke against the provision to force a wartime inquiry. He concluded that "there are many on the minority side of this Chamber who will be disappointed if they do not find something badly wrong with the prosecution of the war. . . ." This opening statement immediately transformed the debate into a name-calling session. Hamilton Fish, also a member of the Rules Committee, attacked Clark: "I do not believe . . . any speech I have heard recently in the House could create more disunity than the remarks of the gentleman from North Carolina." He then turned to discredit the administration for avoiding the Pearl Harbor question for so long.[28]

As the lines of support and opposition were forming, the debate focused on section 2 of the proposed resolution, which called for immediate court-martial proceedings. Dewey Short and his supporters argued that the country could wait no longer for the "truth" about Pearl Harbor, while the administration partisans, especially McCormack and Emanuel Celler (Democrat, New York), countered. As Celler argued, "Any public court martial now, I say would be a sort of grist to Goebbel's mill and would give aid and comfort to Emperor Hirohito."[29]

On June 6 the debate in the House still raged, but the deadline of the 1943 extension was fast approaching and the luxury of extended debate inevitably had to make way for a decision. In a final attempt to deter Short's plan, some of the Democrats tried to exploit the beginning of the Allies' cross-channel invasion of Europe (D-Day) to rally the chamber to a call for patriotism. This was espe-

---

5281–5287; Drury, *A Senate Journal*, pp. 184–186; D. J. Ramsey to James V. Forrestal, May 29, 31, 1944, memoranda, Box 44, Record Group 80, National Archives; conference of Walsh, Hanify, Rugg, May 27, 1944, Box 35, Kimmel Collection.

[28] Congress, *Congressional Record*, 78th Cong., 2d sess., 1944, 90, pp. 5340 ff. See also *New York Times*, June 6, 1944, p. 8.

[29] Ibid.

cially true of Celler, who believed that in light of the events on
Normandy Beach the resolution to extend the statute of limitation
was "inane." He added: "It would be a splendid contribution on the
part of the Members of the House . . . if we would no longer continue deliberations on this bill and discard it. That would be a
fitting tribute to the brave and intrepid commanders of our armed
forces and the boys under them." Despite this desperate ploy, the
supporters of the resolution would have their way. Realizing the
cause was lost, opposition collapsed, and Short's provisions for a
three-month extension and immediate courts-martial passed by a
vote of 305 to 35.[30]

Everyone was aware that the Republican victory was by no
means complete. Since the Senate and the House bills conflicted, a
conference session would have to resolve the dilemma. Less than
seven hours before the 1943 statute extension ran out, the conference struck a compromise over strong Republican opposition. The
joint resolution provided that the statute would be extended six
months—well beyond election day, but not too long to be forgotten
and brushed aside. More importantly, the section demanding immediate courts-martial was toned down. Instead of calling for immediate trials, it directed the War and Navy departments to reopen
the Pearl Harbor case and investigate it with the intent of using the
information for eventual proceedings.[31]

The Democrats succeeded in putting the threat of immediate
trials beyond election day and seemingly deflated a potentially
powerful campaign issue. But the recent agitation over the extension, its public airing, and the directive ordering army and navy
investigations still gave the Republicans something to exploit in
November if they chose. Also, and most significantly, the new resolution raised the possibility of a political issue for future political
advantage, weakened the administration's control over the Pearl
Harbor question, and kept Roosevelt supporters on the defensive.
All in all, the joint resolution was not a clear victory for anyone;
it merely left the question of responsibility open for more specula-

[30] Congress, *Congressional Record*, 78th Cong., 2d sess., 1944, 90, pp.
5402–5415; *New York Times*, June 7, 1944, p. 11.

[31] Congress, *Congressional Record*, 78th Cong., 2d sess., 1944, 90, pp.
5473ff.; *New York Times*, June 8, 1944, p. 14; *Army and Navy Journal* 81
(June 10, 1944): 1235.

tion. As long as no clear answers were available, the administration had something to worry about.

The duty to fulfill the requirements of the resolution fell upon the War and Navy departments. It was a distasteful task for them to begin new inquiries after months of trying to avoid that very action. While the Senate Judiciary Committee was considering the proposed resolution, both departments followed its progress closely. Navy officials for the moment had not felt threatened because Hart was in the field gathering evidence. On May 29 Captain D. J. Ramsey, who was reporting the activities of the Senate committee, informed the secretary: "I am still of the opinion that there is nothing to get excited about."[32]

With the final passage of the resolution, the departments had something to get excited about. In their recommendations to the president both secretaries advised against signing the legislation, and both included proposed veto messages. They expressed apprehension about Congress becoming too intimately involved in military and naval business and restated that the extension was not legally binding. Both draft veto messages also focused on the investigation directive, emphasizing how detrimental such legislation would be to the prosecution of the war.[33]

From the perspective of the White House, the recommendations of the war and navy secretaries were politically dangerous. A veto of the resolution would create a serious liability in an election year by giving the opposition an issue to exploit. The president, having previously accepted the 1943 resolution, was committed by precedent to the concept of *ex post facto* extension. With respect to the proposed investigations, a negative reaction would admit apprehension about the uncovering of information politically detrimental to the administration. Based on these considerations, Roosevelt took

[32] Ramsey to Forrestal, May 29, 30, 1944, memoranda, Box 44, Record Group 80, National Archives; conference of Walsh, Hanify, Rugg, May 27, 1944, Box 35, Kimmel Collection.

[33] Forrestal to Harold Smith, June 9, 1944, and attached veto message; Stimson to Smith, June 9, 1944, and attached veto message, Box 78, Official File 5708, Roosevelt Papers; Cramer to Hugh Cox, June 8, 1944, transcript of telephone conversation, Army Pearl Harbor Board File, Box 26, Record Group 107, National Archives (exhibit in Congress, *Pearl Harbor Attack*, pt. 19, pp. 3925–3928).

the advice of the attorney general, the Bureau of the Budget director, and other high officials and advisers and decided to approve the resolution. In order to protect against the leaking of important information—especially the code-breaking data—and to insure that the investigations would not interfere with the prosecution of the war, the president's statement was worded carefully. He declared that both the secretary of war and the secretary of the navy had advised against signing the resolution largely on the grounds of national security. "If there were any doubt in my mind," he concluded, "that the resolution might require such action by the Secretaries of War and Navy as would interfere with the successful conduct of the war, I would have withheld my approval from the resolution. I am confident, however, that the Congress did not intend that the investigation of this matter or any proceedings should be conducted in a manner which would interrupt or interfere with the war effort. . . ."[34]

In a rather unusual and audacious manner, Roosevelt publicly exposed the differences in administration circles over the resolution, using the War and the Navy departments' recommendations as a foil. Seemingly, he was attempting to make political capital with his acceptance, demonstrating his willingness to accept the decree of Congress despite the risks to the war effort. Since the investigations required by the new legislation were unlikely to affect the election in any substantive way, Roosevelt had chosen a middle position between rejection and unqualified support of the resolution. But the president's actions would not be sufficient to keep the question of Pearl Harbor responsibility out of the election. The Republicans would try mightily to find some way to employ it and discredit the Democratic foreign policy and Roosevelt's drive for a fourth term.

[34] Statement by the president, June 13, 1944; Rosenman to FDR, June 12, 1944, memorandum; Paul H. Appleby to M. C. Latta, June 10, 1944; Biddle to Smith, June 9, 1944, Box 78, Official File 5708, Roosevelt Papers.

6

A Republican Assault Falls Short

ALTHOUGH the Democrats diluted the politically threatening Republican proposals in the June statute of limitations debates, Pearl Harbor remained a potential campaign issue in the months before the November election. That few political analysts have realized the issue's vitality can be attributed not to its insignificance, but to a failure to take account of the persistence of the war responsibility question. It is also a recurring oversight to forget those queries raised by the defeated party and highlight the strengths of the victors. Hindsight can be deadly, and often the success of a candidate and what that success implies can cloud an understanding of the battle and the elements that were influential. Pearl Harbor, of course, did not prove to be a vital matter on which the election turned, but it was an issue which the Republicans desperately wanted to exploit against the man who had captured the nation's top office an unprecedented three times and who would likely win again unless the GOP could convince the nation that changing the proverbial horse in midstream was absolutely necessary.

A wartime election poses particular difficulties to the opposition party, especially on questions of foreign policy, where discrediting an incumbent could be construed as disloyalty. But central to a Republican victory in 1944 was the imperative to uncover weaknesses in Roosevelt's management of foreign affairs in general and to offer redirection without too severely castigating his conduct of the war in particular. The case to be made was that a younger, fresher, more energetic chief executive—in this case Thomas E. Dewey—could not only carry out the obligations of the war effort but also construct a peace settlement acceptable to Americans. The

GOP had to raise questions about foreign policy and draw a clear line between the administration's outlook and their own alternatives. One way to do this, many Republicans believed, was to question the administration's handling of the war responsibility issue. It remained to be seen whether they could convince voters that the administration's intransigence on the issue represented an intentional concealment of the causes of the debacle.[1]

Aside from the congressional debates over extension of the statute of limitations, other sporadic attacks on the Roosevelt administration helped to keep Pearl Harbor in the press before the opening of the presidential campaign. Senator Rufus Holman (Republican, Oregon) declared in a May 7 campaign speech that the White House had "engineered" opposition to his renomination. In mounting his counterattack he alluded to the Hawaiian debacle, charging that the administration failed to prepare adequately for war. "The reason why Admiral Kimmel and Maj. General Walter C. Short . . . have not been court-martialed," he prodded, "is because 130,000,000 people would rise in rage if they realized how the Commander in Chief had blundered."[2]

More blatant attacks on Roosevelt appeared in extreme right-wing publications. A biting editorial in the July installment of *America Preferred* proclaimed that "American nationalists" were prepared to challenge the fourth-term candidate for president, "whose principal supporters are Josef Stalin, Earl Browder, Sidney Hillman and Walter Lipschitz, alias Winchell. . . ." The article especially challenged the notion that the Japanese air raid was unprovoked. Among other things, it quoted from a letter appearing in the *Saturday Evening Post* (April 14, 1942), written by Congressman Hatton W. Sumners (Democrat, Texas), who had been chairman of the House Judiciary Committee: "We have been a very foolish people, which has made it possible for us politicians to get away with murder. This blaming the Pearl Harbor tragedy upon the treachery of the Japs is like the fellow who has been tickling the

---

[1] For a well-balanced treatment of the importance of foreign policy issues in the 1944 campaign, see Robert A. Divine, *Foreign Policy and U.S. Presidential Elections, 1940–1948*, pp. 91–164. See also Herman Edward Bateman, "The Election of 1944 and Foreign Policy" (Ph.D. diss., Stanford University, 1952).

[2] *New York Times*, May 8, 1944, p. 11.

hind leg of a mule trying to explain his bunged-up condition by blaming the mule for having violated his confidence."[3]

During the summer Republican opponents of Roosevelt were planning to exploit the issue of Pearl Harbor. As early as June the chairman of the steering committee of the Conference of the Minority in the Senate, the influential Robert A. Taft (Republican, Ohio), and the committee's secretary, George H. E. Smith, sought to determine the practicality of Pearl Harbor as a campaign issue. Taft directed Smith to prepare a detailed chronology of the background of the attack and the administration's policy toward Japan. After examining what material was available in published form, and desirous of as much inside information as possible, Smith solicited the aid of Charles B. Rugg, Admiral Kimmel's attorney. Rugg was very willing to oblige.[4] About the same time, Smith wrote Republican National Committee Chairman Herbert Brownell, candidate Dewey, and Senator Arthur H. Vandenberg (Republican, Michigan) to convince them that war responsibility should be considered as "a point of major strategy" in the upcoming election.[5] In a letter outlining his recent activity, Smith explained to Taft that he wanted to see a more effective foreign policy strategy in 1944 than the Republicans demonstrated in 1940. His purpose was to counteract Roosevelt's strategy of appealing for unity in the face of war.[6]

Smith knew the task of discrediting the Democrats' foreign policy would be difficult, especially since Dewey had effectively closed the avenue to criticism of the conduct of the war during the campaign. He believed, however, that Dewey could effectively assail the administration's conduct of the war through an indirect route—a critical analysis of American diplomacy before the war. Smith believed that "with telling documentation" it could be shown that Roosevelt's prewar approach to foreign policy was "so stupid and inept that it constituted a danger to American interests and to world peace which contributed to the ultimate outbreak of the war." He concluded: "That is an issue we cannot allow to go by default as

[3] *America Preferred* 2 (July, 1944): 9–12.
[4] Smith to Rugg, June 23, 1944, Box 657, Robert A. Taft Papers, Library of Congress, Washington, D.C.
[5] Smith to Brownell, July 3, 1944, ibid.
[6] Smith to Taft, July 7, 1944, ibid.

Willkie did in the spring and summer of 1940 when he gave a hearty 'Me, too' to the Roosevelt foreign policy. It is an issue we should not permit the New Deal to slide out of with their smart tactics of confining the campaign to 'domestic issues.' "[7]

Smith's ideas appealed to Republicans. Other members of the party sensed the value of using the issue of Pearl Harbor as a backhanded method of discrediting the Democrats' policy without violating the limitations set by Dewey or criticizing the conduct of the war. In September the GOP began to exploit the Hawaii disaster in a major way. Ironically, the Democrats themselves provided the opportunity. In the August 26 issue of *Collier's*, vice-presidential candidate Harry S Truman called for a consolidation of the army and navy. This suggestion was an outgrowth of his work as chairman of the so-called Truman committee which investigated graft in military contracts during the war. As he noted in the article: ". . . The bitter lessons of the last few years . . . make it plain that we can rely no longer upon chance and luck. The nation's safety must have a more solid foundation." Although most of the article dealt with current conditions which needed correction, he prefaced his argument with a discussion of how the Pearl Harbor attack especially revealed "the danger that lies in a division of responsibilities." Truman was particularly critical of Kimmel and Short, insinuating that they had not been on speaking terms before the air raid and had not established sufficient communications between their headquarters in preparation for a possible attack.[8]

Although the bulk of the article dealt with the alleged weakness in the dual systems of the army and navy and the virtues of a unified command and consolidation, Truman's introductory remarks about Kimmel and Short created a controversy which Republican critics could exploit. Admiral Kimmel himself was among the first to challenge the Missouri senator's aspersions. In a letter to Truman, released to the press, he decried the statement about his conduct as commander in chief of the Pacific Fleet. "Until I am afforded a hearing in open court," he snapped, "it is grossly unjust to repeat false

[7] Smith to Taft, July 10, 1944, memorandum, ibid. See also Smith to Taft, July 12, 1944; Smith to Taft, August 8, 1944, ibid.

[8] Truman, "Our Armed Forces Must Be Unified," *Collier's* 114 (August 26, 1944): 16, 63–64.

charges against me, when, by official action, I have been persistently denied an opportunity to defend myself publicly."[9]

Soon the partisan forces began to rally to Kimmel's defense. Broadcaster Rupert Hughes, whose air time was paid for by southern California Republicans, used the publicity over the Truman article to lambaste the administration. Declaring that the Hawaiian commanders' predicament was an "American Dreyfus Case"—an increasingly common comparison used by Roosevelt's critics—Hughes asserted: "Dreyfus was on Devil's Island for four years. Kimmel and Short will have been in purgatory for three years in December. . . ." Hughes also charged the administration with intentionally covering up the case. "Of course," he added, "if Thomas E. Dewey is elected, the fur will begin to fly. . . . It took a new President of France to get Dreyfus out of his cruel inferno."[10]

An opportunity now arose to cultivate voter doubts about the ability of the Roosevelt administration to prosecute the war effectively. Republicans made the most of the opportunity, especially in the House of Representatives. Hugh Scott (Republican, Pennsylvania) singled out the passages in the well-publicized article which dealt with the Hawaiian commanders and charged that Truman—the possible "Assistant Commander in Chief"—had reopened the question of Pearl Harbor responsibility "and had prejudged it, in allocating the blame, before all the facts have been made known." Calling for full disclosure of the incidents surrounding the disaster, Scott criticized the decision to place the fleet at Hawaii and the administration's relations with Japan before December 7. The Pennsylvania representative raised a series of provocative questions: Why had the fleet been stationed at Pearl Harbor? Why had the president not met with the Japanese prime minister, Prince Fumimaro Konoye, in what might have been the last chance to stave off war? Why had Kimmel not received the extra seaplanes he request-

[9] Kimmel to Truman, August 20, 1944, Box 4, Husband E. Kimmel Collection, Division of Rare Books and Special Collections, University of Wyoming Library, Laramie. See also diary of Harry E. Yarnell, August 19, 1944, Harry E. Yarnell Papers, Naval History Division, Department of the Navy, Washington, D.C.; New York Times, August 22, 1944, pp. 1, 32; Washington Post, August 23, 1944, p. 8; Charles A. Beard, President Roosevelt and the Coming of the War, 1941: A Study in Appearances and Realities, pp. 273–276.

[10] Broadcast transcript, August 30, 1944, Box 1, Kimmel Collection.

ed for protection of the Oahu base? What about a supposed ultimatum which Secretary of State Cordell Hull presented to the
Japanese on November 26, 1941? And in a final query Scott wondered why "the acts of commission and omission at Washington"
were so carefully excluded from the Roberts inquiry.[11]

The following day, Congressman Francis H. Case (Republican,
South Dakota) challenged Roosevelt's bid for a fourth term by
raising the war responsibility issue. Arguing that the Truman article
brought that question into the campaign, he stated that the issue
was inescapable, for if the fourth-term bid succeeded it would be
because of the feeling that Roosevelt alone could run the war and
make peace, "that he is indeed a superman, the one indispensable
man, whose talents will be lost to the country if he is not reelect-
ed. . . ."[12]

Scott's and Case's attacks clearly demonstrated that Pearl Harbor could be used effectively as a way to discredit Roosevelt's past
policies. Yet with the war going well for the Allies in 1944, the
partisan charges would have little impact on the public unless some
new revelations could be uncovered to expose weaknesses or even
derelictions on the part of administration officials. This disclosure
would be a difficult and decidedly sensitive undertaking during wartime, but if successful it would be politically advantageous.

Congressman Forest A. Harness (Republican, Indiana) made
the most dramatic challenge. In a September 11 speech before the
House, he announced that General Short had documentary proof
which would demonstrate that he used "all reasonable care and
precaution" in Hawaii and had acted justifiably in view of the information transmitted from Washington. But Harness's most dramatic accusation was that high officials intentionally withheld vital
information regarding the attack from the Hawaiian Command.
Specifically, he asserted that seventy-two hours before the air raid,
the Australian government advised Washington that a Japanese
aircraft carrier task force was sighted heading toward Hawaii. The
American government was supposedly notified a second and a third

---

[11] U.S. Congress, *Congressional Record*, 78th Cong., 2d. sess., 1944, 90,
pp. 7573–7576; *Chicago Tribune*, September 7, 1944, p. 11.
[12] Congress, *Congressional Record*, 78th Cong., 2d sess., 1944, 90, pp.
7588–7590.

time, forty-eight and twenty-four hours, respectively, before the assault. If this was true, Harness argued, an investigation was clearly in order. He also urged courts-martial for the commanders, declaring that Roosevelt wanted Kimmel and Short to take full responsibility for the success of the attack in order to avoid it himself.[13] The Indiana legislator kept the pressure on the administration when, on September 18, he called for a full-scale congressional investigation of Pearl Harbor which would be required to report its findings in thirty days.[14]

An obvious partisan maneuver, Harness's call for an inquiry, coupled with the rumor of advance notice of the attack, created a storm in Washington. The Republicans in the House believed that the time was right to press the case, despite the apprehension of party men like George Smith, who thought that the new leaks would divert attention from the larger issue of responsibility for the war.[15]

The Democrats quickly realized the potential threat of Harness's assault. Congressman George E. Outland (Democrat, California) led the Democratic rebuttal, calling the accusations "a real below-the-belt blow."[16] Congressman McCormack, likewise, realized the gravity of the charges: "A dangerous rumor of this kind cannot be treated lightly, or brushed aside, as most political statements are, with a smile." In order to counteract Harness's rumors, McCormack announced an official denial that the administration received the alleged messages, and he added that the Australian prime minister termed it "a pure invention." "There would appear to be a bottomless cavern," the majority leader concluded, "wherein cheap politics begets unforgivable war rumors."[17]

Instead of quelling the debate over the new revelations, the

[13] Ibid., pp. 7648–7651.
[14] Ibid., pp. 7866ff.
[15] Smith to Taft, September 11, 1944; Smith to Rugg, September 12, 1944, Box 657, Taft Papers; Taft to Rugg, September 12, 1944, Box 4, Kimmel Collection.
[16] Congress, *Congressional Record*, 78th Cong., 2d sess., 1944, 90, pp. 7960–7961.
[17] Ibid., pp. 8110–8112. See also Stimson to Rayburn, September 19, 1944, transcript of telephone conversation, microfilm reel 128, Henry L. Stimson Papers, Manuscripts and Archives, Sterling Memorial Library, Yale University, New Haven, Conn.

House Democrats actually attracted increasing attention from the press and induced even more vehement charges from Republicans. Congressman Ralph E. Church (Republican, Illinois) leveled a broadside at the Democrats. Defending Harness, he challenged the administration to demonstrate that it was not afraid of the truth by investigating the new charges. And in an attempt to counteract the denials of the War, Navy, and State departments, he produced a statement written by Sidney C. Graves, who had reportedly overheard Sir Owen Dixon, the former Australian ambassador to the United States, discuss the alleged warning at a Washington dinner party on December 7, 1943. Dixon supposedly stated that before Pearl Harbor, when he was in charge of coastal shipping in Australian waters, intelligence sources informed him that a Japanese carrier task force was at sea and that Australia should prepare for an attack. Twenty-four hours later sources believed that the force was not aimed at the island continent but directed against some American possessions. Although Graves's statement did not reconfirm Harness's charge that the United States received this warning, and although Dixon denied the statement, Church believed the incident was sufficient grounds for an inquiry.[18] The Graves affidavit in essence diluted the original charges, but it still received wide publicity.[19]

The conflicting evidence about the Australian affair and the administration's denials of the existence of any such advance warnings finally undermined Harness's case. When asked about the seventy-two-hour warning in his September 22 press conference, Roosevelt artfully brushed aside the issue: "Anybody with information of that kind had better submit [it] to one of these boards that is investigating [Pearl Harbor] now, that's the proper place to go. There will be lots of things like that, flocks of them—morning, noon and night—until the seventh of November."[20]

[18] Congress, *Congressional Record*, 78th Cong., 2d sess., 1944, 90, pp. 8132–8134; statement by Graves, September 21, 1944, Army Pearl Harbor Board Files, Record Group 107, National Archives, Washington, D.C.

[19] For example, see radio commentaries, September 21, 1944, Pearl Harbor Investigation Records, Box 1961, Record Group 165, National Archives, Washington, D.C.; transcript of broadcast by Fulton Lewis, Jr., September 21, 1944, Box 37, Kimmel Collection.

[20] Press conference 969, September 22, 1944, *Complete Presidential Press*

Despite the ease with which Roosevelt dismissed the Australian episode, it was only one of many such issues which could ignite a more substantial debate on war responsibility. Administration officials remained concerned that similar rumors might be dredged up as the campaign developed. The Navy Department, for example, sent word to the White House about August 28 that Dewey's first major campaign speech would deal with the Hawaiian debacle. About one week later Steve Early informed Roosevelt that Charles Rugg was passing information about Pearl Harbor on to Republican leaders, especially to Robert Taft and the Republican National Committee.[21]

Public displeasure with the administration's concealment of information about the disaster and its refusal to investigate the possible culpability of high officials inspired increasing amounts of critical mail to the White House. In one such letter an irate citizen questioned the administration's preparedness program in Hawaii: "The American People demand the TRUTH be told about Pearl Harbor before November 7th, 1944. Did Harry Hopkins transfer 250 Navy planes which were needed at Pearl Harbor before the attack?"[22]

What concerned the president most about the question of responsibility for Pearl Harbor was recent agitation for release of the reports of the ongoing army and navy investigations before election day. He feared that a premature disclosure could only give the opposition an exploitable issue. According to Stimson, Roosevelt was "worried for fear there would be an adverse report by the Grunert Committee [Army Pearl Harbor Board] just before Election. . . .

Conferences of Franklin D. Roosevelt, XXIV, 124. See also Dixon to Hull, September 21, 1944; statement by Frank C. Hanighen, September 25, 1944, Army Pearl Harbor Board Files, Box 1, Record Group 107, National Archives.

[21] M. F. Correa to James V. Forrestal, August 28, 1944, Records of the Secretary of the Navy, Record Group 80, National Archives, Washington, D.C.; Forrestal to FDR, undated, President's Secretary File, Box 80, Franklin D. Roosevelt Papers, Franklin D. Roosevelt Presidential Library, Hyde Park, N.Y.; Early to FDR, September 6, 1944, memorandum; Correa to Forrestal, September 5, 1944, memorandum, Box 24, Stephen T. Early Papers, Franklin D. Roosevelt Presidential Library, Hyde Park, N.Y.

[22] Preston Kline Caye to FDR, September 11, 1944, Official File 400, Roosevelt Papers. See other similar letters in Official Files 400 and 5563 for September, 1944.

The President rather characteristically isn't worried at all about the Navy inquiry but is worried about the Army and was anxious to have the termination of the inquiry postponed until after Election. . . ." Stimson did not believe he could interfere with the investigation while it was in progress, but—like the president—he hoped it would not include politically damaging information.[23] Some War Department officials assumed that the report would be partisan and were convinced that the board included members of antiadministration persuasions.[24]

When the army and navy reports were finally submitted in late October, Roosevelt's anxieties were far from alleviated, because they both contradicted the Roberts report and extended blame to Washington. Consequently, Secretary of War Stimson and the new secretary of the navy, James V. Forrestal, decided to keep them secret— at least until after the election and possibly until the end of the war.[25] In his diary entry of November 4, Henry Morgenthau, Jr., indicated Stimson's concern about keeping the army report from becoming publicly volatile. Morgenthau had talked with the war secretary on that day about issues related to the election, and he wrote: "He sounds more tired than ever. Said he was tired out from working the last two weeks on Pearl Harbor report to keep out anything that might hurt the Pres."[26]

With the military and naval reports safely buried until after the election, the administration could concentrate on counteracting the prevailing rumors and making sure the war responsibility question did not grow in intensity. The impetus for raising Pearl Harbor

[23] Diary of Henry L. Stimson, September 21, 1944, XLVIII, 101–102, microfilm; Stimson to FDR, September 26, 1944, microfilm reel 110, Stimson Papers.

[24] Memorandum by Thomas North, September 20, 1944, Pearl Harbor Investigation Records, Box 1962, Record Group 165, National Archives.

[25] Diary of Henry L. Stimson, October 21, 1944, XLVIII, 173; October 26, 1944, XLVIII, 186–187; November 1, 1944, XLIX, 2, microfilm, Stimson Papers; Forrestal to Orin Murfin, October 21, 1944, Records of the Secretary of the Navy, Box 44, Record Group 80, National Archives; Forrestal to Ernest J. King, October 21, 1944, Box 87, James V. Forrestal Papers, Princeton University Library, Princeton, N.J.

[26] Diary of Henry Morgenthau, Jr., November 4, 1944, Box 6, pp. 1457–1459, Henry Morgenthau, Jr., Collection, Franklin D. Roosevelt Presidential Library, Hyde Park, N.Y.

to the rank of a pivotal campaign issue remained with the Republicans, who continued to prod the White House into an open fight. On September 20, Republican vice-presidential nominee John W. Bricker, speaking to an enthusiastic crowd of ten thousand in Wilkes-Barre, Pennsylvania, accused the administration of withholding facts of the "disgraceful Pearl Harbor episode." Bricker charged that the reason for withholding information was to protect Roosevelt's fourth-term campaign. "I do know," he goaded, "that the New Dealers think it would harm their selfish political interests."[27]

The administration could almost ignore Bricker's harangue and others like it because they had become so commonplace in the last few months of the campaign. But the most foreboding Republican assault was at hand in late September. Rumors circulated that the GOP presidential candidate was finally going to speak out on the war responsibility question in his Oklahoma City speech on September 25. Earlier that day Senator Styles Bridges (Republican, New Hampshire) stated that Dewey had been "gathering facts" about the Pearl Harbor disaster and might use them in a major campaign address. "The Democrats are scared to death," he said, "that the Pearl Harbor question will be brought into the campaign further than it has been."[28]

The rumors about Dewey's intentions were true. Indignant over Roosevelt's accusations of Republican "isolationism" in his electrifying speech at the Teamsters banquet on September 21—better known as the Fala speech—Dewey decided to put aside his prepared comments for the Oklahoma City appearance and, among other things, to challenge the Democratic administration on the war responsibility question.[29] In the speech he charged that the White

[27] *New York Times*, September 21, 1944, p. 15; transcript of broadcast by Morgan Beatty, September 21, 1944, Pearl Harbor Investigation Records, Box 1961, Record Group 165, National Archives.

[28] United Press release, September 25, 1944, Pearl Harbor Investigation Records, Box 1961, Record Group 165, National Archives; *New York Times*, September 26, 1944, p. 7.

[29] Samuel I. Rosenman, comp., *The Public Papers and Addresses of Franklin D. Roosevelt*, XIII, 286–290; Robert E. Sherwood, *Roosevelt and Hopkins: An Intimate History*, p. 820; Robert E. Sherwood, *Working with Roosevelt*, pp. 473–474; *New Republic* 111 (October 2, 1944): 413; *Time* 44 (October 2, 1944): 21–22; *New York Times*, September 24, 1944, pp. 1, 36.

House was accountable for "the shocking state of our defense program" in the four months before Pearl Harbor, and he hammered on the lack of preparedness for war. Whipping up enthusiasm for his charges, he added: "Now listen to this: 'When the treachery of Pearl Harbor came we were not ready.' Mr. Roosevelt was that [statement] from Dr. Goebbels? The man who said that was Alben Barkley, your majority leader of the United States Senate. And where do you suppose Alben Barkley said 'When the treachery of Pearl Harbor came we were not ready?' Right in his speech nominating Mr. Roosevelt for a fourth term."[30]

The Oklahoma City speech gained extensive national attention and again put the Democrats on the defensive. Almost immediately Samuel Rosenman and other important advisers prepared a lengthy analysis of and response to Dewey's speech, attempting to demonstrate that he had pulled phrases out of context. Rosenman sent his handiwork to FDR and the Democratic National Committee. Paul A. Porter, director of publicity for the committee, sent the analysis to all Democratic speakers for use in their attacks on the Republicans.[31] On October 14 the Democrats publicly released the whole analysis, but Dewey responded that it merely proved the truth of the statements he made.[32]

Although Dewey's charges were not new, the fact that he had taken his party's leadership on the war responsibility matter this late in the campaign changed the complexion of Pearl Harbor as a political issue. If Dewey could uncover new evidence that would catch the electorate's attention, he might be able to break the Democrats' stranglehold on all queries dealing with the war and its aftermath.

As circumstances unfolded, Dewey's use of Pearl Harbor ended almost as quickly as it arose. In late September, Chief of Staff

[30] *Washington Post*, September 26, 1944, pp. 1, 6; *New York Times*, September 26, 1944, pp. 1, 15; transcript of broadcast by Fulton Lewis, September 26, 1944, Pearl Harbor Investigation Records, Box 1961, Record Group 165, National Archives.

[31] Rosenman to FDR, October 2, 1944; Rosenman to Early, October 2, 1944; open letter by Paul A. Porter, October 4, 1944; analysis of Oklahoma City speech, Box 26, Early Papers.

[32] *New York Times*, October 15, 1944, pp. 1, 39; October 16, 1944, pp. 1, 61.

George Marshall discovered that the Republicans intended to launch "a detailed attack" on the administration, employing the war responsibility issue. He was also aware that someone, presumably someone in the armed services, had informed Dewey of the navy's ability to break the highest Japanese diplomatic codes before the war and that the Republican standard-bearer was prepared to make that fact public. Marshall and other high officials feared the disclosure of the ultrasecret code breaking for reasons of both national security and the immediate political consequences. They could not forget that American cryptanalysts had invested much painstaking effort in analyzing the character of the Japanese machine used to encode diplomatic communiqués and had devised the Magic machine which could decipher them. And although the American codebreakers were cracking other important and newer enemy codes, the Japanese continued to employ the Magic codes originally involved in the Pearl Harbor affair to transmit important messages. The Magic intercepts did not include information about specific military or naval deployments, but they still provided data vital to the war effort. For example, they revealed some of Hitler's intentions regarding Europe, which were gleaned from Japanese diplomatic messages between Berlin and Tokyo. But the protection of the specific codes was secondary to a broader concern that the disclosure of Magic would lead to the elimination of the wide range of secret information that the United States might still acquire from various codes and ciphers. After all, the Japanese were unaware that the American cryptanalysts were reading their messages and continued to transmit important information by means of Magic.[33]

On a baser plane, the high officials realized that publicizing the code breaking also had political ramifications. The opposition party could exploit the administration's foreknowledge of the Japanese diplomatic secrets, which—they could argue—should have prevented the Pearl Harbor attack. And although it was only con-

[33] Marshall to Truman, September 22, 1945, memorandum in diary of James V. Forrestal, p. 501, Forrestal Papers; memorandum by Harry Hopkins (re: Marshall-Dewey letters), undated, Box 141, Harry Hopkins Papers, Franklin D. Roosevelt Presidential Library, Hyde Park, N.Y.; Marshall to Dewey, September 25, 1944, Box 4, Kimmel Collection; Roberta Wohlstetter, *Pearl Harbor: Warning and Decision*, p. 177.

jecture that the intercepts made the air raid predictable, the disclosure of Magic could provide a means to discredit the Roosevelt administration's foreign policy and to question its lack of adequate preparations for war.[34]

Not surprisingly, Marshall sought to keep the vital information secret, as it had been during the time of the Roberts commission. After consulting Admiral King, he decided to confront the Republican presidential candidate by letter "with a frank statement of the situation and the assurance that the President and the Cabinet were unaware of my action. . . ."[35] This was an audacious and unprecedented plan; if poorly executed it could damage the Roosevelt campaign and make the chief of staff appear to be a Democratic partisan who was abusing his high position of authority. However, Marshall felt so strongly about maintaining secrecy about the codebreaking that he was willing to take that chance. The September 25 letter began, "I am writing you without the knowledge of any other person except Admiral King because we are approaching a grave dilemma in the political reactions of Congress regarding Pearl Harbor. . . ." Following the admonition to Dewey to read no further unless he would keep the information confidential, the letter outlined the development of Magic and its continual importance to the war effort (adding that all mention of this had been withdrawn from the Roberts report before the public release). Marshall then implored Dewey to avoid using the information for campaign advantage because of its sensitivity.[36]

In Tulsa on the afternoon following the Oklahoma City speech, Col. Carter W. Clarke of the General Staff Corps, in charge of cryptographic intelligence, called upon Dewey and presented him with the sealed message. Dewey was skeptical of Marshall's motives. Upon examining the chief of staff's letter, he stopped reading it at the point where the confidential data began and returned it to Colonel Clarke. He told the intermediary he would be happy to

[34] Marshall to Truman, September 22, 1945, memorandum in diary of James V. Forrestal, pp. 501–502. Forrestal Papers; Marshall to Dewey, September 25, 1944, Box 4, Kimmel Collection.

[35] Marshall to Truman, September 22, 1945, memorandum in diary of James V. Forrestal, pp. 501–502, Forrestal Papers.

[36] Marshall to Dewey, September 25, 1944, Box 4, Kimmel Collection.

discuss the matter with Marshall, but as the nominee of his party he was not in a position to make "blind commitments."[37]

Unwilling to end the affair so abruptly, Marshall decided to try again, even though Dewey was thoroughly apprehensive of the general's rationale for pursuing the matter. On Thursday, September 28, Clarke delivered a second letter to the executive mansion in Albany. The GOP candidate declined to discuss the subject or read the letter except in the presence of a witness, Elliot V. Bell, his personal adviser and New York superintendent of banks. As a representative of the Republican Party, Dewey did not believe he could act as an individual in this case. After some haggling on the phone, Marshall agreed to let Bell read the letter.[38] Also, in the second letter Marshall made some concessions in order to insure Dewey's compliance. The New York governor had been unwilling to commit himself to not revealing the contents of the letter since he already knew some of the secrets about the code breaking probably referred to therein. Marshall agreed to have him read what came after "with the understanding that you are bound not to communicate to any other person any portion on which you do not now have or later receive factual knowledge from some other source than myself." Furthermore, Marshall tried to assuage Dewey's concern that the letter was actually a presidential ploy to keep Pearl Harbor out of the election. The remainder of the letter was the same as the first one.[39]

When Dewey finally read the letter, he discovered that he knew most of the information disclosed about the codes. "While I have never had access to official information concerning the events leading up to the Japanese attack on Pearl Harbor," he told William D.

[37] Dewey to Mitchell, November 1, 1945, Joint Congressional Committee on the Pearl Harbor Attack, Box 5, Record Group 128, National Archives, Washington, D.C. See also Marshall to Truman, September 22, 1945, memorandum in diary of James V. Forrestal, pp. 501–503, Forrestal Papers; Forrest C. Pogue, *George C. Marshall: Organizer of Victory, 1943–1945*, pp. 471 ff.

[38] Dewey to Mitchell, November 1, 1945, Joint Congressional Committee on the Pearl Harbor Attack, Box 5, Record Group 128, National Archives; Marshall to Truman, September 22, 1945, memorandum in diary of James V. Forrestal, pp. 501–503, Forrestal Papers.

[39] Marshall to Dewey, September 27, 1944, Box 4, Kimmel Collection. See also memorandum by Harry Hopkins, undated, Box 141, Hopkins Papers; Sherwood, *Roosevelt and Hopkins*, p. 827; Pogue, *Organizer of Victory*, pp. 471 ff.

Mitchell (the chief counsel for the postwar congressional investigation of the attack), "it was and is my firm conviction that the national administration was guilty of criminal neglect, costing the lives of thousands of Americans and actually risking invasion and conquest of our country." Believing the administration was responsible for Pearl Harbor, and urged by some Republicans to expose the facts about the codes for political advantage, Dewey was tempted to reject Marshall's exhortations, but in the end he realized the limits imposed by the wartime campaign and, having little choice, promised silence. With a touch of melodrama and a great amount of hindsight, he later confided to Mitchell: "Despite these very grave doubts, I decided, on the basis of General Marshall's letter, that I would rather be defeated for President than run even the slightest risk of injuring any aspect of our military effort." As protection, however, Dewey kept a copy of the letter in his secret file.[40]

The issue of responsibility for Pearl Harbor had been pulled from under Dewey before he had a chance to employ it effectively. Until his Oklahoma City speech he had not raised it in any significant public statement, and then had only done so in response to the Fala speech. Dewey's ability to exploit the controversy was negated when he accepted Marshall's terms. The promised silence kept him from taking the leadership on the Pearl Harbor question— if he indeed wanted it. In its new watered-down form, "war responsibility" offered little attractiveness.

The increasing success of the Allied war effort in Europe in the fall of 1944 worked against Dewey as much as Marshall's pressure did. Disclosure of the decoded intercepts at that time probably would not have served the Republicans well. The Democrats would have castigated Dewey for breaching American security and relinquishing the valuable advantage that the breaking of the codes provided against Japan and Germany in much the same way that the *Chicago Tribune* came under fire when it published one of the United States' most secret war estimates on December 4, 1941. The

---

[40] Dewey to Mitchell, November 1, 1945, Joint Congressional Committee on the Pearl Harbor Attack, Box 5, Record Group 128, National Archives; Marshall to Truman, September 22, 1945, memorandum in diary of James V. Forrestal, pp. 501–503, Forrestal Papers.

political advantage of any such disclosure would have been lost to the Republicans. The American public, anxious to see the war brought to a rapid end, would most likely have overlooked past administration "lapses"—at least for the moment.

By October, vice-presidential candidate Bricker and the Republicans in Congress found no new uses for Pearl Harbor which would loosen the Democrats' increasingly formidable hold on foreign policy issues. The hope of using Pearl Harbor to discredit the administration's conduct of the war dwindled. With major revelations about the attack safely concealed and the determination of the War and Navy departments and the president not to release the findings of the Hart investigation, the Army Pearl Harbor Board, and the Navy Court of Inquiry, the Republicans resorted to name-calling and invective. Nothing novel was found to revive the deflated war responsibility issue, nothing to incite the voters in the last month of the election.[41]

There is little doubt that the Republicans tried every possible way to interject Pearl Harbor into the election—short of disclosing Magic—but they had failed to raise it above open-ended charges. War responsibility was not a nonissue in the 1944 election, but rather a weak issue. It was too nebulous, lacking specific charges supported by ironclad revelations. Also, Dewey had avoided the Pearl Harbor question much too long for his supporters and other Republican candidates to sufficiently develop it. Fearing that sensitive and controversial matters of this type had damaged the Republican cause in 1940, he was reticent at best to exploit war responsibility. Consequently, those supporters who did raise questions about the disaster and preparedness did so at their own risk without the necessary support of the party's standard-bearer. Most significantly, the Republicans sought to use a potentially explosive issue at a time when it might have backfired. Confronted with the war effort and its recent successes, Republican denigration seemed out of place. It was possible that the revelations might have been misconstrued by

---

[41] Most active in the futile effort to raise the war responsibility issue in October was Congressman Melvin Maas. See radio comments, October 20–21, 1944, Pearl Harbor Investigation Records, Box 1961, Record Group 165, National Archives; transcript of radio address by Melvin Maas, October 27, 1944, Box 1, Kimmel Collection; *Time* 44 (October 30, 1944): 16.

voters or used effectively by the administration to demonstrate dis-
loyal acts in time of war.

The war responsibility issue's lack of focus, Dewey's scant—
if at all existent—direction and support for it, and the problem of
timing all plagued the Republicans in 1944 and made Pearl Harbor
ineffective in the campaign. However, that the issue was raised at
all and that it was considered potentially volatile by both sides is a
tribute to the deep impression it had made on many Americans
throughout the war. As the war came to an end, circumstances
could change, and the revelations about the December 7 disaster
might fall on more fertile ground than they had in the autumn of
1944.

7

Threat to the Official Line

WHILE the Democrats and the Republicans squared off in the 1944 presidential campaign, the army and the navy began the new Pearl Harbor investigations ordered by the June congressional resolution. To many political observers it seemed logical to assume that since officials in the executive branch would oversee the new inquiries, they would reflect the same attitudes and conclusions as the Roberts commission of two and one-half years before. Contrary to these estimates, both the Army Pearl Harbor Board and the Navy Court of Inquiry produced reports which challenged the administration's interpretation of responsibility. More than the efforts of the Republicans in the 1944 election, the findings initiated a whole new round of debate over Pearl Harbor, culminating in the long-awaited congressional inquiry.

In assembling the new investigatory bodies, the War and Navy departments were restricted by the intent of the June resolution's charge. At first both considered the possibility of a joint board to examine the evidence. After further consultation with congressional supporters of the legislation, they discovered that the aim of the resolution was for the departments to organize separate investigations under the control of the armed services rather than under the supervision of the president, as in the case of the Roberts commission. Since many congressmen had been dissatisfied with the Roberts board, they tried to avoid another presidential inquiry which might delay the announcement of charges against any officer or officers. These presumptions, however, did not take into account that the

War and Navy departments had just as much influence over the Roberts commission as did the president, and possibly more.[1]

The specific purpose of these inquiries was to provide the army and navy with definitive evidence and information for bringing charges and specifications against any culpable party—that is, to give sufficient justification for possible courts-martial. The services would have a free hand in setting up boards they considered appropriate to the task proposed. These new investigations were to be narrower in scope than the Roberts commission, but it was hoped that they would be more detailed. The nature of the directive restricted them largely to examining issues within their own spheres— army investigating army responsibility, navy investigating navy responsibility. This arrangement would not duplicate the generalized conclusions of the Roberts report, but it also would be unlikely to produce comprehensive findings.[2]

In organizing its Army Pearl Harbor Board, the judge advocate general, although predisposed to a broad inquiry, had to settle for a body which would examine the activities of the army and the War Department only and make recommendations. The board was to be composed of three generals assisted by a recorder from the JAG Office and a technical adviser familiar with the military problems involved in the case. The department hierarchy determined that the composition of the board should be a regular army lieutenant general as chairman, an air officer, and a nonregular officer.[3]

Lt. Gen. George Grunert was selected as chairman. Grunert was a typical professional soldier, commissioned from the ranks. He was considered close to General Marshall and was a great favorite in the

1 McNarney to Cramer, June 15, 1944, transcript of telephone conversation, Army Pearl Harbor Board Files (hereafter cited as APHB), Box 57, Record Group 107; Gatch to Forrestal, June 15, 1944, Records of the Secretary of the Navy (hereafter cited as Sec Nav), Box 44, Record Group 80, National Archives, Washington, D.C.

2 Gatch to Forrestal, June 17, 1944, Sec Nav, Box 44, Record Group 80; Cramer to Stimson, June 24, 1944, APHB, Box 57, Record Group 107, National Archives.

3 Cramer to Stimson, June 24, 1944, APHB, Box 57, Record Group 107; White to Craig, September 27, 1945, Pearl Harbor Investigation Records (hereafter cited as PHI), Box 1962, Record Group 165, National Archives, Washington, D.C.

War Department. At the time of his appointment, Grunert was in charge of the Eastern Defense Command, after having served as commander of the Philippine Department before Gen. Douglas MacArthur. With respect to the Pearl Harbor case the new chairman believed that Short had failed in his mission and must bear the consequences. His great desire to vindicate the War Department waivered somewhat during the investigation, but he remained a staunch supporter of Marshall.[4]

The Army Air Forces nominated Maj. Gen. Walter H. Frank, who was attached to Army Air Force Headquarters. The West Point graduate—the only one on the board—had an independence of thinking and action but had one fixed opinion: Short must suffer the charge of dereliction of duty, since he had enough information available at Hawaii to make the right decision.[5]

Gen. Henry D. Russell was the nonregular appointment. He had been in command of a National Guard division until he was relieved in May, 1942. For that action he became bitter toward Marshall, whom he blamed for the anti–National Guard policy which arose during the war. Russell had little prior knowledge of the Pearl Harbor affair; he had read the Roberts report superficially and had accepted its conclusions at the time. Of the three members of the board, he was closest to Short, who was his first corps commander during the war. They had differed over policy, but Russell had a very high regard for Short and was most interested in determining if his alleged derelictions justified court-martial. However, the National Guard commander had been very reluctant to serve on the board. He believed his selection was unwise, since he had conducted a manpower survey of General Frank's command and had made some unfavorable comments about its administration. He also winced at a task which would likely result in controversy over the army's role in the Hawaiian fiasco. Yet Russell's presence on the

[4] Henry D. Russell, unpublished manuscript, undated, pp. 4–6, Box 14, George Morgenstern Collection, Division of Rare Books and Special Collections, University of Wyoming Library, Laramie; *Time* 45 (September 10, 1945): 25–27.

[5] Russell, unpublished manuscript, pp. 6–7, Box 14, Morgenstern Collection; *Time* 45 (September 10, 1945): 25–27; White to Craig, September 27, 1945, PHI, Box 1962, Record Group 165, National Archives.

army board gave it a degree of balance necessary for a fair hearing of the case at hand.[6]

The board convened on July 20, 1944, and remained in continuous session from July 24 through October 20. It was administrative instead of punitive in nature, lacked the power of subpoena, and restricted itself largely to interrogating military personnel or civilians under the jurisdiction of the War Department. Since the board was not a trial body, it could not grant General Short or anyone else the right to sit in on the proceedings with counsel or participate in any manner other than as a witness. Furthermore, the board confined its investigation to the Pearl Harbor disaster exclusively. The only extraneous element introduced beyond the general issue of army responsibility was the so-called Col. Theodore Wyman, Jr./Hans Wilhelm Rohl case dealing with the noncompletion of a permanent aircraft warning system before December 7, 1941, which some officials felt contributed to the lack of readiness for the Japanese raid.[7] Despite the limitations, no potential witnesses ignored the board's invitation to testify, and the members ultimately had the authority to make substantive recommendations based on their findings.[8]

The Grunert board conducted a massive undertaking, examining more witnesses than did any other Pearl Harbor inquiry. In all, the members formally interrogated 151 witnesses and interviewed many other individuals. About 55 percent were army personnel, 38 percent were civilians, and 7 percent were navy personnel. Short, Stimson, and Marshall were the most noteworthy witnesses. Because of his predilections, Russell remained very critical of Marshall's per-

[6] Russell, unpublished manuscript, pp. 9–10, Box 14, Morgenstern Collection; White to Craig, September 27, 1945, PHI, Box 1962, Record Group 165, National Archives; Stimson to FDR, September 26, 1944, microfilm reel 110, Henry L. Stimson Papers, Manuscripts and Archives, Sterling Memorial Library, Yale University, New Haven, Conn.; *Time* 45 (September 10, 1945): 25–27.

[7] For more information about the case, see U.S. Congress, *Pearl Harbor Attack: Hearings before the Joint Committee on the Pearl Harbor Attack*, 79th Cong., 1st sess., pts. 27–31, 39; *Newsweek* 23 (June 26, 1944): 43–44.

[8] Minutes of the Army Pearl Harbor Board meetings, July 20, 25, 1944; McNarney to Grunert, July 20, 1944, transcript of conversation; Grunert to assistant chief of staff, July 26, 1944; J. A. Ulio to Stimson, August 3, 1944, APHB, Box 7, Record Group 107, National Archives; "Report of Army Pearl Harbor Board," in Congress, *Pearl Harbor Attack*, pt. 29, p. 24.

formance and highly sympathetic to Short, while Grunert especially seemed unsympathetic toward the Hawaiian commander.[9]

Like the Roberts commission, the Army Pearl Harbor Board was not privy to all the documentation necessary for the most thorough investigation. The generals did not have the opportunity "to comb personally and exhaustively" the official files, but instead called for the designated groups to provide the pertinent materials. Although they received much of what they wanted, a few files had important papers missing. Through cross-checking of other files and sources, most of the missing information materialized.

Of course, the Army Pearl Harbor Board—like its predecessors—did not have the necessary access to intercepted Japanese messages, including those in the controversial "Winds" code, which the Japanese had devised to be used in an emergency when the severing of diplomatic relations with its enemies or the cutting off of international communications was imminent. A warning in the form of a weather forecast was to be included in the middle and at the end of the daily Japanese-language shortwave broadcast (also in the general intelligence broadcasts) using one of three phrases: "east wind, rain," in case of danger to U.S.-Japanese relations; "north wind, cloudy," in case of danger to U.S.S.R.-Japanese relations; or "west wind, clear," in case of danger to British-Japanese relations. If any of these signals were transmitted, the Japanese envoys were to destroy all code papers and the like. Documents clearly demonstrated the existence of the Winds code and American awareness of it, but a debate raged over whether it was executed before Pearl Harbor and intercepted by American cryptanalysts. Although the code did not pinpoint the attack upon Hawaii and could hardly be considered evidence that would have "saved the day," its existence could have raised some serious doubts about American intelligence gathering and disseminating.[10] The inability of the army board to examine the Winds code evidence and com-

[9] Russell, unpublished manuscript, pp. 12ff., Box 14, Morgenstern Collection; list of witnesses in Congress, *Pearl Harbor Attack*, pt. 27, pp. 1–4.

[10] Congress, *Pearl Harbor Attack*, pt. 12, pp. 154–155. For contrasting views on the significance of the Winds code, see Roberta Wohlstetter, *Pearl Harbor: Warning and Decision*, pp. 51 ff., 214ff.; Robert A. Theobald, *The Final Secret of Pearl Harbor: The Washington Contribution to the Japanese Attack*, pp. 134ff.

prehensively study other decoded Japanese messages hampered the members in acquiring a fuller perception of the circumstances surrounding the attack. And a skeptical General Russell, in particular, assumed that the exclusions were intentional to protect the army and navy high commands from recriminations.[11]

Given the investigation's various limitations, it was fortunate that the army board was involved in a minimum of interdepartmental haggling. The only point of contention—and it was a mild one—occurred when Secretary Stimson attempted to acquire the transcript of the Hart inquiry for the board. James V. Forrestal, the new secretary of the navy, would not release the transcript on the grounds that the judge advocate of the Navy Court of Inquiry was using it to prepare evidence and testimony for the members. He also suggested that handing over the information would violate the congressional directive for separate investigations. The War Department officials naturally were perturbed and felt that the navy must have had something to hide. But aside from this incident, the relations between the departments remained relatively cordial.[12]

To Stimson, the maintenance of amicable ties with the navy was vital. As the investigations were drawing to a close, he began to consider seriously the upcoming reports and their political consequences. On October 12 he made arrangements to see Forrestal to discuss the respective inquiries "which have been going on without any coordination for some time and are on the point of reaching the time for making their reports." Stimson believed that a conference could help the boards avoid reaching diverse conclusions, which could be publicly damaging. Although he felt the navy had been "rather offish" about his proposal, the two secretaries met the following day, and Stimson suggested that he and Forrestal order the boards to meet and exchange data, but that they not intervene personally. After further discussion they parted without resolving their dilemma. Returning to his office, Forrestal asked Adm. Orin Murfin,

---

[11] "Report of Army Pearl Harbor Board," in Congress, *Pearl Harbor Attack*, pt. 39, pp. 24–25; Russell, unpublished manuscript, pp. 87–92, Box 14, Morgenstern Collection.

[12] Forrestal to Stimson, September 5, 1944; Stimson to Forrestal, undated; John J. McCloy to Nelson, September 16, 1944, transcript of telephone conversation, APHB, Record Group 107, National Archives.

the chairman of the Navy Court of Inquiry, if he thought it advisable to hold a conference. Unlike Grunert, who was quite willing to exchange information, Murfin was extremely reluctant to do so because his board was a statutory court which did not make provision for such acts. Forrestal's aide, Maj. Mathias F. Correa, argued that it was highly doubtful whether the secretary could act as a convening authority to direct the navy court to meet with the army board and exchange information before the official reports of both bodies were submitted. Based on those opinions, the navy secretary decided against a joint session, but as a way of appeasing Stimson he did agree to exchange reports after the completion of the investigations.[13]

On October 20 the Army Pearl Harbor Board submitted its report. Despite the lack of some important documentary evidence and the restrictions imposed by the resolution's charge, the Grunert board conducted a thorough examination of army involvement in the Hawaiian debacle. The conclusions were well balanced and judicious, and most significantly they assessed responsibility over a much wider spectrum than did the Roberts report. A rather lengthy document, the army report not only included a list of findings, but also provided a scenario on United States relations with Japan before December 7, 1941, and a chronology of events leading to the attack. As might be expected, the report insisted on the aggressiveness and deception of Japanese policy in the Pacific, and it noted that the lack of American preparedness for war arose out of the confusion and conflict of a nation unwilling to acquire a "war mind," to which isolationist feelings contributed greatly. The nation's general policy during these sensitive times, it concluded, was a perplexing duality: American policy makers wanted to avoid offending Japan—a form of appeasement—while simultaneously adhering to an offsetting plan of commercial restrictions. The net result was a "do-don't" attitude which the War Department transmitted to the

---

[13] Diary of Henry L. Stimson, October 12, 13, 1944, XLVIII, 137, 142, microfilm; Stimson to Grunert, October 12, 1944, transcript of telephone conversation, microfilm reel 128; Stimson to Forrestal, October 14, 1944, transcript of telephone conversation, microfilm reel 128, Stimson Papers; diary of James V. Forrestal, October 13, 14, 1944, pp. 35–39, James V. Forrestal Papers, Princeton University Library, Princeton, N.J.

Hawaiian Command. This explanation strongly implied that decisions to be made with respect to Japan, at all levels, were liable to be rife with contradictions in an atmosphere already convoluted and uncertain.

Recognizing a more complex and contradictory series of events and issues which affected the coming of the Pacific war than did either the Knox or the Roberts report, the army board's conclusions ostensibly indicated a wider range of culpability. The board determined that the extent of the disaster was due primarily to a combination of the failure of General Short to adequately alert his command for war and the failure of the War Department—with knowledge of the type of alert Short had ordered—to direct him to implement a more appropriate warning based on its knowledge of the deterioration of Japanese-American relations in late 1941. In addition to those conclusions the board briefly assessed the role of the State Department in the affair, judging that the interchange of information between it and the War Department was as complete as could be expected under the circumstances. However, Secretary Hull's so-called November 26 ultimatum to Japan, which allegedly hastened the attack, "was in conflict with the efforts of the War and Navy Departments to gain time for preparations for war," even though war was inevitable at that point.[14]

The most startling findings dealt with the conduct of the chief of staff, Gen. George C. Marshall. The report charged that he failed in his relations with the Hawaiian Department in a number of ways. He had not kept Short completely advised about the growing tenseness of the Pacific situation, "of which information he had an abundance and Short had little," and he had not sent sufficient instructions to Short when he evidently failed to realize that the Hawaiian commander had inadequately alerted his command for war. These were serious charges which could arouse intense skepticism about the chief of staff's preparedness program.[15]

Although the Grunert board castigated Marshall rather severely, it did not automatically exonerate Short. The report dispelled the notion that relations between Kimmel and Short were strained, and

[14] "Report of Army Pearl Harbor Board," in Congress, *Pearl Harbor Attack*, pt. 39, pp. 23–178.
[15] Ibid., pp. 144–146.

it stated that the Hawaiian commander had made an "earnest and honest" effort to implement the plans which would result in the services working as a unit in an emergency—although this was not accomplished by the time of the attack. Yet they especially criticized Short for not sufficiently placing his command in a state of readiness for war—adopting a sabotage alert only. The warnings he received may have been incomplete and confusing, but they did notify him of the seriousness of the situation in general. The board also charged that Short had failed to reach an agreement with Kimmel to implement the joint army/navy plans, had failed to inform himself of the effectiveness of the navy's long-distance reconnaissance, and had overlooked replacing inefficient staff officers.[16]

Short's lapses paled in comparison with the criticisms leveled against Marshall and the War Department, especially since the board prepared top secret findings in addition to the major report which emphasized some significant high-level culpability. The supplemental report essentially reinforced the general findings, pointing out the importance of evidence and documents "which for reasons of security should not be incorporated in the General Report"— especially Magic. The board felt even more compelled than in the major report to insist that Washington had possession of crucial data which should have been transmitted to the Hawaiian Command but was not. "All [the War Department] had to do," it stated, "was either to give it to Short or give him directions based on it." The board further concluded that the variety of information available in Washington made it evident that by December 4 or 5 the imminence of war breaking out on December 6 or 7 was clear-cut and definite, implying strongly that the War Department was capable of warning Hawaii much more completely than it did.[17]

The Army Pearl Harbor Board had gone much further than the Roberts report had in assessing blame for the attack. Whereas the president's commission had mentioned some of the faults originating in Washington, it had concluded that these were of little consequence in comparison with the responsibilities of the local commanders. The army board weighted the various lapses more evenly and determined that neither side was completely free of guilt. Of

[16] Ibid., pp. 175–176.
[17] Ibid., pp. 221–230.

course, it did not thoroughly examine Washington's responsibility beyond the War Department or the role of the navy. For what it did study, it took a decidedly more equitable position than did the Roberts report, which had ignored the role of Washington officials almost completely. The army board did not make any recommendations based on the findings, but Secretary Stimson and his aides realized that the shift in emphasis away from Hawaii to Washington was foreboding enough. The findings of the Navy Court of Inquiry would pose the same kind of dilemma for the high officials in the Navy Department.

In form, the Navy Court of Inquiry was quite different from the Army Pearl Harbor Board, although its conclusions ran parallel to the army panel's. It was a formal hearing much like a trial, and it was a prelude to an official court-martial. The men selected to sit on this investigation followed in the tradition of such proceedings. All were retired admirals with lengthy service records. The chairman was Orin G. Murfin, who had particular qualifications for the task. A former judge advocate general, he had also served as commander in chief of the Asiatic Fleet and from 1936 to 1940 had been commandant of the Fourteenth Naval District, Hawaii.[18] Also sitting on the court was Adolphus Andrews, a Republican who had been a former aide to three presidents. In recent years he had held assignments in the Atlantic—first as commandant of the Third Naval District in charge of the North Atlantic Frontier and then as commander of the Eastern Sea Frontier responsible for protecting the East Coast during the early years of the war.[19] The final member was Edward C. Kalbfus, who was best known as the president of the Naval War College from 1934 to 1937 and from 1939 to 1942. He was also the most sympathetic to Kimmel's case, believing that the Hawaiian commander should not be held solely accountable for the Pearl Harbor disaster.[20] The combined records of these three

[18] National Cyclopedia of American Biography, XLIII, 99; New York Times, October 24, 1956, p. 37.

[19] National Cyclopedia of American Biography, XLVIII, 467–468; New York Times, June 20, 1948, p. 60.

[20] New York Times, September 7, 1954, p. 25; Kimmel interview with Admiral E. C. Kalbfus, December 7, 1944, memorandum, Box 33, Husband E. Kimmel Collection, Division of Rare Books and Special Collections, University of Wyoming Library, Laramie.

admirals gave the inquiry a solid stature, but their conclusions based on the conflicting evidence were as hard to predict as those of the army board.

When the court convened in July, 1944, the first duty of Murfin, Andrews, and Kalbfus was to select the interested parties in the hearing—those individuals who were specifically under inquiry. They named Admiral Kimmel, Adm. Harold R. Stark, the former chief of naval operations (CNO), and Adm. Claude C. Bloch, the former commandant of the Fourteenth Naval District and Pearl Harbor defense officer. Aside from the interested parties, the board interrogated thirty-six other witnesses in Washington, San Francisco, and Hawaii. Of these witnesses, twenty-four had been examined by other inquiries: sixteen by the Roberts commission, fifteen by Hart, and seventeen by the army board. Seventy-seven percent of the witnesses were high navy personnel, 15 percent were army personnel, and 8 percent were State Department officials, including Ambassador to Japan Joseph C. Grew. This was a decidedly less expansive hearing than the army board, but it was sufficient to fulfill its primary function of determining "whether any offenses have been committed or serious blame incurred on the part of any person or persons in the naval service."[21]

The inclusion of interested parties and the formality of the court produced more immediate tensions for the navy court than were experienced by the army board, which worked without these pressures. The interested parties attended the interrogations with counsel. Stark remained only through his testimony and then returned to his command in London. He left his fate in the hands of his counsel and friend, Thomas Hart. By the time of the inquiry, the relationship between Kimmel, Stark, and Bloch was not strong. The Pearl Harbor investigations had especially bruised the friendship of Kimmel and Stark. Kimmel had broken off his personal correspondence with "Betty," as the former CNO had been fondly nicknamed, because after the Roberts proceedings he believed Stark had walked away from the incident unscathed while he shouldered all of the blame.[22] Stark seemed hurt by the break in their friendship, confid-

[21] See precept, pt. 32, pp. 5–6, "Report of Navy Court of Inquiry," in Congress, *Pearl Harbor Attack*, pt. 39, pp. 297ff.

[22] See Kimmel-Stark correspondence, 1941–1942, Kimmel Collection.

ing in Hart that the Hawaiian commander should not take all the responsibility for the Pearl Harbor disaster. About his testimony before the court he told Hart that he wished he had "just gone in and expressed [his] thoughts." Then he added: "Perhaps I was tired. Perhaps part of the trouble was my fondness and loyalty to Kimmel, my actual desire to share the burden and protect him so far as I could, and trying too hard to be so one-hundred-percent-plus honest, so that in spots I may have made more or less a mess of it. . . ." Hart, however, remained suspicious that Kimmel had tried to exonerate himself before the court by casting doubt on Stark. He felt Bloch had done as well.[23] Fearing the worst, the principals were understandably uncomfortable with what conclusions the navy inquiry might render.

On October 20 the Murfin court submitted its report. As a court of inquiry it concentrated on the guilt or innocence of the interested parties and thus it did not analyze the background of the attack comprehensively or assess the responsibilities of Washington officials thoroughly. It did, however, clearly assert that the defense of Pearl Harbor was basically the responsibility of the army, with the navy only assisting. This decision could have repercussions later between the services. And, like the army board's report, the navy report was at variance with the Roberts findings; it was clearly favorable to Admiral Kimmel, almost exonerating him, and it contradicted nearly all the adverse comments made about his performance in the Roberts report. Because of the lack of specific information available to predict when and where the attack would come, the navy court presumed that the air raid was unpreventable. Kimmel, therefore, could not be blamed for something he could not expect, especially when he did not receive all available information from Washington. On the positive side, the court asserted that the Hawaiian commander—despite the various handicaps—followed the proper procedures available to him and that his relations with Short were "friendly, cordial and cooperative," allowing for reasonable

[23] Stark to Hart, September 20, 1944; Hart to Stark, September 28, 1944, series I, Thomas C. Hart Papers; Stark to Richmond K. Turner, November 30, 1944, series II, Harold R. Stark Papers, Naval History Division, Department of the Navy, Washington, D.C.; reminiscences of Thomas C. Hart, Naval History Project, 1962, pp. 212–214, Columbia University, New York (*New York Times* microfiche).

actions under the circumstances. Likewise, any aspersions against
Bloch were quickly dismissed, because the examining admirals believed he performed his task satisfactorily.[24]

The only area of personal remissness of any consequence discussed in the report was directed at Admiral Stark. The court believed that he failed to display "the sound judgment expected of
him" by not transmitting to Hawaii the important information available in Washington. In an addendum to the findings outlining the
importance of the decoded messages, the court reinforced the view
that Washington officials, including Stark, had significant data
which should have been sent to Kimmel. Since the board did not
believe that the attack could have been prevented under the prevailing circumstances, Stark was not severely reprimanded for his role
in the debacle. In fact, the general conclusion was that in the case
of all interested parties "no offenses have been committed nor serious blame incurred." Murfin, Andrews, and Kalbfus recommended
no further proceedings against anyone.[25]

Both the navy and the army reports altered the findings of the
Roberts commission and clearly removed much of the stigma from
the local commanders, although they relieved Kimmel more than
Short. Because these latest reports did not parrot the official line,
they posed a serious problem to the War and Navy departments,
and to the president himself. Administration officials would have to
readjust their point of view or suppress the new findings.

Stimson confided in his diary at the end of November that the
"confounded Pearl Harbor case which ought never to have been
loaded upon us by the Congress in the middle of the war" had taken
an immense amount of his time and a great amount of his strength
because it was "such a rasping, hard, annoying matter." He added:
"It has worried me a great deal. The mistake made by the Pearl
Harbor Board and the attacks that they have made upon the men
who are invaluable in the war are things which ought never to have
happened."[26]

From the outset, the war secretary had been disgruntled about

[24] Forrestal to Murfin, October 20, 1944, Box 87, Forrestal Papers; Congress, *Pearl Harbor Attack*, pt. 39, pp. 297ff.

[25] Congress, *Pearl Harbor Attack*, pt. 39, pp. 297ff.

[26] Diary of Henry L. Stimson, November 27, 1944, XLIX, 51, microfilm,
Stimson Papers.

the imposition of the investigation. In his diary he complained about the unnecessary time-wasting of ". . . this never-ending problem of testimony before the Pearl Harbor Board. It is just a sample of how a move in Congress instigated by purely political motives can successfully tie up at a very critical moment the activities of an official like myself who is pretty important to the war effort." The political ramifications of the investigation weighed heavily upon him, especially since Roosevelt wanted to adjourn the committee until after the 1944 election. And although the secretary was unwilling to intervene in this way while the board was in session, his concern about the implications of the report lingered.[27]

When the generals presented their report to the War Department, Stimson's worst anxieties had come true, for it contradicted the standard departmental position. According to his aide, Harvey Bundy, Stimson referred to the Grunert board's handiwork as "a very poor report," and although not criticized directly in it, he was disturbed that the chief of the War Plans Division, Gen. Leonard T. Gerow, and particularly Chief of Staff Marshall had been. Feeling that the report posed "a big problem," he not only conferred with the JAG Office, but also appointed a committee to examine the report and determine what action to take, especially on the top secret information discussed in the supplementary findings. On November 1 the committee recommended not releasing the report to the public during the war, and Stimson quickly accepted this recommendation. He now had a rationalization, at least for the present, to hold the report out of the press.[28]

The preliminary maneuvers out of the way, Stimson still needed to determine what further action to take, short of a public disclosure. Early in November he conferred with Forrestal to keep their actions consistent. The war secretary also oversaw the formulation of criticisms of the report and the checking of facts which aides Bundy and Allen Klots had begun. It was the "pinpricks" in the conclusions about Marshall which seemed to concern him most.

[27] Ibid., September 18, 19, 24, 26, 1944, XLVIII, 87–88, 104, 107.
[28] Excerpt from press conference of Henry L. Stimson, October 26, 1944; memorandum for the press, APHB, Box 26, Record Group 107, National Archives; diary of Henry L. Stimson, October 21, 26, 1944, XLVIII, 173, 186–187; November 1, 1944, XLIX, 2, microfilm, Stimson Papers.

"That's what makes all the trouble," he felt. Marshall was held in such high regard in the army and throughout the administration by virtue of his steady leadership as chief of staff that any aspersions cast on him as the result of the Pearl Harbor inquiry seemed only to retard the war effort. Also, criticisms of the chief of staff brought Pearl Harbor culpability uncomfortably close to other high administration officials, namely the president and the secretary himself. To Marshall, who had only heard about the contents of the army board report in November, the conclusions were shocking, and he became despondent. He told Stimson that because of the report he believed his usefulness in the army was destroyed. Although Stimson assure him that was nonsense, the pressure on the war secretary was mounting greatly.[29]

On November 14 Stimson submitted the report to the Judge Advocate General's Office. In a subsequent memorandum General Cramer assailed the army report and largely reconfirmed the findings of the Roberts commission while possibly softening the original criticism of Short. He flatly stated that the conclusions about Marshall's performance were "unjustified and erroneous," and he argued that Gerow's errors did not warrant disciplinary action, especially since he had demonstrated great qualifications for field command during the remainder of the war. With respect to Short, he reasserted that the Hawaiian commander had been adequately warned about coming circumstances, but he concurred with the board that Short had made mistakes of judgment but had not neglected his duty. Reiterating his apprehension about a trial or any punitive action against Short, he recommended that the department make a public statement giving their views of the proceedings "and pointing out that General Short was guilty of errors of judgment for which he was properly removed from command, and that this constitutes a sufficient disposition of the matter at this time."[30] Cramer's suggestions demonstrated unwillingness to alter his original interpretation of the question of responsibility and also indicated a desire

[29] Diary of Henry L. Stimson, November 6, 11, 14, 1944, XLIX, 6, 22, 25, microfilm, Stimson Papers; diary of James V. Forrestal, November 14, 1944, p. 58, Forrestal Papers.
[30] Cramer to Stimson, November 25, 1944, memorandum in Congress, *Pearl Harbor Attack*, pt. 29, pp. 231–269.

to place the department's welfare above that of the individual, that
is, General Short. The earlier promise of a court-martial as a means
of obtaining a waiver from the former commander was fairly well
laid to rest at this point. The department hierarchy believed the
Army Pearl Harbor Board report had eliminated its necessity, and a
court-martial could only stir up adverse attention.

In the Navy Department, Secretary Forrestal began to formulate his policy on the knotty problem of the Pearl Harbor report in
late October. Since he was strongly supportive of the administration's war policy and Roosevelt's leadership in general, it was unlikely that he would allow the new report to significantly challenge
the official policy on guilt. Forrestal had come to the government as
a highly successful investment banker who had little political experience but much organizational ability. His first position in Washington was as an administrative assistant to FDR in the spring of
1940. With the passage of the Government Reorganization Act in
that year, Roosevelt was looking for men with a "passion for ano-
nymity" who would bring efficiency and effectiveness to government during a time of national emergency. Forrestal fit that require-
ment well, impressing Roosevelt sufficiently to be named to the new
post of undersecretary of the navy. His specific task was to aid in
the building of a large two-ocean naval force. Forrestal's rapid
ascendancy in the New Deal administration was probably enhanced
by his connection with the Dutchess County (New York) Democratic organization, which had helped elect young Franklin Roosevelt to a seat on the state senate in 1910. The undersecretary's excep-
tional work in the Navy Department made him a natural heir to the
secretaryship when Knox died in 1944. His passion for naval expan-
sion and his tenacious adherence to keeping the Navy Department
at cabinet rank, despite wartime pressure to unify the armed services, made Forrestal a strong addition to the Democratic administration.[31]

His handling of the latest Pearl Harbor inquiry, not surprisingly, followed the pattern of his War Department counterpart. Like

[31] *New York Times*, May 23, 1949, pp. 1, 3; *National Cyclopedia of
American Biography*, XLII, 10–11. See also Robert G. Albion and Robert H.
Connery, *Forrestal and the Navy*; Arnold A. Rogow, *James Forrestal: A Study
of Personality, Politics, and Policy.*

Stimson, Forrestal decided to separate the material into secret and top secret classifications; the top secret segment included information about the intercepts and other sensitive materials. Murfin disagreed with this decision and told Forrestal that he had understood that the material now designated as secret was not to be classified at all and supposedly would be made public. As he concluded in his October 21 letter, "The Court is of the opinion that its report on Finding of Facts, (without the "Addendum") Opinions, and Recommendations contains nothing of a confidential nature, and had no intention of giving any impression to the contrary." Despite Murfin's steady protests, the navy secretary wanted time to decide what to do, insinuating that the total document was too sensitive to release. He then began the process of gathering departmental advice about the report.[32]

After the election, both departments realized pressure would continue to mount for release of the reports. If they withheld the information completely, they stood the chance of a public incident which could prove more catastrophic than some mild criticisms engendered by a well-planned partial disclosure. Such an orchestrated policy demanded close cooperation between the departments—a difficult proposition in view of what each body believed were its own interests. And inevitably a schism developed. General Surles, who had met with Stimson on November 20, feared that if the secretary publicized the army report, the navy would try to "ride behind" the disclosure, let the War Department bear the whole burden, and escape criticism themselves. Stimson's present thinking was that the War Department had to publicize the report in some way before administration opponents exploited the information about General Marshall. He believed the department could simultaneously release a vindication of the chief of staff with the disclosure of the board's findings.[33]

[32] Murfin to Forrestal, October 21, 1944; Forrestal to Murfin, October 21, 1944, Sec Nav, Box 44, Record Group 80, National Archives; conference of Murfin, Lavender, and Rugg, July 27, 1945, Box 33, Kimmel Collection; diary of James V. Forrestal, October 3, 1944, pp. 29–30; Forrestal press conference, October 18, 1944, Box 7; Forrestal to King, October 21, 1944, Box 87, Forrestal Papers.

[33] Diary of Henry L. Stimson, November 20, 1944, XLIX, 36, microfilm, Stimson Papers.

Stimson was still troubled about what the navy was considering. In a telephone call to Forrestal, he inquired about the navy's planned action on their report. Much to his surprise, navy officials had met with the president a week before, and subsequently Forrestal was preparing a short public statement about the Navy Court of Inquiry findings. When Stimson discovered that the Navy Department was not going to take further action against any officer, he was appalled. The secretary feared that a full disclosure of the army report without similar action by the navy would throw all the unfavorable criticism against the War Department. He concluded that it was time to go to the White House. At their meeting Roosevelt told him that the less said the better. This was a crushing blow to Stimson, who had planned elaborate publicity to vindicate Marshall and keep criticism away from the department. He nonetheless made his case to the president, who reacted to those criticized by saying, "Why, this is wicked; this is wicked." Yet Roosevelt still wanted silence. The secretary then tried to convince him that Congress would pounce on that decision, but the president reiterated that they should take every step against that happening and insisted on keeping the reports secret until after the war. Leaving the White House without changing Roosevelt's mind, Stimson was disappointed, his pride was hurt, and he resented allowing the navy to set the standard for the disclosure. He reluctantly complied with the order to prepare a shorter news release but stubbornly included that there had been delinquencies in the War Department and strongly emphasized that Short was blameworthy.[34] In the cover letter accompanying the revised statement, he told the president that the new draft went as far as he could properly go. "To say merely that I believe that the facts do not warrant the institution of any proceedings . . . ," he stated, "inevitably [would] give the impression that I was trying entirely to absolve all Army officers from any criticism including General Short. . . . That is an impression I am unwilling to father."[35]

[34] Ibid., November 21, 22, 1944, XLIX, 38–42.
[35] Stimson to FDR, November 22, 1944, and attached statement, President's Secretary File, Box 104, Franklin D. Roosevelt Papers, Franklin D. Roosevelt Presidential Library, Hyde Park, N.Y.

The forced concession required of Stimson apparently lightened the tensions between the War Department and the Navy Department. After talking with Forrestal on November 23, the war secretary found him "not as stiff as the draft statement which he sent me the other day. . . ." But Stimson was not completely reassured, since persistent rumors that the navy would whitewash its men filtered back to him, and he again called Forrestal to get reassurances. By this time the navy secretary was willing to compromise somewhat, and he promised to mention the guilt of some of his officers in his statement. "I have an uneasy feeling," Stimson concluded, "till the thing is done, but it seems to be on the right track now." [36]

Forrestal and the Navy Department were not as insensitive to Stimson's views as he thought. The secretary of the navy realized that criticism of Stark would reflect unfavorably upon Marshall, who held a parallel position to the CNO in the War Department. He found himself forced to choose among the conflicting possible policies of no publicity, public censure of Kimmel and Stark, or censure of Kimmel only. And like Stimson, divergent recommendations about what to do with the report still plagued him. Some advisers believed that the report was completely inadequate and should be discarded and a new investigation begun; others suggested a new joint army/navy inquiry; still others argued that the Navy Department not make an immediate announcement about a further investigation, but only release an innocuous statement about the recent report with no mention of the details; and a few believed that the department should make a recommendation to Congress that the statute of limitations be extended two years because war security did not allow for an immediate disclosure. These alternatives posed a true dilemma for Forrestal. He had not been secretary of the navy during Pearl Harbor and thus was in a different position than Stimson, who had a personal stake in the affair. Forrestal confided in his diary how difficult it was to analyze the situation from hindsight, but he concluded in his own mind that officials in the

---

[36] Diary of Henry L. Stimson, November 23, 24, 1944, XLIX, 45–47, 49, microfilm, Stimson Papers.

Navy Department and the Hawaiian Command had not taken adequate precautions for the attack—and saw both groups guilty to a degree.[37] Of course, in his associations with the War Department these views were guarded. His first duty was to protect the navy's reputation. After the lengthy negotiating, however, the secretaries' compromise seemed to come as a temporary hiatus in the Pearl Harbor debates.

At the direction of the president, Stimson and Forrestal made their brief announcements on December 1. They acknowledged that officials in Hawaii and Washington had committed errors in judgment. Forrestal remained very general on this point, but Stimson stated that he did not concur with all the conclusions of the army board and, in order to justify previous action taken against Short, specifically singled him out. Stimson did not mention anyone else by name. The secretaries—reciting the old line—also declared that the reports could not be made public during the war for security reasons. But most significantly, they concluded that based upon the evidence "now" available, no individual had committed a serious enough error to justify a court-martial. Since both Stimson and Forrestal were dissatisfied with the results of their investigations, they left the option open for further inquiries.[38]

The announcements fell short of full disclosure of the reports but at the same time were not absolute vindications of high officials in the War and Navy departments. Stimson and Forrestal were walking a fine line between their duty to protect their respective departments from criticism and avoidance of the charge of whitewashing the investigations. With their strong proclivities for the former, this was a trying task. On November 30, after they received Roosevelt's directive to release their statements, Stimson wrote in his diary that he felt as if he had "a burden off my back for the present." But he reluctantly concluded: "It is not a final settlement I fear, I think it was a great mistake not to go more into a frank full statement of

[37] Diary of James V. Forrestal, November 22, 26, 27, 1944, pp. 62, 70–72. See also diary of Henry Morgenthau, Jr., November 13, 1944, Book 794, p. 15, Henry Morgenthau, Jr. Collection, Franklin D. Roosevelt Presidential Library, Hyde Park, N.Y.; Kimmel interview with Gatch, December 7, 1944, memorandum, Box 33, Kimmel Collection.
[38] New York Times, December 2, 1944, pp. 1, 5.

what has happened and what we have done, but it is as much as Forrestal and I could accomplish under the President's direction that we should not go too far." [39]

Stimson instincts were accurate, for the news releases only increased curiosity and did nothing to stifle the demands for a complete explanation of the recent findings. Newspapers and magazine reaction went strongly against the administration on this issue. In a report on nationwide editorial reaction to the December 1 announcements, conducted by the Navy Department's Office of Public Relations, 75 percent of the newspapers reacted negatively. [40]

The announcements also set off another round of partisan debate in Congress. Democrats defended the releases as all that could be disclosed during the war, while Republicans admonished the administration for suppressing vital information. As early as November 21, Senator Homer Ferguson tied a demand for a Senate investigation of Pearl Harbor to his new resolution to further extend the statute of limitations. Although there was faint hope of a congressional investigation while the war continued, the secretaries' announcements were added fuel to sustain the political fires. [41]

The findings of the Army Pearl Harbor Board and the Navy Court of Inquiry had been filed away while the administration once again tried to ride out the new round of public criticisms. Postponement was a persistent feature of the Pearl Harbor controversy. How-

[39] Diary of Henry L. Stimson, November 30, 1944, XLIX, 62, microfilm, Stimson Papers.

[40] Office of Public Relations, Navy Department, "Special Report on Editorial Reaction to the December 1 Stimson-Forrestal Statements on Pearl Harbor, December 20, 1944," Sec Nav, Box 44, Record Group 80, National Archives. See also *Time* 44 (December 11, 1944): 23; *Newsweek* 24 (December 11, 1944): 49; (December 4, 1944): 47; *Kiplinger Washington Letter*, December 9, 1944; diary of Henry L. Stimson, December 6, 1944, XLIX, 68, microfilm, Stimson Papers.

[41] U.S. Congress, *Congressional Record*, 78th Cong., 2d sess., 1944, 90, 8224ff.; Allen Drury, *A Senate Journal, 1943–1945*, pp. 297, 303; departmental endorsements of Senate Joint Resolution No. 156, December 8–13, 1944, Official File 5708, Roosevelt Papers; D. J. Ramsey to Forrestal, November 29, 1944, Pearl Harbor File, Record Group 128, National Archives, Washington, D.C. See also George H. E. Smith to Homer Ferguson, August 21, 1945, Box 657, Robert A. Taft Papers, Library of Congress, Washington, D.C.

ever, with reports as politically devastating as those of the army board and the navy court, the end of the war offered serious forebodings for the administration. Once the veil of wartime security was removed, public and congressional pressure could possibly force the president to accede to the demands for a dramatic open inquiry.

8

Prying Open Pandora's Box

THE continuation of the war into 1945 shielded the Roosevelt administration from releasing the army and navy reports for a while longer. The rationale of national security remained the most effective way of avoiding a public confrontation over the question of war responsibility. As cautiously as the secretaries of war and the navy monitored the disclosure of information about Pearl Harbor in December, 1944, the very existence of the reports posed a continual aggravation. Once the war ended little could be done to effectively withhold that information or completely counteract its impact. While time remained, both departments intended to soften the reports' most serious charges against the high command and reestablish the conclusions of the Roberts commission as the standard by which to assess blame for the disaster.

Since 1942 Secretary Stimson had been quite willing to accept the findings of the Roberts report as definitive because it had limited responsibility for the Pearl Harbor attack to the lowest levels in the chain of authority. When the Army Pearl Harbor Board suggested that guilt for the debacle extended beyond the Hawaiian Command and into the office of the chief of staff, the long-accepted plan that Kimmel and Short should bear total blame was effectively challenged, and the secretary's own credibility was placed in jeopardy. Stimson had escaped criticism for Pearl Harbor in the Roberts and Army Pearl Harbor Board reports, but as secretary of war during 1941 and after he was ultimately responsible for the actions of the War Department. And as recriminations turned toward Washington, he might eventually be held personally accountable. At the moment, his concern was the protection of the War Department hierarchy in general and of Marshall in particular. As one of the most respected leaders in the Roosevelt administration, the chief of staff's reputation could not afford to be smirched lest his discreditation should reflect upon department and administration officialdom. Believing that the army board had gone too far in its assessment of blame in Washington, and supported by corroborating opinions from many of his advisers, he quickly decided to regain the balance by calling for a further investigation.

Stimson was deeply concerned about the army board's charges that General Marshall had failed to adequately evaluate General Short's preparations for air attack and had failed to keep him completely informed of the gravity of the situation developing in the Pacific. The crucial factor in making these charges ironclad was the Magic intercepts. Although the army board only came upon this information in the final stages of its inquiry, the members realized that the existence of a large number of deciphered high-level Japanese diplomatic messages and other similar material raised significant questions about whether Washington knew more about the coming attack than had been assumed and whether such information was transmitted to the local commanders. If it could be determined that high-level Washington officials had information which might have given warning about the attack and they had not disseminated it, the case against Marshall would be sealed. The war secretary therefore ordered an inquiry to determine the role of the Magic intercepts and other important decoded material in the Pearl Harbor affair. If the new inquiry could discover that Short had more information available to him than the army report implied, and that Marshall had less, the case against the local commanders could be reestablished while the chief of staff could be exonerated.[1]

The secretary assigned Maj. Henry C. Clausen (soon to be pro-

---

[1] Diary of Henry L. Stimson, November 30, 1944, XLIX, 61–62, microfilm, Henry L. Stimson Papers, Manuscripts and Archives, Sterling Memorial Library, Yale University, New Haven, Conn.; John F. Sonnett to Mathias F. Correa, December 14, 1944, Pearl Harbor File, Record Group 125, National Archives, Washington, D.C.; Cramer to Stimson, November 25, 1944, memorandum in U.S. Congress, *Pearl Harbor Attack: Hearings before the Joint Committee on the Pearl Harbor Attack*, 79th Cong., 1st sess., pt. 39, pp. 321 ff.; Richard N. Current, *Secretary Stimson: A Study in Statecraft*, pp. 178–179; *New York Times*, December 2, 1944, pp. 1, 5.

moted to lieutenant colonel) to follow up the Army Pearl Harbor Board investigation in late November, 1944. He was suitably qualified for his task. He had been an attorney in private life and was currently serving in the Office of the Judge Advocate General. He also was well acquainted with the army board, on which he served as assistant recorder.[2] During the course of his investigation, from November 23, 1944, to September 12, 1945, Clausen traveled over fifty-five thousand miles to gather evidence. He spent a great portion of his time tracking down leads about the interchange of information between Washington and Hawaii and the manner in which officials handled the information gleaned from the decrypted messages. In all, he interviewed ninety-two army, navy, and civilian personnel, many of whom had not been interviewed by any previous Pearl Harbor investigatory body.[3]

Throughout the investigation Clausen periodically reported his findings to Stimson's aide, Harvey Bundy. The tenacious investigator believed he was uncovering important evidence which demonstrated that General Short actually had more information available about the approaching hostilities with Japan than he had previously admitted. On March 3, 1945, Clausen informed Bundy that the Hawaiian commander apparently had received information about the existence of the so-called Winds code and advance notice of the Japanese decision to destroy their secret codes and papers at various important embassies preceding the air attack. "[I]t follows," Clausen asserted, "that there may have been available in the Hawaiian Department the same information possessed by the War Department."[4]

Clausen's analysis, however, was not based upon a complete study of the circumstances under which Washington transmitted information to Hawaii or what data the navy might have contributed

---

[2] Congress, *Pearl Harbor Attack*, pt. 9, p. 4301; interview with Clausen, January 3, 1964, Box 29, Charles C. Hiles Collection, Division of Rare Books and Special Collections, University of Wyoming Library, Laramie.

[3] Clausen to Stimson, September 14, 1945; Cramer to Clausen, December 5, 1944, in Congress, *Pearl Harbor Attack*, pt. 35, pp. 1–2, 6–7; Clausen testimony in *ibid.*, pt. 9, pp. 4301–4303, 4421–4423, 4500–4501.

[4] Clausen to Bundy, March 3, February 17, May 23, August 1, September 14, 1945, memoranda, Army Pearl Harbor Board Files, Box 7, Record Group 107, National Archives, Washington, D.C. (exhibits in Congress, *Pearl Harbor Attack*, pt. 35, pp. 114–121, 127–129); interview with Clausen, January 3, 1964, Box 29, Hiles Collection.

to the local commander's knowledge. The curious Winds code issue still remained unresolved. Clausen had not determined if the Japanese executed the code or who might have been informed if they had, and he still did not have a clear notion about what the War Department had done to direct Short to order an appropriate alert to keep him fully informed of developments in the crumbling Japanese–United States negotiations. It would be Stimson's duty to determine how Clausen's analysis materially affected the official department position on the question of responsibility.

To the hierarchy of the War Department the new findings were sufficient to discredit portions of the army board report that they did not support. Although Clausen had not substantially altered the board's overall assessment of army responsibility, he had been able to cause some doubt about the extent of Short's knowledge of the coming disaster. Placing special emphasis on that impression, the judge advocate general and Stimson both agreed that Short should continue to assume the brunt of the guilt. In a written opinion, Cramer told Stimson that the Clausen investigation sustained his original evaluation of the army board's findings. He added that Clausen uncovered no evidence to prove that War Department officials ever received a Winds execute, implying that they had even less vital information than previously had been assumed.[5]

The clearest explication of Stimson's views on the extent of army culpability—which included the findings of the Clausen inquiry—was his own statement accompanying the public version of the Army Pearl Harbor Board report of August 29, 1945. The war secretary emphasized that the "primary and immediate" responsibility for the protection of Hawaii rested with the commanding officer, General Short; it was not the function of the chief of staff to supervise or direct in detail the duties of the various sections of the General Staff. "It would hopelessly cripple the performance of these great and paramount duties [that is, to advise the president and the secretary of war and to supervise the overall organizational and strategic duties of the department]," he stated, "should a Chief of Staff allow himself to become immersed in administrative details by which the plans for defense are carried out in our many outposts."

[5] Cramer to Stimson, September 14, 1945, memorandum in Congress, *Pearl Harbor Attack*, pt. 39, pp. 270–295.

By establishing this criterion for responsibility, Stimson contradicted the army board's assessment almost categorically—although it might not seem so on the surface. Conceding that the War Plans Division made an error by failing to transmit more information than it did to General Short, he still insisted that the Hawaiian commander had been warned but did not take adequate precautions. Stimson did not recommend any further disciplinary action, but he had rationalized the former commander's relief from duty and retirement. Every other potentially guilty party, most especially Marshall, was freed from blame.[6]

The Clausen investigation had not materially affected Stimson's opinion of the Pearl Harbor incident. It did raise some serious doubts about the extent of information available in Hawaii, and it eased the secretary's mind that there was no perceivable blockbuster which could implicate General Marshall. That Stimson chose to amplify the faults of General Short and minimize those of the chief of staff and the War Plans Division was an attempt to have his own view of culpability prevail. He could not and did not, however, rewrite the conclusions of the army board with the findings of the new inquiry. It remained to be seen if his challenge to the Army Pearl Harbor Board would succeed.

Like the secretary of war, Chief of Staff Marshall realized that the findings of the Army Pearl Harbor Board might produce serious repercussions for the high command. After the release of the top secret Japanese intercepts to the board, he became especially concerned about the possible impact, personally and departmentally, that this startling information might have on determining blame for Pearl Harbor. And he had long feared as well that a public disclosure of Magic would irreparably damage American security. In order to determine how Washington and the Hawaiian Command dealt with the code messages before the surprise attack, he decided to conduct his own confidential investigation. In September, 1944, he directed Col. Carter W. Clarke, deputy chief of the Military Intelligence Service and soon to be intermediary between Marshall and Governor Dewey, to determine "the manner in which certain Top Secret communications were handled." On September 14 through 16 Clarke interrogated a number of high-level military personnel privy

[6] Statement by Stimson in ibid., pt. 35, pp. 13–19.

to Magic. He also examined thirty-eight of the decoded Japanese messages which the Tokyo government had sent to its various embasses from October to early December, 1941. In his September 20 report Clarke outlined the manner in which top secret code information was dispersed and concluded that Marshall and the high command dealt appropriately with this sensitive material. Clarke further suggested that the highly controversial Winds codes was not a factor in the Pearl Harbor episode. "I am unable to find," he stated, "that a Japanese message using the 'Winds' code was intercepted by the F.C.C. or the Army Signal Corps until after Pearl Harbor." He intimated that if the navy had information concerning this code, it was not brought to Marshall's attention.[7]

Marshall quickly dispensed with the Clarke inquiry in late September but reopened it in July, 1945, after hearing rumors that he allegedly tampered with the secret intercepts. Testifying before the navy's Hewitt investigation, William F. Friedman, the principal cryptanalyst of the army's Signal Intelligence Service before Pearl Harbor and at the time of the investigation director of communications research for the War Department's Signal Security Agency, declared that in 1943 Col. Otis K. Sadtler, chief of the Army Communications Service, told him that General Marshall had apparently ordered the destruction of a decoded Winds message.[8] All parties accepted the existence of the Winds code, but the interception of an actual Winds message which executed the code was still in dispute. If the rumor gained any credence, it would imply that the code was implemented and thus gave the United States some advanced warning of a Japanese attack somewhere in the world. It also might imply that Marshall destroyed the evidence to cover up the failure to transmit such an important piece of evidence to Hawaii.

Clarke set out to uncover the source of the rumor about Marshall and to prove it erroneous. Friedman repeated his story to Clarke, asserting that although he could not "believe, swallow, or give credence" to the rumor, Sadtler was "pretty firm in his statement and, there was no checking him in that." Sadtler denied Fried-

[7] Clarke to Clayton Bissell, September 20, 1944, memorandum in ibid., pt. 34, pp. 2–7.
[8] Clarke to Marshall, August 13, 1945, memorandum, in ibid., pt. 34, pp. 75–76; Friedman testimony before the Hewitt inquiry in ibid., pt. 36, pp. 305ff.

man's story, stating that Gen. Isaac Spalding of the War Department had told him—and in turn had been told by Col. John T. Bissel of the Military Intelligence Division—that all documents pertaining to Pearl Harbor were being or had been destroyed. And so went the inquiry, with the rumor attributed to first one officer, then another, and with denial after denial of Marshall's involvement. To Clarke's satisfaction the potentially destructive rumor was squelched, and it seemed as if the curiosity over the intriguing Winds code message was momentarily abated.[9]

The Navy Department was not immune to the challenges raised by its own court of inquiry. After the submission of its report, Forrestal remained unconvinced that Admiral Kimmel could be completely exonerated of previous charges against him, even though he believed some culpability might reside in Washington.[10] Although Forrestal had not been secretary of the navy at the time of the Pearl Harbor incident, and thus had no direct personal stake in the matter, he felt obligated to defend the Navy Department from unwarranted criticism in much the same manner that Stimson felt compelled to protect the War Department. But Forrestal was less determined to shield all the high officials in Washington than was the secretary of war. Most significantly, he would not protect former Chief of Naval Operations Stark, who had been Chief of Staff Marshall's counterpart in the navy. Besides his detachment from the Pearl Harbor incident and a limited working relationship with Stark, Forrestal, along with other high Navy Department officials, did not consider the admiral as indispensable to the war effort as Marshall was. Stark had been removed from his position as CNO soon after Pearl Harbor and had been sent to London as commander of the U.S. Naval Forces in Europe, and according to Admiral King, "It appeared that this assignment had been made originally because the President wished, for political reasons, to have Stark out of Washington."[11] Unlike Marshall, who continued to serve in the same position he held in December, 1941, Stark had been "kicked upstairs" either to protect him from recrimination or to shelve him.

[9] See testimony before the Clarke inquiry in ibid., pt. 34, pp. 77ff.

[10] Diary of James V. Forrestal, November 27, 1944, pp. 71–72, James V. Forrestal Papers, Princeton University Library, Princeton, N.J.

[11] King and Walter Muir Whitehill, *Fleet Admiral King: A Naval Record*, p. 632.

The secretary of the navy's own predilections were reinforced by Judge Advocate General Gatch and Fleet Admiral King, whose endorsements lent support to his desire to pursue the Pearl Harbor investigation further in order to untangle the unclear aspects. Gatch defended the high command from the charge of withholding vital information from the local commanders. He also translated the report's conclusions about Stark to mean that the evidence did not prove that the former CNO's failure to transmit some important information to Kimmel was the "proximate cause" of the disaster, and he concurred with that finding.[12] King's endorsement dealt much more explicitly with personal culpability, and he disagreed with the tone of the navy report. While admitting that there was inadequate evidence to support general courts-martial of the responsible parties, he did not believe that the navy could evade a share of responsibility for the disaster. After all, he argued, Pearl Harbor "cannot be regarded as an 'act of God,' beyond human power to prevent or mitigate. . . ." King surmised that the derelictions of Stark and Kimmel were "faults of omission rather than faults of commission." He asserted, "In the case in question, they indicate lack of the superior judgment necessary for exercising command commensurate with their rank and their assigned duties, rather than culpable inefficiency." Since court-martial was not warranted, he believed that the appropriate administrative action would be to relegate the officers to positions in which "lack of superior judgment may not result in future errors."[13]

The final decision for initiating the new inquiry, however, was Forrestal's alone. Despite his concurrence on Kimmel and Stark's qualified guilt, Admiral King told the secretary that he saw little need for any further investigation. He argued that the material to be uncovered was unlikely to influence any decision made by the Court of Inquiry. For example, part of the reason for the renewed investigation was to take additional testimony on matters touched upon in the army report but not in the navy report, such as the discovery that Japanese carriers had been reported in the region of the Marshall Islands before the attack. King did not believe disclosures

[12] Gatch to King, November 2, 1944, in Congress, *Pearl Harbor Attack*, pt. 39, pp. 330–332.
[13] King to Forrestal, November 6, 1944, in ibid., pp. 335–345.

of this type warranted a formal inquiry. But Forrestal overrode King's recommendation and, without notifying the judge advocate general, signed a precept for the investigation. Even before this encounter, King had been on poor terms with the navy secretary. But this incident clearly inflamed the fleet admiral, who feared that the charge for the new inquiry was too broad and gave the designated investigator too much authority and responsibility.[14]

Despite the objections, Forrestal had made his decision and directed Adm. H. Kent Hewitt in May, 1945, to conduct a special investigation of Pearl Harbor. He advised Hewitt that based upon the evidence before the navy court (not necessarily the conclusions) and all the other proceedings, he had determined that certain officers in Hawaii and Washington—namely Kimmel and Stark—had committed errors in judgment, but all possible leads had not yet been exhausted.[15] Like Stimson, Forrestal hoped new evidence would reinforce his own conclusions about culpability rather than the Navy Court of Inquiry's.

Admiral Hewitt was a logical choice to head the new navy probe. He was the first ranking flag officer released from the war zone who had no direct interest in the Pearl Harbor affair. The assignment would prove to be a very disagreeable one for Hewitt because he had been associated favorably with Kimmel in the past as his former division commander. Hewitt later recalled: ". . . I was very fond of him and a great admirer of him. . . . He did more than anyone I'd ever seen at getting his cruisers ready for war, first, and the fleet after that. . . ." He believed Kimmel had been placed in a difficult position in Hawaii, had decided that air attack was improbable, and had made a wrong guess—something he believed anyone was capable of doing. Despite Hewitt's friendly association with Kimmel, the former Hawaiian commander was not allowed to

[14] Kimmel interviews with King, May 18, December 7, 1945, Box 33, Husband E. Kimmel Collection, Division of Rare Books and Special Collections, University of Wyoming Library, Laramie; King and Whitehill, *Fleet Admiral King*, pp. 632–633; Arnold A. Rogow, *James Forrestal: A Study of Personality, Politics, and Policy*, pp. 103–104; Robert G. Albion and Robert H. Connery, *Forrestal and the Navy*, pp. 150–151.

[15] Forrestal to Hewitt, May 2, 1945, in Congress, *Pearl Harbor Attack*, pt. 36, pp. 259–260; diary of James V. Forrestal, April 18, 1945, p. 304, Forrestal Papers.

appear before the board, even though he was anxious to do so. The new investigator did not believe Kimmel could add anything to his previous testimony but was willing to have him appear. Forrestal ruled against it.[16] Once again Kimmel assumed that the Navy Department had thwarted his chance to exonerate himself. His patience was wearing thin, and his cynicism was growing deeper.[17] Hewitt's leadership in the investigation, however, might in some way counteract Forrestal's less sympathetic reaction toward the former Hawaiian commander.

From early May until mid-July Hewitt conducted his inquiry, reviewing previous data and interrogating more than thirty witnesses, 90 percent of whom were navy officers.[18] He uncovered additional detailed information about the transmission of top secret code data, and he even faced charges that one of his subordinates on the investigating team pressured key witnesses to change their previous testimony, but the results of the inquiry were not startling. "Secretary Forrestal had some very set ideas about the thing," Hewitt noted some years later, "and he wanted me to find certain things which I wouldn't find and didn't find. I think he was disappointed that I didn't make a report in accordance with some of his ideas."[19]

Hewitt's report was a fairly extensive document which fell midway between the Roberts report and the Navy Court of Inquiry report in assessing blame. Hewitt believed that the system of defense in Hawaii, a system which depended upon mutual cooperation between the services instead of the more sensible practice of unifying command and centralizing authority under a single leader, was inadequate to meet the attack. Because of the lack of command unity

16 Reminiscences of H. Kent Hewitt, Naval History Project, 1962, Columbia University (New York Times microfiche), pp. 411 ff.

17 Kimmel to Yarnell, January 19, 1945; Kimmel to Rugg, July 12, 1945, Harry E. Yarnell Papers, Naval History Division, Department of the Navy, Washington, D.C.; Lavender to Kimmel, January 31, 1945; Rugg to Kimmel, February 10, 1945; Kimmel to Rugg, February 12, 1945; Yarnell to Kimmel, April 26, 1945; Forrestal to Kimmel, May 14, 1945; Yarnell to Kimmel, August 2, 1945, Box 5, Kimmel Collection; Correa to Gatch, May 28, 1945; Kimmel to Forrestal, May 24, 1945, Records of the Secretary of the Navy (hereafter cited as Sec Nav), Box 44, Record Group 80, National Archives, Washington, D.C.

18 See witness list in Congress, Pearl Harbor Attack, pt. 36, p. 1.

19 Reminiscences of H. Kent Hewitt, Naval History Project, pp. 411–412.

as well as the absence of a well-organized intelligence system, the theoretically sound war plans were not placed into operation. With respect to department responsibilities, Hewitt—reiterating previous conclusions—stated that while there was a full exchange of important information in Washington and within the Navy Department, not all of it was transmitted to Hawaii. He singled out Admiral Stark for this lapse, but he also charged that Admiral Kimmel had sufficient data to indicate a serious situation developing in the Pacific and should have employed what means, although meager, he had available. Somewhat muting his criticism of Kimmel, Hewitt added that while the carrier attack probably could not have been prevented, a prior warning might have reduced its effects. These conclusions were not as charitable toward the Hawaiian Command as those of the navy court, yet they were by no means a whitewash of the Navy Department and were not meant to make Kimmel a scapegoat. The Hewitt investigation differed in degree from the Murfin inquiry without refuting its findings.[20]

Forrestal nonetheless believed the Hewitt report sustained his own misgivings about the conclusions of the court of inquiry. With King and Gatch largely in agreement, the navy secretary prepared what was to be the official department position on culpability. Outlined in a statement accompanying the public version of the Murfin report, his viewpoint was essentially a modification of the Roberts findings. Forrestal found nothing in the various investigations to justify negligence on the part of Washington officials with respect to withholding vital information which before December 6 clearly indicated an attack on Hawaii. He especially denied the existence or interception of the Winds message. His criticisms were individual rather than departmental. Clearing Admiral Bloch of any charges, he criticized Admirals Kimmel and Stark for failing to demonstrate "the superior judgment necessary for exercising command commensurate with their rank and their assigned duties." The Navy Department would not recall Kimmel and Stark (who had recently been retired on Forrestal's order) to active duty, especially to any position requiring superior judgment.[21]

[20] Congress, *Pearl Harbor Attack*, pt. 36, pp. 523ff.
[21] Endorsement by Forrestal, August 13, 1945; King to Forrestal, August

122   THE SHADOW OF PEARL HARBOR

Forrestal had applied the same principles to his analysis as had the Roberts commission—that is, that individuals, not the system of defense, were to blame for the breakdown at Hawaii. The inclusion of former CNO Stark was less a barb cast at the Navy Department than an attempt to isolate culpability in Washington to the one person directly charged with keeping the Hawaiian Command informed. Although the criticism of Kimmel and Stark did not carry any penalty beyond forced retirement, the implication of the secretary's words alone was sufficient to place the onus of guilt on their backs. Like the War Department, the navy had interpreted Pearl Harbor responsibility in the narrowest sense possible. Therefore, Secretary Forrestal had little interest in withholding the report of the Navy Court of Inquiry from the public much longer. Indefinite in the actual timing of such a release, he authorized his staff to fully inform the appropriate committees of Congress of the navy investigations and declared that there would be a public disclosure of the facts, less the information on Magic.[22]

As the war in the Pacific finally ended in the late summer of 1945, the major criterion for concealing the details of the Pearl Harbor attack and the subsequent army and navy investigations evaporated. Unaware that Forrestal was considering some kind of public disclosure, antiadministration forces in Congress began to pressure the service departments to loosen their grip on the heretofore secret reports. Sen. William Langer (Republican, North Dakota), a perennial foe of the administration and a staunch isolationist, presented a fifteen-thousand-name petition to the Senate demanding the publication of the results of the navy court and insisting upon punishment for all guilty parties. The originator of this petition was the Reverend Arthur W. Terminiello of Huntsville, Alabama. A southern version of Father Charles Coughlin, Terminiello sought to discredit the recently deceased President Roosevelt and his administration while simultaneously aiding Admiral Kimmel in his attempt to obtain a public hearing. The former Hawaiian commander was skeptical of the Huntsville minister, but he welcomed the publicity and was intrigued by Terminiello's determination to make Pearl Harbor

13, 1945; Gatch to King, August 10, 1945; Forrestal to Gatch, July 25, 1945; Hewitt to Forrestal, July 12, 1945; in ibid., pt. 39, pp. 355–391.

[22] Endorsement by Forrestal, August 13, 1945, in ibid., pp. 371 ff.

a major postwar issue, even to the extent of organizing "Truth about Pearl Harbor" clubs. Terminiello had a small following, but his petition was just the kind of vehicle that administration critics could use effectively to force the War and Navy departments to disclose the reports.[23]

When the petition was referred to the Senate Committee on Naval Affairs, Chairman David Walsh used it and the announcement of Japan's surrender on August 14 as levers to obtain copies of the complete files of the Navy Department's inquiries. As he told Forrestal in an August 16 letter: ". . . when Congress reconvenes there is certain to be a strong demand from Members of the Congress for information. . . . With the war in Japan ended, the explanation of military expediency, which Congress agreed to be desirable while the war was in progress, cannot be seriously urged as reason for now keeping the matter secret."[24] In response to Walsh's prodding, the official word from the Navy Department was that nothing would be done about the report until after the formal surrender of Japan. Despite the secretary's private commitment to disclosing the navy report, he wanted to choose the time and place.[25]

Roosevelt's successor, Harry S Truman, was unwilling to have the Pearl Harbor issue interfere with postwar planning. On August 17 he told Secretary Forrestal that he was disposed to meet the request for a full disclosure of the reports to avoid adding to the mystique already surrounding the December 7 disaster. The former vice-president straddled the fine line between perpetuating the traditional administration position on Pearl Harbor, which he had long supported, and attempting to detach himself and his administration from the issue. In his *Collier's* article that appeared before the 1944 election, Truman placed himself squarely in the camp of those who felt Kimmel and Short should bear major blame for the disaster. But aside from that outburst he had avoided becoming

[23] U.S. Congress, *Congressional Record*, 79th Cong., 1st sess., 1945, 91, p. 7429; Terminiello to Kimmel, July 21, 1945; Forrestal to Hanify, July 21, 1945; Kimmel to Yarnell, August 6, 1945, Yarnell Papers; *The Crusader: The Voice of the Union of Christian Crusaders* and attached petition, January, 1945, Box 41, Kimmel Collection.

[24] Walsh to Forrestal, August 16, 1945, Sec Nav, Box 44, Record Group 80, National Archives.

[25] *New York Times*, August 18, 1945, p. 4.

caught up in the controversy. Not personally involved with setting prewar policy, he was not faced with having to defend his own actions. Instead, as a strong party man and a loyal Roosevelt supporter, he tried to protect the Democratic administration from any new assaults without inciting further debate. The best way to accomplish this was to terminate the whole issue expediently; a disclosure of the secret army and navy reports was a good initial step. His apparent magnanimity was possible because the war was over. Protecting the Pearl Harbor data for the sake of national security was no longer a justification for concealment of the evidence. Given the political realities, Truman took the only logical course.[26]

After their August 17 meeting Forrestal confided in the president that his own mind was "veering toward your advice." His major concerns were that the security question surrounding the deciphering of the Japanese codes had to be resolved and that the War Department had to agree to a concurrent disclosure "so that the Navy should not bear the full brunt, which it does now, of responsibility for the Pearl Harbor disaster. . . ." The navy secretary tenaciously held to the belief that the public disclosure of the breaking of the codes would be disastrous even with the war all but formally concluded. It would take considerable convincing for the secretary to accept publication of the navy report with the details of Magic included. As for the willingness of the War Department to agree to a simultaneous release of its report, Forrestal remained uncertain about what Stimson would decide. He discussed the proposition with Assistant Secretary of War John J. McCloy, who was in charge of the War Department during Stimson's absence. Forrestal told McCloy that he realized "there were some oblique references" to General Marshall in the army report, but he felt the chief of staff's war record would make the present time the most favorable atmosphere for disclosure. The War Department officials, however, were not yet willing to commit themselves.[27]

Despite the growing sentiment in the administration for public

[26] Diary of James V. Forrestal, August 17, 1945, p. 440, Forrestal Papers. See also Truman to Harley M. Kilgore, September 14, 1945, Official File 400, Harry S Truman Papers, Harry S Truman Presidential Library, Independence, Mo.

[27] Diary of James V. Forrestal, August 18 and 19, 1945, pp. 445–446, Forrestal Papers.

disclosure of the army and navy reports in the last days before the formal surrender of Japan, Pearl Harbor data created some shock waves. At the end of August, Maj. Mathias Correa, special assistant to the navy secretary, learned through Harvey Bundy that journalist and zealous Roosevelt critic John T. Flynn planned to disclose some top secret materials relevant to the disaster. On August 27 Correa further discovered that Flynn had given the material to the *Chicago Tribune* for publication. Bundy was quite disturbed by the news and recommended that both departments send representatives to see the publisher and urge that "no publication prejudicial to security be made." He also suggested that the president be apprised of the situation. As a result, the information was passed along to Truman's naval aide, Commodore James K. Vardaman. Even General Marshall became concerned enough to recommend that Secretary of State Hull call on the publisher.[28] The incident eventually dissipated when the sensational release failed to materialize, but not without demonstrating the heightened anxieties of the War and Navy departments, most likely brought on by the long period of concealing information from a public which they believed was not prepared to receive it. The fear of leaks made it more imperative that the departments release the materials on their own terms.

On August 29 the high officials in Washington decided to release the reports—but not without some final pulling and hauling. On that morning the president, his important advisers, and officials from the War and Navy departments hammered out the details. According to Truman's senior military adviser, Adm. William D. Leahy, the president wanted the full story to be released immediately "to anticipate a political attack" by the McCormick newspapers in Chicago.[29] But Forrestal, fearful that the administration was being "stampeded" into taking action, raised a dilemma he faced over the disclosure: Because of the formal nature of the Navy

[28] Correa to Vardaman, August 27, 1945, memorandum; Correa, Mr. Byrd, and Captain Taylor, August 27, 1945, transcript of telephone conversation, Sec Nav, Box 44, Record Group 80, National Archives. See also *Washington Post*, August 28, 1945, concerning speculation that a late August meeting between Justice Owen Roberts and President Truman portended something about the release of information about Pearl Harbor.

[29] Diary of William D. Leahy, August 28, 1945, p. 153, William D. Leahy Papers, Library of Congress, Washington, D.C.

Court of Inquiry and the critical tone of his and Admiral King's endorsements with respect to Kimmel, he was concerned that release of the department's findings might make it impossible for the Hawaiian commander to receive the unbiased court-martial which Knox had promised in 1942. On the other hand, withholding publication of the navy court findings could expose the department to charges of a coverup.

Faced with these unpalatable alternatives, the secretary recommended that Truman either order courts-martial for Kimmel and Short or name a new commission to study the case. He also suggested that the army publish its report as it was and that the Navy publish nothing, but simultaneously announce the trial of the commanders. Aware that Forrestal was trying to protect his department from bad publicity at the expense of the War Department, Harvey Bundy and Acting Secretary of War Robert P. Patterson objected vigorously. Since Stimson had previously claimed that the facts of the Pearl Harbor affair were not sufficient to base any charges against Short, the alternative of a court-martial was rejected. The War Department officials were also unwilling to accept any proposal which placed more emphasis upon army culpability than they deemed absolutely necessary. President Truman intervened and terminated the debate since he had already made up his mind in favor of disclosing the reports. He assured the group that Kimmel could receive a fair trial despite the publicity, although the admiral deferred his demand for a hearing until after the public congressional inquiry. The only remaining point of major contention was the issue of the secret code material. Not wanting to disclose what many of the officials believed to be a continuing source of information that needed protection—and most likely undesirous of making public a weapon which many people might assume should have given Washington advance warning of the attack—the group decided to omit any reference to Magic or related code data from the public version of the reports.[30]

At his morning press conference on August 29, Truman an-

[30] Diary of James V. Forrestal, August 29, 1945, p. 453, Forrestal Papers. See also Forrestal to Kimmel, August 28, 1945; Kimmel to Forrestal, September 8, 1945, Sec Nav, Box 44, Record Group 80; McCloy to Correa, August 21, 1945, memorandum, Pearl Harbor File, Record Group 125, National Archives.

nounced his decision to release the reports with the accompanying statements of the secretaries and the pertinent endorsements. The president was particularly sensitive about the criticisms of General Marshall and avidly supported Stimson's disclaimer concerning the chief of staff's alleged guilt. "Indeed," he concluded, "I have the fullest confidence in the skill, energy and efficiency of all our war leaders, both Army and Navy."[31]

On August 30 Truman held another press conference at which he faced a number of pointed questions about the disclosures: Was there any reason for putting out the report on the day American troops entered Tokyo? Were the reports a whitewash as certain individuals had suggested? Would he order the army and navy to institute court-martial proceedings against anyone? Staving off this inquisition with his characteristic terseness, Truman responded to a question about the alleged breakdown in communications between Washington and Hawaii with his standard analysis of the cause of the December 7 disaster: ". . . I came to the conclusion that the whole thing is the result of the policy which the country itself pursued. The country was not ready for preparedness. . . . I think the country is as much to blame as any individual in this final situation that developed in Pearl Harbor."[32]

The president's assessment did not quell the suspicion that the complete story remained untold. There were too many complexities and inconsistencies in the available public evidence to pass judgment so easily. There was also a growing feeling that the administration had been less than candid in revealing the essential information about Pearl Harbor. Many questioned the timing of the recent disclosures, which coincided with the American troop landings in Japan. A significant number in the press corps were disgruntled that White House officials gave them so little time—about two hours— to examine the army and navy reports before publication. In this climate of skepticism the press, radio, and general public reacted critically to the disclosure.

A majority of journalists and radio commentators were dissatisfied with the August 29 release. According to a report prepared

[31] Press conference 21, August 29, 1945, in *Public Papers of the Presidents of the United States: Harry S. Truman, 1945*, pp. 243–245.
[32] Press conference 22, August 30, 1945, in ibid., pp. 246–248.

by the Evaluation Section of the Navy Department's Office of Public Information, 64 percent of the editorials, 54 percent of the columnists, and 68 percent of the radio commentators sampled reacted unfavorably.[33] Many newsmen would not accept Truman's analysis that the whole country was to blame for Pearl Harbor. According to an editorial in the *Nashville Banner*: "President Truman pulled a boner when he laid the blame for Pearl Harbor on the American people. . . . The attempt to place the blame on the American people is a national insult." The most fervid of the administration critics screamed "Cover-up!" as in the case of the *Kiplinger Washington Letter*: "These higher-ups are now sitting in judgment on their own acts. They are ducking all blame, and applying the whitewash to each other, and tell partial truths. This may be natural but it is not honest. . . ."[34]

In seeking an alternative to Truman's blanket indictment, commentators focused on Washington. According to the *Providence Evening Bulletin*: "A careful reading . . . leaves one with the impression that the fault did not lie mainly with the ranking naval and military command in Pearl Harbor but with the authorities in Washington." The more disgruntled editors of the *Washington Times-Herald* and the *New York News* leveled salvos more pointedly against an old foe: "Of course Hull was wrong. Of course Stimson was wrong. Of course Marshall was wrong. They were wrong because the whole system in Washington was wrong. The whole system was wrong because it was centered in and dominated by one man, Franklin D. Roosevelt. . . ."[35]

By 1945 these attacks on Roosevelt and other Washington officials were standard responses to the administration's assessment of the Pearl Harbor affair. The only new stir about personal guilt was the case of General Marshall. Although the army and navy reports expanded the web of responsibility to include Stark, Hull, Gerow, and others, the strong criticism of the chief of staff in the army re-

[33] Press and Radio Reaction to the Pearl Harbor Reports, September 7, 1945, Sec Nav, Box 44, Record Group 80, National Archives.

[34] *Kiplinger Washington Letter*, September 1, 1945; Press and Radio Reaction to the Pearl Harbor Reports, Sec Nav, Box 44, Record Group 80, National Archives.

[35] Press and Radio Reaction to the Pearl Harbor Reports, Sec Nav, Box 44, Record Group 80, National Archives.

port, and the equally vehement defense by Stimson and Truman, brought the chief of staff's case in particular to public attention. Despite General Marshall's great stature, there was fear in governmental circles that he might be subjected to devastating reprisals by his most ardent critics. An Office of War Information press summary distributed to a great many high-ranking American officials overseas reported: "There is no getting away from the fact that the public reputation of General Marshall has been smirched. . . . his name has been bracketed with Kimmel and Short, the two men whom the American public has long been led to believe were primarily responsible for the Pearl Harbor tragedy."[36] There were even rumors that because of the recent public disclosures, Marshall planned to retire and seek a court-martial to clear his name. Although officials labeled the story as "poppycock," the shock of Marshall's implication reverberated throughout Washington.[37]

The personal recriminations were not the only issues undertaken in the heightened dialogue on Pearl Harbor. Since the army and navy reports—plus the endorsements—offered evidence and opinions complicating instead of illuminating the affair, some commentators tried to analyze the intricacies of a defense system which failed. As the *New York Times* stated, ". . . in point of fact, the most important element in the reports is the plain evidence that Pearl Harbor was not so much the fault of men as the fault of a system that was not geared to cope with such an eventuality. . . ."[38] The most often discussed solution to the problem of inadequate defenses seemed to be unifying command at strategic American bases and possibly consolidating the armed services into a single Department of Defense to increase efficiency and centralize authority and responsibility. These were issues which the service branches were considering throughout the war and which were a constant source of discussion whenever Pearl Harbor was publicly debated. As the *New York Herald Tribune* asserted: "Out of [the Pearl Harbor af-

[36] British Division Daily Summary, August 31, 1945, Box 334, Stanley K. Hornbeck Collection, Hoover Institution on War, Revolution, and Peace, Stanford, Calif.

[37] *New York Times*, August 30, 1945, p. 5; August 31, 1945, p. 6. See also favorable radio reactions about Marshall and Hull, August 29, 1945, Box 78, Cordell Hull Papers, Library of Congress, Washington, D.C.

[38] *New York Times*, August 31, 1945, p. 1.

fair] emerges at least one overwhelming lesson. As long as a possibility of war remains, this country cannot meet it with the kind of diplomatic, military and naval machinery in existence in 1941."[39] The army and navy reports helped foster, in part at least, a public discussion of American defense policy that made the controversy over Pearl Harbor something more than a mud-slinging contest.

Yet more questions were raised by the army and navy reports than answers were given. If they had done anything, the disclosures had confused and complicated the debate. In the press and on the radio the demand for a congressional investigation became increasingly popular. As radio commentator Gabriel Heatter argued: "Whether any investigation can fix responsibility, on any one or half-dozen men, time alone will tell. . . . Those whose sons were killed at Pearl Harbor . . . owe it to the memory of their sons."[40]

Public opinion surveys demonstrate that the majority of Americans also wanted the Pearl Harbor story to be thoroughly aired. Although it is unlikely that many Americans digested the highly complex reports—or were capable of doing so because of lack of expertise—the four-year controversy had produced conflicting theories of responsibility which had yet to be reconciled. An American Institute of Public Opinion (AIPO) survey indicated that 73 percent of those polled had heard about the reports; of that group 55 percent favored further investigation.[41] Similar polls conducted by Roper-Fortune showed that a majority or a plurality of the respondents were at least mildly interested in a continuation.[42] Most significantly, when cross-tabulated with political party preference, the responses demonstrated that Americans of Republican persuasion were substantially more interested in further investigation than were their Democratic counterparts.[43] These results would seem to

[39] Press and Radio Reaction to the Pearl Harbor Reports, Sec Nav, Box 44, Record Group 80, National Archives; *New York Times*, August 30, 1945, p. 1; August 31, 1945, p. 6; *U.S. News* 19 (September 7, 1945): 42.

[40] Press and Radio Reaction to the Pearl Harbor Reports, Sec Nav, Box 44, Record Group 80, National Archives.

[41] AIPO Poll, September 26, 1945, in Hadley Cantril and Mildred Strunk, eds., *Public Opinion, 1935–1946*, pp. 1144–1145.

[42] Roper-Fortune Poll 50 (question 21), September, 1945; Poll 51 (question 14), October, 1945, Roper Public Opinion Research Center, Williams College, Williamstown, Mass.

[43] Roper-Fortune Poll 50 (question 21), September, 1945, ibid.

indicate that those individuals who were least pleased with the pro-administration findings of Secretaries Stimson and Forrestal were most desirous of discovering how valid their narrow interpretation of culpability really was.

Considering the excitement engendered by the recent termination of the war and the number of years that had passed since the attack on Hawaii, the desire for further investigation affirmed by about 50 percent of those surveyed is significant. Furthermore, the polls indicate that as of late 1945 no consensus on guilt had emerged. Responsibility was spread among a variety of individuals, ranging from Roosevelt to Kimmel and Short, although more Americans blamed politicians than military men—much to the chagrin of the administration.[44]

This ambivalence worked to the advantage of the War and Navy departments, and the whole administration, which had been very anxious about the public reaction to the recent disclosures. Although an open congressional investigation loomed ahead, the decision to release the army and navy reports, and the manner in which the release was accomplished, was likely to protect the Washington hierarchy from serious recriminations. The complexity of the Pearl Harbor issue worked to their advantage, as did the ability of the war and navy secretaries to tone down the criticisms of Washington with their supplemental inquiries and public disclaimers. Also, the withholding of information about the top secret code data kept out of the hands of critics a possible weapon to use for political advantage. What a public investigation could do to the Washington officials' scenario was uncertain. All they knew was that the question of war responsibility had not yet been laid to rest.

[44] Roper-Fortune Poll 50 (question 20), ibid.

9

Hope and Trepidation

THE surrender of the Japanese and the reawakened interest in Pearl Harbor induced by the release of the army and navy reports provided the ideal conditions for the much-anticipated public investigation. For the first time since mid-1944, Congress took the initiative to resolve the controversy over the December 7 attack. There was little that the Truman administration could do to forestall the public inquiry or maintain complete control over the issue. As *Newsweek* stated in late August, 1945: "In the fury of transition, Congress appeared cast for a larger role. No longer would the military and other war agencies dictate their own terms on the basis of wartime emergency. Inevitably, demands for investigation of the conduct of many aspects of the war would bear fruit."[1]

However, the sides in the debate had long since polarized, and the possibility that the public congressional inquiry could rise above partisanship seemed remote. Democratic supporters of the Roosevelt administration and its foreign policy were apprehensive about further probing into the Pearl Harbor matter and remained quite willing to adhere to the standard administration view that the local Hawaiian commanders should bear the guilt for America's lack of vigilance. Republican critics of Roosevelt, on the other hand, saw the new investigation as a unique opportunity to challenge the Democratic hierarchy's claims of innocence and possibly garner some political advantage for the future. Given these motivations, it was unlikely that congressional action would resolve the controversy.[2]

[1] *Newsweek* 26 (August 27, 1945): 29.
[2] *New York Times,* September 2, 1945, sect. 4, pp. 3, 6; September 4, 1945, p. 4.

With an eye to discrediting the Roosevelt administration in particular and the Democratic party in general, Republicans in the Senate and House were first to call for a congressional hearing to fix responsibility for what Sen. Robert A. Taft called "the greatest disaster in our history." On September 4 Sen. Alexander Wiley (Republican, Wisconsin) called for courts-martial for Kimmel and Short and implored the Truman administration "to cease its cover-up activities and allow the lid to be completely taken off the whole stench-ridden, bungling mess of December, 1941." On the same day, the Republican steering committee in the Senate approved Homer Ferguson's resolution calling for a public inquiry. In the House, Congressman Forrest Harness also prepared to submit a similar resolution, and Minority Leader Joseph W. Martin (Republican, Massachusetts) declared that he wanted "no more whitewashing."[3]

During the Republican blitz the Democrats remained cautious and quiet. When Speaker of the House Sam Rayburn (Democrat, Texas) was asked if he had discussed the congressional undercurrents about the surprise attack with the president, he replied: "That always comes up; however unfortunate that might be, it is up. I wish we could forget about Pearl Harbor, but we can't." Rayburn probably reflected the attitude of many Democrats, who, while interested in resolving the controversy, feared the political repercussions. If Roosevelt and his high advisers were discredited publicly, it would reflect upon them whether they had been avid supporters of the former president or not. Furthermore, the resurgence of the Pearl Harbor issue, directed by GOP legislators, could prove to be a serious political liability in the upcoming congressional elections of 1946 and possibly in the presidential election of 1948. Democrats in both houses of Congress, either for the sake of protecting the reputation of the Roosevelt administration and the Democratic party or simply to protect their own political careers, had to devise some way to counteract the Republican onslaught.

Before Ferguson or Harness could formally introduce their resolutions, the Democratic leadership, under the direction of Majority Leader Barkley, decided to coopt the Republicans' plan and offer their own resolutions. With the approval of President Truman, Bark-

[3] U.S. Congress, *Congressional Record*, 79th Cong., 1st sess., 1945, 91, pp. 8389–8390, 8412–8413; *U.S. News* 19 (September 7, 1945): 34.

ley introduced legislation on September 6 calling for a public joint congressional investigation of Pearl Harbor. The proposed committee would consist of five senators and five congressmen on a ratio of three Democrats to two Republicans for each house. The committee was to produce a report no later than January 3, 1946. In presenting the resolution, Barkley contended that popular demand and the contradictions and inconsistencies of the previous inquiries made an open investigation necessary. "This inquiry," he proclaimed, ". . . should be of such dignity and authenticity as to convince the Congress and the country and the world that no effort has been made to shield any person who may have been directly or indirectly responsible for this disaster, or to condemn unfairly or unjustly any person who was in authority, military, naval or civilian, at the time or prior thereto."[4]

Barkley's announcement took the Republican senators completely by surprise, but they were well aware of the majority's strategy. As Ferguson told *Time* correspondent Frank McNaughton, "[The administration] caught over a barrel not only took the stave but the whole barrel."[5] Outmaneuvered, the Michigan senator and his GOP colleagues put up only mild resistance to the Democratic plan. They had forced an investigation even if they would not get credit for introducing the official legislation.[6]

As might be expected, the new developments in the Pearl Harbor political saga attracted more lively debate in the House than in the Senate. House Republicans, not to be outdone by their opponents, decided to make some political capital of their own. On September 6, minority leaders prepared an amendment to the Senate resolution which would balance the membership on the Pearl Harbor committee between the two political parties. Joseph Martin confided to McNaughton that if the Democrats went ahead and passed the resolution for three Democrats and two Republicans from each

[4] Congress, *Congressional Record*, 79th Cong., 1st sess., 1945, 91, pp. 8338–8339; Alben W. Barkley Oral History Interview, November 1, 1953, Harry S Truman Presidential Library, Independence, Mo.; *Newsweek* 26 (September 17, 1945): 32.

[5] McNaughton to Don Bermingham, September 6, 1945, Frank McNaughton Papers, Harry S Truman Presidential Library, Independence, Mo.

[6] Congress, *Congressional Record*, 79th Cong., 1st sess., 1945, 91, pp. 8340 ff.

chamber and then whitewashed the whole affair, the GOP political position would be enhanced. He added: "We can really go to the people on this issue. If we get equal representation, we can block any whitewash. We are going to make a record, and if they won't agree to equal representation then the responsibility is on them."[7]

Responding to the minority's attempt to gain advantage from the Barkley resolution, House Democrats initiated a name-calling debate on September 11. Congressman Adolph J. Sabath (Democrat, Illinois) attacked the Republicans for attempting to circumvent congressional tradition by denying the Democrats majority representation on the proposed investigatory body. He charged that the minority's "attacks, harangues, charges, and insinuations" were politically motivated. "I question," he said, "whether the Republicans are seeking the truth. It appears to me that what they want is some publicity that they can use in the next campaign. . . ." Despite attempts by Minority Leader Martin to defend the amendment on the grounds that the surprise attack was a special case which demanded equal representation, congressmen from both sides of the aisle were drawn into the dispute, which was characterized by accusations of partisanship. Inevitably the Democrats won out. The equal-representation amendment was defeated on a party-line vote, 163–136. When that Republican challenge crumbled, the Barkley resolution passed unanimously.[8] *Newsweek* astutely noted that although temporarily outmaneuvered, the Republicans "had little reason to complain. They were getting what they had wanted—an investigation with all stops pulled."[9] The congressional investigation was now a reality, and the maneuverings over the resolution were merely preliminary to a political confrontation which would consume the remainder of 1945 and half of 1946.

The selection of members for the joint congressional inquiry insured that the partisan debate which began on the floor of the House and the Senate would extend into the committee room. In general, the legislators brought adequate qualifications to the investigation.

[7] McNaughton to Arthur Monroe, September 7, 1945, McNaughton Papers.

[8] Congress, *Congressional Record*, 79th Cong., 1st sess., 1945, 91, pp. 8494–8510; *New York Times*, September 12, 1945, pp. 1, 6.

[9] *Newsweek* 26 (September 17, 1945): 32.

The members were not exceedingly old or young; the average age was fifty-seven. There was a rough geographical balance of representation, with a slight advantage to the Midwest, the South, and the border states. All ten members were lawyers; some had been prosecuting attorneys and judges. The group averaged thirteen years' experience in Congress; the most experienced member, Barkley, had thirty-three years. Only one member sat on a permanent service committee. The rationale for not selecting more legislators from the army and navy committees was to avoid conflicts of interest. But the decision also meant that most of the members were novices with respect to the intricate aspects of the Pearl Harbor issue.[10]

The general qualifications of the committee members did not highlight the obvious partisan backgrounds of most of them. The senatorial selections—Democrat and Republican—were largely party stalwarts. Leading the Democratic delegation, and selected as chairman of the proceedings, was Majority Leader Alben W. Barkley. A professional politician of the old school, he was a "faithful Democratic wheelhorse" who had been a main spokesman of the New Deal in the Senate and a staunch defender of Roosevelt's foreign policy. Whether Barkley was willing to defend the memory of FDR, however, was uncertain. A controversy between the White House and Congress over tax legislation in early 1944 had led Barkley to resign as majority leader. Although he was unanimously re-elected by the Democratic caucus, the relationship between president and Barkley was damaged. Nevertheless, Barkley, a man of great endurance and personal charm, was certain to keep the best interests of his party in mind as he wielded the gavel.[11]

The remaining two Democratic senators were also sure to defend the majority's view of Pearl Harbor. Scott W. Lucas (Democrat, Illinois) was a steadfast New Dealer who was regarded as one of the "fairhaired boys" by the White House even though he had

[10] *Biographical Directory of the American Congress, 1774–1971,* pp. 553, 635, 743, 783, 935, 992, 994–995, 1215, 1313, 1456; *New York Times,* September 15, 1945, pp. 1, 5; *Newsweek* 26 (September 24, 1945): 38.

[11] *National Cyclopedia of American Biography,* vol. H, 9–10; McNaughton to David Hulburd, Jr., September 14, 1945, McNaughton Papers; *Biographical Directory of the American Congress,* p. 553; *New York Times,* May 1, 1956, p. 26; Richard Polenberg, *War and Society: The United States, 1941–1945,* pp. 197ff.

incurred FDR's ire for denouncing his court-packing scheme in 1937. Lucas had consistently supported the administration's internationalist foreign policy.[12] The third Democratic senator was the highly conservative Walter F. George (Democrat, Georgia). The archetype of the Southern Democrat, he perennially voted with his Southern colleagues and had difficulty adhering to party regularity. As powerful chairman of the Finance Committee, he had not been a strong supporter of FDR. One of the prime subjects of the president's famed 1938 congressional election "purge," the graying but fearless Georgian had run a vigorous campaign, repelling the assault successfully. On international affairs he was a reluctant convert to the administration's foreign policy. Before World War II he had favored the neutrality legislation that restricted the power of the president, and he opposed the cash-and-carry formula. But when war broke out in Europe, George returned to the fold. Although he was not as closely tied to the Roosevelt or the Truman administrations as Barkley and Lucas, he was unlikely to side with the Republicans to criticize a foreign policy he had come to accept.[13]

The Republican senators were as strong advocates of their party affiliation as Barkley and Lucas were of theirs. Homer Ferguson was the committee member with the longest history of involvement in the Pearl Harbor controversy—save possibly Barkley, who had spoken for the administration's point of view since December 7— and he had continually tried to prod the administration into a public inquiry for some years. The soft-spoken, white-haired Michigan senator had acquired a reputation as an able interrogator in his home state and especially as a member of the Mead committee, which investigated graft in military contracts as did its predecessor the Truman committee. Although he was by no means an isolationist, Ferguson had actively opposed the suppression of information about Pearl Harbor and believed that guilt resided in Washington.[14] Ralph

[12] *Newsweek* 26 (September 24, 1945): 38; *National Cyclopedia of American Biography*, vol. G, pp. 136–137; *Biographical Directory of the American Congress*, p. 1313; McNaughton to Hulburd, September 14, 1945, McNaughton Papers; *New York Times*, February 23, 1968, p. 33.

[13] *Biographical Directory of the American Congress*, pp. 994–995; *New York Times*, August 5, 1957, p. 21; McNaughton to Hulburd, September 14, 1945, McNaughton Papers.

[14] McNaughton to Hulburd, September 14, 1945, McNaughton Papers; *National Cyclopedia of American Biography*, vol. G, pp. 508–509.

Owen Brewster (Republican, Maine) was the senior minority senator on the committee and a staunch party man. Called by his opponents a "Republican needler," the brazen-voiced, aggressive politician was an antagonist of the New Deal although he supported Roosevelt as commander in chief when the war broke out. He was the only committee member who sat on a service committee—the Naval Affairs Committee.[15]

The congressmen selected for duty on the investigating committee were not as well known as their senatorial counterparts, but they did display the same degree of party attachment. The senior member of the Democratic entourage, and the vice-chairman of the investigation, was Jere Cooper (Democrat, Tennessee). The shy, quiet, cautious Tennessean—nicknamed "the Sphinx" by reporters —was a strong party man who acted as Democratic troubleshooter in the House.[16] J. Bayard Clark (Democrat, North Carolina), a contemporary of Cooper, was the second-ranking Democratic congressman on the committee. He, too, was "silent as a casket" and generally supported the administration line, defending the Pearl Harbor policy during previous congressional debates. Like George, he often voted with the Southern conservatives but never had any serious disputes with the party leadership, especially since he was a close friend of Speaker Rayburn. Clark had a reputation as an able questioner with a sharp, judicial mind.[17] The final Democrat was the forty-three-year-old John W. Murphy (Democrat, Pennsylvania), a liberal who faithfully supported his party. Despite his short tenure in the House, he had already proved himself to be a keen interrogator in other congressional investigations. He would direct much of the Democratic examination of witnesses during the Pearl Harbor hearings.[18]

The two Republican congressmen were not particularly influen-

[15] *New York Times*, December 26, 1961, p. 25; McNaughton to Hulburd, September 14, 1945, McNaughton Papers.

[16] *Newsweek* 26 (September 24, 1945): 38; McNaughton to Hulburd, September 15, 1945, McNaughton Papers; *New York Times*, December 19, 1957, p. 31.

[17] McNaughton to Hulburd, September 14, 1945, McNaughton Papers; *Biographical Directory of the American Congress*, p. 743.

[18] *New York Times*, March 29, 1962, p. 33; *Biographical Directory of the American Congress*, p. 1456; McNaughton/Beal to Hulburd, September 15, 1945, McNaughton Papers; *Newsweek* 26 (September 24, 1945): 38.

tial in House affairs but shared an active dislike for the Democratic administration, past and present. Bertrand W. Gearhart (Republican, California) was an anti–New Dealer and an isolationist. The chunky, rather affable Californian did not have a sparkling record in the House; he was best known for his advocacy of Iceland as the forty-ninth state. During the investigation he would demonstrate a strong personal attachment to Admiral Kimmel.[19] Frank B. Keefe (Republican, Wisconsin), a six-foot, three-inch, 250-pound congressman, generally shared the political sentiments of his colleague from California, although he had at one time broken with the Republican party over the issue of the National Youth Administration program of the New Deal. He had the capacity for biting cross-examination and would likely give the Democrats a difficult time.[20]

Leading the four-man legal staff was the quiet and methodical William D. Mitchell of New York. The seventy-one-year-old lawyer was a compromise choice. A nominal Democrat, he had served as solicitor general under Calvin Coolidge and attorney general under Herbert Hoover. It was hoped that he could act as a balance wheel between the opposing factions of the committee. The remainder of the staff selected to aid Mitchell consisted of Gerhard A. Gesell (chief assistant), Jule M. Hannaford (assistant), and John E. Masten (assistant). According to Gesell, the committee counsels remained detached from the politics of the investigation. Although that may have been true about himself and the assistant counsels, Mitchell wittingly or unwittingly became embroiled in numerous political disputes. As the investigation proceeded, his consistent support of the majority cause would alienate him from the Republicans.[21]

[19] *Biographical Directory of the American Congress*, p. 992; *New York Times*, October 13, 1955, p. 31; McNaughton to Hulburd, September 14, 1945; McNaughton/Beal to Hulburd, September 15, 1945, McNaughton Papers.

[20] *Newsweek* 26 (September 24, 1945): 38; *Biographical Directory of the American Congress*, p. 1215; McNaughton to Hulburd, September 14, 1945; McNaughton/Beal to Hulburd, September 15, 1945, McNaughton Papers; *New York Times*, February 6, 1952, p. 29.

[21] Gerhard A. Gesell interview with author, May 16, 1974, Washington, D.C.; *Newsweek* 26 (October 8, 1945): 39; *U.S. News* 19 (November 16, 1945): 89; 20 (January 11, 1946): 55–56; *New York Times*, September 9, 1945, p. 4.

Almost as soon as the committee convened, controversy arose. Both sides began to maneuver for advantage to insure that the inquiry would reflect its own point of view. The focus of the debate before the November 15 opening date was the question of access to pertinent files and materials. The Democratic position—expressed by Barkley and reinforced by committee counsel—was that the investigatory body as a whole should request essential data; the Republicans—especially the senators—demanded that governmental and other important files be open to individual members. The majority members objected to the Republican alternative, branding it as an attempt to conduct "fishing expeditions." They feared that the individual investigations would retard the process of inquiry and allow the minority to pursue leads meant solely to discredit the administration. The minority members believed their method would protect them from being "spoon fed" information by the committee counsel and the majority members.

From the moment the committee members were appointed until the end of the inquiry, the debate over access to materials dragged on. The catalyst was President Truman's August 28 directive, which had been distributed immediately preceding the release of the army and navy reports. The order stated that appropriate departments of the government and the Joint Chiefs of Staff were directed to prevent release of information regarding the technique or specific results of any cryptanalytic unit.[22]

When chief committee counsel Mitchell discovered this directive, he realized it would prevent the committee from obtaining copies of the decoded Japanese messages or using their texts during the hearings. As a result, he attempted to have the order rescinded. In discussing the matter with the War and Navy departments, he tried to convince them that the members were interested only in the substance of the messages and not the technique used to crack the codes. Both departments were very hesitant—especially the navy —because they felt the public disclosure of the intercepts would lead to a complete examination of intelligence operations, which might cause the loss of continuing sources of secret data and the

[22] Memorandum by Truman, August 28, 1945, in U.S. Congress, *Pearl Harbor Attack: Hearings before the Joint Committee on the Pearl Harbor Attack*, 79th Cong., 1st sess., pt. 1, p. 8.

disclosure of valuable decoding methods. Mitchell argued with the intelligence branches of both services for a week and persuaded all but the Office of Naval Intelligence that the August 28 directive had to be terminated. Finally he "appealed to Caesar" and went to the White House for a conference. Until that moment he had not informed the members of the committee of his actions; he finally discussed the matter with Barkley and asked for his support. After conferring with Truman in late October, Mitchell prepared a "wide open order" which the President signed. The new directive lifted the ban on the availability of the decoded intercepts for committee use.[23]

Satisfied with his action, Mitchell was not prepared for the Republican criticism that followed. Ferguson and other minority members were dissatisfied with the chief counsel's explanation of the situation, believing he was closely tied to the majority and was acting as the executor of its wishes to keep the Republicans from uncovering important leads. Seeking public attention for their complaint, the GOP members brought this latest point of contention to the floors of the House and the Senate. On November 2 Ferguson and Brewster complained that individual members could not examine the pertinent files in the War and Navy departments under the present directive, nor could naval and military personnel furnish tips or talk individually with the members. Barkley and George attempted to counter the charges, but the adamant minority senators persisted.[24]

Republicans raised the same issue in both houses again on November 6. But other more specific demands convoluted the debate.

[23] Mitchell to C. R. Mason, November 10, 1945, Box 657, Robert A. Taft Papers, Library of Congress, Washington, D.C.; Mitchell to Colclough and H. Duncombe, October 15, 1945; Duncombe to Howard C. Petersen, October 29, 1945, and attachments, Army Pearl Harbor Board Files, Box 35, Record Group 107, National Archives, Washington, D.C.; Forrestal to Barkley, November 25, 1945; reminder by Correa, October 8, 1945; King to Forrestal, September 28, 1945, memorandum, Records of the Secretary of the Navy, Box 44, Record Group 80, National Archives, Washington, D.C.; memorandum by Truman, October 23, 1945, in Congress, *Pearl Harbor Attack*, pt. 1, p. 8; diary of James V. Forrestal, October 5, 1945, p. 531, James V. Forrestal Papers, Princeton University Library, Princeton, N.J.
[24] Congress, *Congressional Record*, 79th Cong., 1st sess., 91, pp. 10340–10357.

The most significant of them was the desire to gain access to Roosevelt's private presidential papers. Some news accounts highlighted rumors that White House war records had disappeared or were carefully hidden and that the personal papers of FDR contained valuable information with respect to prewar Japanese-American relations. Except for the fact that the personal papers may have contained some significant information about Japanese-American relations, the rumors were patently untrue, yet they were believable enough to attract more attention to the Republicans' case. Regarding the challenge, Lucas asserted: "I hope I never have to debate Pearl Harbor again until we can bring in the report. But I am satisfied we shall have it on the floor of the Senate every day. It is an unfortunate thing. . . ."[25]

Despite Lucas's lament, the Democrats had their way on the issue of individual access to files. On November 7 Truman signed a directive ordering every person in the relevant departments or agencies—if interrogated by the committee—to give any information bearing on the investigation and authorizing them, whether interrogated or not, to voluntarily come forward and disclose what information they had acquired. On November 9 Truman enlarged on the directive slightly to include disclosure of pertinent information to individual members of the committee.[26] Although these orders broadened the original directive, they did not meet the demands of the Republicans for free access to departmental files, personal files, and governmental personnel. The president and the majority members of the committee were unwilling to go that far, fearing that the inquiry could be dragged out indefinitely. In fact, some of Truman's advisers, especially Sam Rosenman and Attorney General Tom C. Clark, believed he had gone too far with the November 9 directive.[27]

The Republican reaction to the new directive was predictable. They grumbled about the viselike grip that the Democrats held on

[25] Ibid., pp. 10431–10439, 10444–10450; *U.S. News* 19 (November 16, 1945): 15, 89–92.

[26] Memoranda by Truman, November 7 and 9, 1945, Official File 400, Harry S Truman Papers, Harry S Truman Presidential Library, Independence, Mo. (exhibit in Congress, *Pearl Harbor Attack*, pt. 1, p. 9).

[27] Rosenman to Truman, November 9, 1945, memorandum, ibid.

the committee—setting policy without considering the minority sentiments. And they tried to refute the charges of obstructionism their demands engendered. Ferguson seriously challenged the November 7 directive, which he believed did not extend immunity to departmental witnesses or authorize them to furnish individual members of the committee with leads or tips. But even the revisions incorporated into the November 9 directive did not satisfy him or other minority members. As Brewster concluded, "The only distinction between the majority and the minority [on this issue] is that the majority are investigating themselves while the minority are conducting the long-established function in connection with Anglo-Saxon parliamentary government of investigating the actions of those in administrative control. . . ."[28] Pious phrases could not take the sting out of the Republican defeat.

The tone of the investigation was clearly established in the maneuverings before the opening of the hearings. Almost every issue raised had its political antecedents; every point of contention had its partisan overtones. Daily, revelations of various sorts filled newspapers and magazines or appeared in antiadministration pamphlets. News that the United States had cracked the Japanese codes was among the most important stories of November, 1945. As *Newsweek* announced: "In an atmosphere surcharged with politics, the joint Congressional committee investigating Pearl Harbor stumbled last week onto a sturdy acorn of truth from which a mighty oak may grow. . . . Plainly, with this as a starting point, the investigation might lead anywhere in official Washington—to the State Department and the White House, as the GOP committeemen openly prayed, or to lesser shoulders, namely the military, as Democratic members fervently hoped."[29]

Related to the disclosure of the breaking of the codes was John Chamberlain's exposé of the 1944 Marshall-Dewey affair in *Life*. He referred to the election incident and other important issues to demonstrate that the previously accepted notion that the United

[28] Congress, *Congressional Record*, 79th Cong., 1st sess., 1945, 91, pp. 10583–10594; McNaughton to Hulburd, November 9, 1945, McNaughton Papers; *U.S. News* 19 (November 16, 1945): 89–92.

[29] *Newsweek* 26 (November 26, 1945): 37.

States had been "slugged without warning" by the Japanese was "a radical distortion of the truth." He contended that Roosevelt knew in advance that the Japanese would attack.[30] Of course, this theme was already a staple claim of the anti-Roosevelt forces, especially John T. Flynn, who advanced it very strongly in his two bitingly critical pamphlets *The Truth about Pearl Harbor* (1944) and *The Final Secret of Pearl Harbor* (1946), and Col. Robert R. McCormick of the *Chicago Tribune*, who had scathingly attacked the Democratic administration and planned a series of critical Pearl Harbor editorials for the fall of 1945.[31] Other gossip gained public attention as well. For example, some argued that Secretary Hull allegedly gave the Japanese an "ultimatum" on November 26, 1941, which precipitated the war. And there were numerous stories that important documents bearing on decisions made in Washington just before the attack now were missing, and that an Army officer who had testified before a previous Pearl Harbor board was "browbeaten" into signing an affidavit changing his testimony. These rumors, disclosures, and revelations contributed substantially to the already politically charged atmosphere preceding the public phase of the committee's investigation.[32]

On November 15 the public hearings began with much anticipation. Not since the Pecora banking investigation of 1933 had a running congressional story received so much attention from the press and radio. Although the "crush of sightseers" in the committee room was not as overwhelming as some of the crowds who swarmed to see Charles Lindbergh testify on the prewar neutrality legislation or Wendell Willkie speaking in favor of lend-lease, the substantial number of interested onlookers, the hum of the newsreel cam-

[30] John Chamberlain. "Pearl Harbor," *Life* 19 (September 24, 1945): 110 ff.

[31] McCormick to Leon Stolz, October 6, 1945; George Morgenstern to McCormick, October 25, 1945; McCormick to Morgenstern, October 25, 1945, Pearl Harbor File (P316-h), University of Wyoming Library, Laramie.

[32] *U.S. News* 19 (November 16, 1945): 89–92; *New Republic* 113 (September 10, 1945): 303–304; *Catholic World* 162 (October, 1945): 1–7; *Christian Century* 62 (October 3, 1945): 1117; George S. Montgomery, Jr., "The People and Pearl Harbor: The New Scapegoat Declines the Role," November 1, 1945, Box 41, Husband E. Kimmel Collection, Division of Rare Books and Special Collections, University of Wyoming Library, Laramie.

eras, the drone of the more than one hundred reporters, and the general opening-day confusion added to the drama of the moment.[33]

Despite the ubiquitous partisanship, the joint congressional committee would provide one of the most comprehensive records of a historical event ever attempted by an investigatory body. Although the inquiry was more heavily weighted toward the military than the diplomatic aspects of the Pearl Harbor disaster, and despite the regrettable lack of testimony from such witnesses as Franklin Roosevelt, Harry Hopkins, and Frank Knox, the committee supplied extensive documentation of prewar events. It even uncovered important information about the controversy over war responsibility. In the seventy days of the proceedings, from November 15, 1945, to May 31, 1946, the committee compiled more than sixty-seven volumes of testimony (comprising about fifteen thousand pages) and more than 6,750,000 words of exhibits and transcripts/exhibits of all of the previous inquiries and publicly questioned forty-three witnesses. Of these, 57 percent were navy personnel, 31 percent were army personnel, and 12 percent were civilians.[34]

In the first phase of the public hearings, which lasted until mid-December, the committee largely focused upon the question of high-level Washington responsibility. The committee approached this task by examining key prewar diplomatic policy makers and those familiar with American intelligence operations. The key witnesses on prewar policy making were Secretary of State Hull and Chief of Staff Marshall. Because of his poor health, Hull could not testify for long periods and consequently was not subjected to the arduous cross-examination that Marshall sustained. Both men stood firmly by previous explanations of their actions before Pearl Harbor. Hull adamantly denied forcing the Japanese to attack by issuing an ultimatum on November 26, 1941. In order to test his contention, the committee questioned Joseph Grew, former ambassador to Japan, who allegedly had stated that the secretary of state had "pushed the war button" with his November 26 note. Grew denied saying it, but

[33] McNaughton to Bill Chapman, November 20, 1945, McNaughton Papers; *Time* 46 (December 3, 1945): 57.

[34] U.S. Congress, *Report of the Joint Committee on the Investigation of the Pearl Harbor Attack*, 79th Cong., 2d sess., 1946, pp. xiv, 278–279.

asserted that he had been warning Washington since 1940 about growing bellicosity in Japan. Like Hull, General Marshall insisted upon the propriety of his actions and reaffirmed that army officials had adequately informed the Hawaiian Command about the approaching danger of war.[35]

Supporters and detractors of the Democratic administration debated the sincerity of Hull's and Marshall's testimony, with special attention to what role Roosevelt himself may have played in establishing American policy in the prewar years. The minority members actively sought to determine whether he had intentionally drawn the Japanese into attacking Hawaii. They uncovered no evidence to support that thesis, but some eyebrows were raised when Adm. J. O. Richardson, the former commander in chief of the U.S. Fleet and the Pacific Fleet, intimated that Roosevelt had an aggressive attitude toward Japan well before December 7, 1941. Richardson contended that in October, 1940, the former president considered blocking Japanese trade with Americans if Japan took drastic action against the British reopening of the Burma Road. He added that he had warned Roosevelt that economic sanctions would constitute an act of war and would cause great losses of ships. The former commander also testified about his disagreement with FDR over the disposition of the fleet at the mid-Pacific base as opposed to the West Coast. The implication was that the admiral had the foresight to perceive that the fleet stationed in Hawaii would be a target of Japanese aggression, not a deterrent. Richardson created a tremendous stir which resulted in the parading of a number of witnesses who refuted his claims, including Adm. William D. Leahy and Undersecretary of State Sumner Welles.[36] The attack on Roosevelt's leadership caused Eleanor Roosevelt to write Harry Hopkins: ". . . I

[35] Hull testimony in Congress, *Pearl Harbor Attack*, pt. 2, pp. 403–457, 551–560, 605–615; Grew testimony, ibid., pt. 2, pp. 560–603, 615–773; Marshall testimony, ibid., pt. 3, pp. 1049–1439, 1499–1541; Waldo H. Heinrichs, Jr., *American Ambassador: Joseph C. Grew and the Development of the United States Diplomatic Tradition*, p. 383; McNaughton to Hulburd, December 13, 1945, McNaughton Papers; transcript of radio broadcast, December 11, 1945, Elmer Davis Papers, Library of Congress, Washington, D.C.; *Nation* 161 (December 1, 1945): 565–566.

[36] Richardson testimony in Congress, *Pearl Harbor Attack*, pt. 1, pp. 253–340; Leahy testimony, ibid., pt. 1, pp. 341–368; Welles testimony, ibid., pt. 2, pp. 458–473, 477–549; *Time* 46 (December 3, 1945): 24–25.

have been greatly disturbed and still am about the Pearl Harbor investigation because I have a feeling that none of those people are
looking after the President's interests. I thought Leahy's testimony
was pretty feeble. I am sure, in the long run, it will all come out all
right but you have got to remember that all of the witnesses are
going to look after themselves." [37]

The disclosure of the breaking of the Japanese high-level codes
and the implications this had for predicting hostilities with Japan
also created a flurry of interest. On the first day of the hearings
Chief Counsel Mitchell announced that the United States had broken the codes, thus revealing that officials in Washington knew in
midsummer of 1941 the basic Japanese war plans, and he presented
379 pages of evidence.[38] By December, 1945, it was becoming clear
that the decoded information had not been put to maximum use by
Washington officials and that much of it remained beyond the local
commanders' grasp. The testimony of Maj. Gen. Sherman Miles, former chief of the Military Intelligence Service, indicated that a substantial amount of the detail in the decoded intercepts was kept
from General Short for fear that the ultrasecret story of the cracking
of the Japanese diplomatic codes would leak out. Miles also indicated that the intelligence services of the army and navy had not
been well integrated before Pearl Harbor; a joint army-navy intelligence committee approved in October, 1941, did not begin its function until after December 7. Despite the decentralization of the
intelligence services and the uneven flow of information from Washington to Hawaii, Miles defended his performance with the Military Intelligence Service and placed the blame for the inadequate
defense preparations on Generals Gerow and Short. Gerow himself
also testified that the policy of denying Short details of the decoded
messages was to prevent them from being made public. On the
navy side, Rear Adm. Richmond K. Turner, former chief of the Navy
War Plans Division, testified that for a year before the Japanese attack, he, Admiral Stark, and others mistakenly assumed that the

---

[37] E. Roosevelt to Hopkins, November 20, 1945, Box 297, Harry Hopkins
Papers, Franklin D. Roosevelt Presidential Library, Hyde Park, N.Y. For Hop-
kins's reaction to the investigation, see Robert E. Sherwood, *Roosevelt and
Hopkins: An Intimate History*, p. 930.

[38] Congress, *Pearl Harbor Attack*, pt. 1, pp. 23ff.; *New York Times*, November 16, 1945, pp. 1, 4.

Hawaiian Command had facilities for breaking the highest Japanese codes. Whether the indequate flow of intelligence information from Washington to Hawaii would prove negligence on the part of high officials remained to be determined by the examination of other witnesses, including the local commanders, and the resolution of the confusion over the Winds message.[39]

The testimony gleaned from these first important witnesses emphasized the complex state of affairs existing before the attack, but it also exposed too many contradictions to provide a consensus on the question of war responsibility. Tactically, the Republican members tried to draw out from each witness some morsel of evidence which would prove that Roosevelt—through design or negligence—exposed the U.S. Fleet to the disastrous sneak attack, or, if that failed, to implicate his immediate subordinates. The Democrats, on the other hand, were faced with the task of protecting the former Democratic president and defending the official administration explanation of the Pearl Harbor affair which they had largely come to support. As such, their strategy was low-key; that is, it was aimed at discrediting the GOP charges by highlighting testimony which supported the administration's point of view or, in the last resort, directly challenging the minority members through public denunciations. In this setting the Republicans attracted much more press attention because they had taken the offensive. Of course, when they failed to obtain the damaging testimony necessary to prod the Democrats, they were susceptible to serious criticism. The Democrats, who controlled the investigation through their majority status, could afford to play a more passive role, exerting their clout only when the Republicans seemed to be going too far.

Every important issue before the committee became subject to this partisan battle. From the first day, the minority members charged Barkley and his cohorts with trying to rush the investigation, giving the Republicans little time to examine the piles of evi-

[39] Miles testimony in Congress, *Pearl Harbor Attack*, pt. 2, pp. 777–982; pt. 3, pp. 1360–1375, 1541–1583; Turner testimony, ibid., pt. 4, pp. 1911–2063; Gerow testimony, ibid., pt. 3, pp. 983–1048; pt. 4, pp. 1592–1673; *New York Times*, December 14, 1945, pp. 1, 2, 13; *Time* 46 (November 12, 1945): 23.

dence. At a press conference on the second day of the public hearings they denounced the Democratic investigation plan as an attempt to shield the Roosevelt administration from blame. The majority members replied that their opponents wanted to "smear" the former president, or as Sen. James M. Tunnel (Democrat, Delaware) charged, they were trying to carry out "a sneak attack upon the grave of Franklin D. Roosevelt." With this political schism shrouding the proceedings, the interrogation of almost every witness became a forum for political bickering.[40]

The culmination of the destructive partisan quibbling was the resignation of Chief Counsel Mitchell and his staff in mid-December. In his official statement of December 20, he said: "The point we have reached in the hearings makes it evident that a complete replacement of the Committee's legal staff is necessary." His rationale for this decision was that the proceedings were moving too slowly —only eight witnesses had been completely examined to date, and there remained possibly sixty more. When he accepted the post, Mitchell added, he assumed his services would not be needed beyond early January.[41] Of course, the enmity between Mitchell and the Republicans—especially the senators—had forced the counsel's decision. From the beginning of the inquiry they had not gotten on well. To the minority Mitchell was a turncoat who sided with the Democrats on all important issues. To Mitchell the GOP members were obstructionists who were merely trying to acquire political advantage from every bit of evidence, something he did not ascribe to the majority members. Mitchell clearly supported the Democrats' basic assumptions about Pearl Harbor culpability. He was particularly critical of Kimmel's and Short's performance before the committee. He told Seth Richardson, his successor as chief counsel, that the press reports of the former Hawaiian commanders' testimony

[40] See Congress, *Pearl Harbor Attack*, pt. 1, pp. 1 ff., 81 ff., 197ff., pt. 2, pp. 679ff., 741 ff., 919ff., pt. 3, pp. 983ff., 1105ff., 1307ff., 1377ff., pt. 4, pp. 1585ff., 1719ff. See also *New Republic* 113 (November 26, 1945): 710; *Catholic World* 162 (February, 1946): 393–394; Blair Bolles, "Isolationists Use Pearl Harbor to Attack FDR Policies." *Foreign Policy Bulletin* 25 (November 30, 1945): 4; *Newsweek* 26 (December 24, 1945): 37.

[41] Statement by Mitchell, December 20, 1945, Army Pearl Harbor Board Files, Record Group 107, National Archives.

were giving the public the impression that few men in the War and Navy departments had conspired to make Kimmel and Short scapegoats. This conclusion, he believed, was untrue.[42]

Directly precipitating the chief counsel's decision to resign was the lengthy and aggressive Republican cross-examination of General Marshall, who was anxious to begin his important trip to China. Mitchell viewed the minority tactics employed against the chief of staff as intolerable. Almost simultaneously, Barkley declared that he, too, might resign, and there were rumors that Lucas and George were considering that option. At this point the hearings came to an abrupt halt, as the holiday break offered at least a brief respite from politics. It was becoming increasingly uncertain whether the joint congressional committee could conduct the kind of inquiry that many people had anticipated a few months before.[43]

The hearings began afresh in January with a new chief counsel and a new legal staff. Mitchell's replacement was North Dakota lawyer Seth W. Richardson, a Republican with a record as a Roosevelt critic. In the course of his political life he had been associated with his state's isolationist senators, Gerald P. Nye and William Langer. President Hoover had appointed Richardson assistant attorney general under William Mitchell, and since 1933 Richardson had practiced law in Washington. Despite his background, the Democratic members of the committee were not concerned that Richardson would prove harmful to their cause. They assumed that his selection might give the hearings an air of impartiality which they had lacked thus far. The Dakota attorney got along well with the majority members. In fact, he had been approached for the Pearl Harbor job before Mitchell and was personally approved by Barkley and recommended by Lucas, his frequent golf partner. Only one member of the Mitchell staff remained with Richardson—John E. Masten. The new members were Samuel H. Kaufman (associate general

[42] Mitchell to Richardson, January 31, 1946, Records of the Joint Committee Investigating Pearl Harbor, Box 5, Record Group 128, National Archives, Washington, D.C.; Mitchell to Mason, November 10, 1945; Mason to Taft, November 13, 1945, Box 657, Taft Papers.

[43] McNaughton to Hulburd, December 15, 1945, McNaughton Papers; transcript of radio broadcast, December 23, 1945, Davis Papers; Alben W. Barkley, *That Reminds Me—*, pp. 264–265; Barkley Oral History Interview, November 1, 1953; *Newsweek* 26 (December 24, 1945): 31.

counsel), Edward P. Morgan (assistant), and Logan J. Lane (assistant).[44]

In the final stages of the investigation the daily interrogations were characterized by the same kind of partisan maneuvering as in 1945, although much the drama and excitement of the previous months had begun to wane. As the weeks went by, the committee sought to bring the inquiry to an end and get on with the writing of the report. The focus of the 1946 hearings included the examination of other principals in Washington who were closely associated with the Pearl Harbor affair—such as Admiral Stark and Secretary Stimson—the interrogation of the former Hawaiian commanders, and the unraveling of the Winds episode.

Finally allowed to state their cases publicly, Kimmel and Short attracted considerable public attention. And both officers made it very clear that they believed blame for the attack rested squarely upon Washington—not Hawaii. After more than four years of public silence and professional disgrace, they did not equivocate in their indictment of high officials. Short declared that the War Department, especially Marshall, Gerow, and Miles, had denied him essential information about the developments in the Pacific and had made him a scapegoat for the whole Pearl Harbor affair.[45] Kimmel made similar charges against the Navy Department. Although unswerving in his profession of innocence and disgusted with the treatment he had received after December 7, the former commander of the Pacific Fleet believed his testimony could rectify some of the wrongs which had befallen him. As he stated in a personal letter:

. . . I believe that the evidence so far presented to this Committee is only a very small part of the evidence that is in existence. It is most unfortunate that we had a Committee composed of partisans. . . .

However, I have had a chance to present my story about Pearl Harbor completely and had it not been for the Congressional Investigation I am confident that the Navy Department would never have permitted me to disclose this story. They would have kept it under wraps on the plea that any disclosure would jeopardize our code breaking activities and

[44] *Newsweek* 27 (January 14, 1946): 29–30; *U.S. News* 20 (January 11, 1946): 55–56. For some transitional correspondence between Mitchell and Richardson for 1946, see Records of the Joint Committee Investigating Pearl Harbor, Boxes 5 and 11, Record Group 128, National Archives.

[45] Congress, *Pearl Harbor Attack*, pt. 7, pp. 2921–3231.

that would have left me hanging in the bight. So I suppose I should be thankful for small favors and certainly telling my story in public has relieved my mind and reduced my blood pressure considerably.[46]

Both Kimmel and Short, however, were apprehensive about the conclusions the committee would reach in its report. They would have to wait a while longer for what seemed to be the final verdict in their case.[47]

The code-breaking issue was another compelling interest of the committee, especially as it pertained to the elusive Winds message. To the Roosevelt critics, the existence of the intercepted Winds message would be proof that Washington had sufficient advance warning of an attack against the United States. The local commanders, especially, assumed that the transmittal of such a piece of information to Hawaii would have given them the warning they needed to prepare an adequate defense. As might be expected, the Democrats played down the significance of the Winds message, doubting its existence and convinced that even if the Japanese did transmit the message Washington would not have learned anything it did not already know.

Confronted with the widespread attention that the issue had raised, committee counsel had no choice but to investigate the Winds code and message thoroughly and to interrogate knowledgeable witnesses on the subject after the Christmas break. In a memorandum from Mitchell to Richardson the out-going counsel stated that previous testimony and available information still left the existence of the message in doubt. He believed that instead of trying to determine if it was misplaced in navy files, the committee should investigate if the message was ever transmitted. "Our first reaction to the whole winds code episode," he stated, "was, and still is, that

---

[46] Kimmel to Manning Kimmel, January 25, 1946, Box 6, Kimmel Collection. See also Kimmel to Singleton Kimmel, January 25, February 15, 1946; Kimmel to Rugg, January 30, 1946; Memo of Events in Connection with the Pearl Harbor Investigation, June 6, 1946, Box 6, Kimmel Collection; Congress, *Pearl Harbor Attack*, pt. 6, pp. 2497–2663, 2701–2915; diary of Harry E. Yarnell, January 21, 1946, Harry E. Yarnell Papers, Naval History Division, Department of the Navy, Washington, D.C.; Kimmel, *Admiral Kimmel's Story*, pp. 166–167, 169; *Newsweek* 27 (January 28, 1946): 25.

[47] Kimmel to Yarnell, September 13, 1946; Yarnell to Rugg, July 25, 1946; Rugg to Kimmel, December 12, 1946, Box 6, Kimmel Collection.

it is all much ado about nothing, because even if such a signal was
sent out in a broadcast by the Japs and [had] been received by the
War and Navy Departments, it would have added nothing to what
our people already knew." For that reason he had hoped the matter
could be dropped, but he knew that the sensational publicity surrounding the issue gave the committee no other choice but to continue its search for evidence.[48]

The key witness who had constantly supported the claim that
the Japanese had transmitted the Winds message was Capt. Laurence F. Safford, who had been chief of the radio intelligence unit
in the Office of Naval Communications. His testimony was the catalyst for an extensive examination of witnesses familiar with American intelligence during the war. Safford claimed that the message of
execution was received and decoded in Washington on December
4, 1941. He further suspected that the War and Navy departments
plotted and caused the destruction of the information to cover up
mistakes that they had made in protecting against the attack on
Hawaii.[49] But after a variety of army and navy officials denied that
they had seen the message, Safford stood virtually alone in his contention.[50] The issue of the Winds code quickly dissipated at this
point, now barren to the Republicans as an issue with which to prod
the Roosevelt administration. Yet the hint of conspiracy that Safford
raised lingered in the minds of those who were willing to believe
the worst about the wartime Democratic leadership.

When the taking of testimony ended in early 1946, many doubts
remained about what had transpired in those days preceding the
war. The committee had uncovered important documentation about
the manner in which the United States conducted its foreign policy
and prepared its military and naval installations and had bared
some of the most important intelligence secrets. But the political

[48] Mitchell, Memo for Succeeding Counsel, December 22, 1945, Pearl
Harbor File, Record Group 125, National Archives, Washington, D.C.

[49] Congress, *Pearl Harbor Attack*, pt. 8, pp. 3555–3813, 3842–3893.

[50] Kramer testimony in ibid., pts. 8 and 9, pp. 3893–4221; Ingersoll testimony in ibid., pt. 9, pp. 4221–4300; Bratton testimony in ibid., pts. 9 and 10,
pp. 4508–4628; Sadtler testimony in ibid., pt. 10, pp. 4628–4659; Rochefort
testimony in ibid., pt. 10, pp. 4672–4710; Noyes testimony in ibid., pt. 10, pp.
4710–4792, Hart testimony in ibid., pt. 10, pp. 4797–4828; McCollum testimony in ibid., pt. 8, pp. 3381–3448.

haggling which accompanied the important testimony left in doubt the ultimate responsibility for the Pearl Harbor disaster. Everyone waited for the committee's report, hoping that it would distill the essential information and bring an end to the controversy that had raged for more than four years.[51]

The inquiry itself had exposed clear divisions in thinking about Pearl Harbor along political lines, and so did the written reports. The hope that the joint congressional committee would somehow reach a compromise which would please most Americans was never more than a dream. The climax of many months of inquiry was a majority and a minority report. The former surprisingly garnered wider committee support than might have been expected. In addition to all of the Democrats, both Republican congressmen signed it. The sudden change of heart of Frank Keefe has baffled all followers of the Pearl Harbor controversy, especially since the Wisconsin representative consistently had been one of the most critical questioners of administration witnesses. As a means of clarifying his position he wrote a statement modifying his support for the majority report. In his "additional views" he acknowledged agreement with most of the conclusions in that report, but objected to its marshaling facts "perhaps unintentionally" with the idea of conferring blame on the Hawaiian officers and minimizing the blame that should be assigned to Washington officials. He also stated that the committee did not have all the information necessary to make a definitive conclusion about Pearl Harbor. In essence, Keefe drew a clear line between himself and the Democrats, but by signing the report he became a traitor to the opponents of the Roosevelt administration. Why he decided upon this method of expressing his views remains a mystery. In the case of Gearhart, a logical explanation

[51] For information about the preparation of the reports, see memorandum by Samuel H. Kaufman, 1946, Records of the Joint Committee Investigating Pearl Harbor, Box 14, Record Group 128, National Archives; Edward Hanify to Rugg, February 27, 1946; Rugg to Kimmel, June 18, 1947, Box 6, Kimmel Collection; Percy L. Greaves, Jr., "The Pearl Harbor Investigations," in *Perpetual War for Perpetual Peace*, ed. Harry Elmer Barnes, pp. 459ff; Richardson, "Why Were We Caught Napping at Pearl Harbor?" *Saturday Evening Post* 219 (May 24, 1947): 20; Greaves to Hiles, June 15, 1962, Harry Elmer Barnes Collection, Division of Rare Books and Special Collections, University of Wyoming Library, Laramie.

seems possible. Unlike Keefe, Gearhart made no additional remarks about his position but publicly accepted the majority report as it stood. Some observers believed that the Californian, representing a district where he depended upon Democratic support, was politically motivated by the upcoming congressional election. An additional reason for Gearhart's and Keefe's defection was suggested by Percy L. Greaves, Jr., aide to the Republican senators on the congressional committee; the minority congressmen may have been unduly influenced by the committee Democrats. According to Greaves, the committee seating arrangement placed Gearhart and Keefe next to the Democrats and separate from Ferguson and Brewster, who were more extensively briefed and who received the bulk of the data which the Republicans used to interrogate witnesses.[52] Of course the Republicans had had a difficult time proving the guilt of Roosevelt, and Gearhart and Keefe merely may have decided to moderate their previously strong antiadministration views.

The majority report clearly reflected the administration's position on the Pearl Harbor affair as it had been moderated by the reports of the Army Pearl Harbor Board and the Navy Court of Inquiry. It was an extensive document which discussed the diplomatic background of the attack, the air raid itself, and the Hawaiian and Washington responsibilities. Like most of the previous reports, it branded the Japanese policy in Asia and the Pacific as "a career of conquest no less ambitious nor avowed than that of the Nazis." And it characterized United States policy as "no provocation whatever." In reciting its evaluation of responsibilities, it accepted Stimson's and Forrestal's 1944–1945 evaluation that Kimmel and Short suffered from "errors of judgment" rather than disregard of obligations or indifference to their duties—"[T]hey were blinded by the self-evident." The disaster, the report concluded, was caused by the failure of the army and the navy to put into effect measures to detect "an approaching hostile force," to institute a state of readiness based

[52] Percy L. Greaves, Jr., interview with author, April, 1974, Austin, Texas; John T. Flynn to Harry Elmer Barnes, April 12, 1951; Greaves to Barnes, November 3, 1950, Barnes Collection; Congress, *Report of the Joint Committee*, pp. 266A–266W; Gearhart to Charles Parsons, February 22, 1946; Emily C. Yarnell to Gearhart, August, 1946, Box 6, Kimmel Collection; Charles A. Beard to Morgenstern, May 7, 1948, George Morgenstern Collection, Division of Rare Books and Special Collections, University of Wyoming Library, Laramie.

on the realization that war was at hand, and "to employ every facility at their command in repelling the Japanese." Less one-sided than the Roberts findings, the majority report blamed the War Plans Division in Washington for not giving careful consideration to intercepted messages transmitted from Tokyo to Honolulu dealing with the berthing of the fleet. The president; the secretaries of war, navy, and state; the chief of staff; and, to a lesser extent, the chief naval operations escaped direct criticism. The Washington high command, aside from the noted exceptions, had adequately warned the Hawaiian commanders of approaching danger.[53]

The majority report also included a list of recommendations to improve United States defense posture. Among these "administrative adjustments" were unity of command for all military and naval outposts, the integration of army and navy intelligence agencies, and other supervisory, administrative, organizational, and statutory changes. Ironically, these recommendations dealt with reforming the defense institutions, while the conclusions of the report implied the human errors of judgment were largely responsible for the disaster. This inconsistency was never adequately resolved.[54]

Senators Brewster and Ferguson, consistent with their opposition to the Democrats throughout the investigation, filed a separate report. They prefaced it by declaring that they found it impossible to concur with the findings and conclusions of the majority report because "they are illogical, and unsupported by the preponderance of the evidence before the Committee. The conclusions of the diplomatic aspects are based upon incomplete evidence." The senators' strong language belied the radical departure from the majority report one might have suspected. The fundamental difference—by no means hairsplitting—was that Washington was not blameless for the success of the attack and should be held as accountable as the local commanders. (Keefe's reservations to the majority report were on the same lines.) Declaring that the record of the inquiry was "far from complete," they argued that the committee had gathered enough evidence to indicate that high Washington officials were well informed from intelligence sources by late November and

[53] Congress, *Report of the Joint Committee*, pp. 1 ff., 251–252. See also Alben Barkley Oral History Interview, November 1, 1953.
[54] Congress, *Report of the Joint Committee*, pp. 252–266.

should have known that some kind of attack was imminent. However, instead of taking appropriate action to warn Hawaii, administration officials waited for the Japanese to fire the first shot before going to war. In other words, they failed in their opportunity to adequately prepare Pearl Harbor for possible assault, having the time and information to prepare directives in language not open to misinterpretation by the local commanders. Ferguson and Brewster further charged that Washington failed to allocate adequate material to the Hawaiian Command which it had requested to improve the island's defenses. With respect to Kimmel and Short, the minority report surprisingly did not advocate complete exoneration. In a backhanded manner, the GOP senators suggested that whatever errors of judgment the local commanders committed and whatever mismanagement they displayed ultimately rested upon the responsibility of the Washington high command, who had designated these men for their posts. While reemphasizing Washington's obligation to prepare adequate defenses, the minority report still indicted the Hawaiian commanders by inference. It concluded by suggesting that the tragedy of the surprise attack was primarily due to the failure of men, not laws or powers, and it singled out the following by name: Roosevelt, Stimson, Knox, Marshall, Stark, Gerow, Kimmel, and Short. Hull was not included because the report contended that he had no authority in military decisions regarding preparations for possible attack. Furthermore, the committee did not examine the diplomatic record deeply enough to determine the secretary of state's long-range responsibilities.[55]

Both reports—majority and minority—were surprisingly free of invective or extreme condemnations. The majority report did not crucify the local commanders beyond criticism of their alleged errors in judgment, nor did it completely ignore the lack of adequate communications between Washington and Hawaii. It even indicated the need for some structural changes. At the same time, the minority report did not offer a blanket indictment of the Roosevelt administration without taking into consideration responsibilities that existed in Hawaii. Ferguson and Brewster made no statement indicating that Roosevelt intentionally exposed the fleet at Pearl Harbor to

[55] Ibid., pp. 493ff.

bring the United States into the war. Even though the gap between the reports was not as wide as the polar positions which had evolved during 1941–1946, a gap remained; that gap was emphasis upon the guilt of the Hawaiian Command versus the Washington officials as the foremost reason for the disaster. The products of the committee's labors, therefore, perpetuated the fundamental schism in opinion which had begun on December 8, 1941, and continued after the war.

Soon after the release of the reports to Congress on July 20, the *Chicago Tribune* declared, "The majority and minority reports, which in varying degree held the Roosevelt administration to blame for the Pearl Harbor attack, were generally accepted as the verdict that is likely to stand for some time to come."[56] For the great majority of people who did not demand the heads of Kimmel and Short or the unqualified discrediting of Roosevelt, the reports provided a choice of views of the Hawaiian affair. In its front-page story about them, the *New York Times*, a long-time supporter of the general features of the administration's thesis of war responsibility, emphasized how the joint committee, by a vote of 8–2, had found Roosevelt blameless, lauded the performances of Knox and Stimson, indirectly blamed high military officials, and directly criticized the actions of Kimmel and Short. In the *Chicago Tribune* story the opposite was true. That perpetual critic of the Roosevelt administration emphasized the distinction between the two reports and highlighted the criticisms of the Washington officials. In an editorial the *Tribune* suggested that the majority report was "another New Deal contribution to the canonization of Franklin D. Roosevelt."[57]

In political circles Democrat and Republican partisans formed ranks behind the appropriate report. Eminent Republicans like Robert Taft lauded the minority report, while others half-heartedly threatened that they would demand a further investigation when the GOP wrested power from the Democrats. In general, the Democrats found the majority report to be as definitive a statement on Pearl Harbor as they believed possible. Barkley wrote in his mem-

[56] *Chicago Tribune*, July 22, 1946, p. 1.
[57] Ibid., July 21, 1946, pp. 1, 8–10; July 22, 1946, p. 16; *New York Times*, July 21, 1946, p. 1; sec. 4, p. 8. See also *Newsweek* 28 (July 29, 1946): 22–23; *Kiplinger Washington Letter*, September 7, 1946; *Forum* 106 (September, 1946): 264–265.

oirs, "The investigation into the Pearl Harbor disaster . . . while it
may not have resulted in specific legislation, was useful in clarifying
a confused public opinion, and fixing some degree of responsibility
for the disaster. . . ."[58]

The joint congressional committee produced two reports which
reflected in a moderate fashion the opposing opinions in the Pearl
Harbor debate but did not resolve that controversy. For those who
envisioned a public investigation as a means of acquiring the "truth"
about the surprise attack and firmly affixing blame on Roosevelt and
the high Washington officials, the end results of the hearings were
disappointing. For those who supported the administration line, the
hope that guilt could be exclusively restricted to the Hawaiian commanders was likewise shattered. If nothing else, the joint congressional committee had demonstrated that blame is not indivisible; it
may reside at many levels and in varying degrees depending upon
the perspective one takes. Those who believed the Pearl Harbor
issue could provide ammunition for future elections were also to be
disappointed, especially because the diffusion of responsibility indicated in both reports made it difficult to uncover dramatic issues
which could inspire voters to turn against one party or the other.
Furthermore, the issues surrounding the surprise attack were becoming less relevant to a peacetime America. At the very least, the
principals who had garnered so much attention for their roles in the
affair were dead or out of power—Roosevelt, Hopkins, Hull, Stimson, Knox, Kimmel, Short, Stark, and the others. Public opinion
polls reflected the inability of most people to determine the "true
culprit" for Pearl Harbor.[59]

The reports of the joint committee had brought an end to the
wartime debate over Pearl Harbor. From late 1946 forward the
issue would be perpetuated largely by avid critics of the Roosevelt
administration who were dissatisfied with the minority report's mild
criticism of high Washington officials, especially the former president. As a public issue and as a partisan political question, Pearl
Harbor was essentially dead. Little more could be said to change
anyone's mind. Each side selectively employed the plethora of evidence to justify its own thesis. And not without the most penetrating

[58] Barkley, *That Reminds Me—*, pp. 88–89.
[59] See *Public Opinion Quarterly* 9 (Winter, 1945–1946): 511.

and painstaking of searches could more startling evidence be un-covered which might conceivably turn the issue around. Inevitably, people were going to believe what they wanted to believe, and in an attempt to rationalize how the mighty United States could be brought to its knees by a tiny island nation they chose those indi-viduals or groups whom they held responsible for the American de-fense. In the search for scapegoats, few remained above suspicion.

10

Conclusion

DESPITE the popular myth, American entry into World War II did
not usher in a period of domestic unity. While making concessions
to the war effort and readjusting their lives to produce the essential
provisions for the armed services, most Americans continued to face
many of the prewar problems and political antagonisms. Politicians
extolled the virtue of "national unity," but isolationists were still
pitted against interventionists, Republicans against Democrats.
Thus, it was not surprising that the Pearl Harbor affair would be
interjected into the wartime political milieu. Because the attack
was so unexpected and its results so dramatic and tragic, the desire
to uncover why and how it had succeeded led to vast speculation
and widespread accusations. Inevitably, eyes turned to the president
for an answer.

For the Roosevelt administration, the Pearl Harbor disaster
was a volatile issue which had to be treated very carefully. The
high officials believed a simple disclosure of all the facts surrounding the affair would jeopardize the war effort by informing the
enemy of the extent of American losses and uncovering our most
secret intelligence weapon—our ability to break the Magic code.
Beyond this immediate concern was a deeper fear that a public
disclosure that would highlight American unpreparedness and lack
of vigilance would also expose the administration to severe criticism
and unleash a political storm of recriminations. Such a result was
unpalatable, especially since the president and the secretaries of
war and the navy were convinced of the correctness of their own
actions preceding the war. They assumed that if there were to be
accountable officials for the disaster, they resided at the lowest

echelons of authority—namely, the Hawaiian Command. Yet creating scapegoats for the disaster was not the original intention of the administration; instead, it sought to steer a middle course between full disclosure and blatant reprisals or punitive action against the local commanders. That compromise backfired.

In dealing with the Pearl Harbor incident, the administration chose a policy which unwittingly initiated and sustained a major controversy over the question of war responsibility instead of averting it. Public and congressional pressure, plus the need to assess the losses at the Hawaiian base, led to the Knox inquiry. The navy secretary's subsequent report did not dwell on personal culpability, but both Knox and Stimson concluded that the local commanders, General Short and Admiral Kimmel, had failed in their mission and had to be relieved from command. Aware that courts-martial were too drastic without further documentation of negligence or dereliction, and believing that keeping the officers at their posts flirted with attracting adverse reactions, their proposed solution seemed to be the best way to bury the Pearl Harbor affair. But that decision—condoned by the president—placed the administration on record against Kimmel and Short and thus accentuated the issue of guilt. The administration created scapegoats who then attracted the attention of those who wished to discredit Roosevelt and his supporters.

The findings of the Roberts commission reconfirmed the Democratic administration's stand against the commanders but also opened the way for a lingering suspicion of conspiracy festering in Washington. The executive branch's careful monitoring of the inquiry and its prohibition against examining questions of Washington's responsibility made its motives suspect. With the decision to place Kimmel and Short on the retirement list while the threat of punitive action was held over their heads, critics quickly assumed that the president and his subordinates had something sinister to hide or at least were withholding the whole truth about the disaster for some secret reason. Ironically, singling out the commanders resulted in turning accusations on the Washington officials. Faced with such charges, the administration became more defensive and less willing to reevaluate its interpretation of the December 7 fiasco.

Personalizing responsibility was the Democratic administration's most serious error in dealing with the Pearl Harbor question. Instead of quietly transferring Kimmel and Short to some innocuous positions in the service bureaucracy, they created a focal point on which critics could prey. Little chance remained to carefully analyze the complexities that contributed to the disaster. Pearl Harbor culpability was now cast in blacks and whites. Thus, it was not surprising that the controversy, after a brief dormancy in 1942 and through most of 1943, reemerged within the context of a debate over the extension of the statute of limitations on Kimmel's and Short's alleged derelictions. The result of that debate was to place tremendous pressure on the administration for a full disclosure of the Hawaiian debacle. The pressure emanated from a Republican attempt to make Pearl Harbor a political issue in the presidential election of 1944 and from congressional legislation that demanded further investigation of the army and navy roles in the disaster. The administration successfully thwarted the former pressure, but was forced to submit to the latter. It was these investigations by the Army Pearl Harbor Board and the Navy Court of Inquiry which further entrenched Washington officials in their indictment of the local commanders. Although the army and navy inquiries could only examine the Pearl Harbor incident from the narrow perspectives of their departments, their mild treatment of the local commanders and more critical views of the high command in Washington— especially Admiral Stark and General Marshall—threatened the administration's explanation of the affair. When Secretaries Stimson and Forrestal decided to withhold the reports from the public for as long as possible, and ordered further inquiries to rectify the army and navy boards' conclusions, little ground for a serious debate remained. The sides were clearly drawn between those favoring the administration's position and those actively in opposition.

The end of the war brought hope that the controversy would be resolved. That dream was not fulfilled. The shroud of mystery surrounding the army and navy reports was lifted, but the war and navy secretaries, by now firmly committed to a policy of making Kimmel and Short scapegoats, tried to water down the criticisms of Washington officials in the reports with endorsements and disclaimers published simultaneously. The reports had forced the administration to modify its criticism of Kimmel and Short by dropping the charge of dereliction of duty, but it continued to justify the retirement of the local commanders on the grounds that they, while not guilty of errors of commission, were to blame for errors of omission.

The publication of the army and navy reports also forced an open congressional investigation of Pearl Harbor—something that almost everyone believed would clear the air of the dispute. But the public inquiry proved not to be a panacea for years of uncertainty and heated debate. The Democratic-controlled hearings, despite their disclosure of a plethora of data, became a partisan circus. The sides were too polarized for any other course. Like the previous inquiries, the congressional investigation tried to resolve the unresolvable question of personal guilt. Consensus was impossible, and blame proliferated instead of being narrowed.

Although the original intent of the Roosevelt administration's policy was to keep Pearl Harbor from interfering with the war effort and the hoped-for national unity, it mutated into a destructive cover-up, which became prohibitive of a dispassionate examination of the disaster and its causes. It was not a cover-up in the sense that Roosevelt and his cohorts concealed some vital secret that could ultimately lead to an indictment of Washington officials, but it was a cover-up brought on by fear that administration opponents would read too much into the available data and employ it for unscrupulous political attacks. In this environment it became necessary to adhere tenaciously to the line that the local commanders were mainly responsible for the Hawaii disaster. And like the boy who cried "wolf" too often, by 1946 the administration's credibility on the issue was clearly challenged, and the hope for a resolution of the controversy was dashed.

What effect did the Pearl Harbor controversy and the administration's policy have upon the nation? In general, they challenged the credibility of the president's preparedness program and his conduct of the war, and they perpetuated the debate over the direction United States foreign policy should take. Isolationists viewed Pearl Harbor as an example of inadequate home defenses; a Fortress America would have thwarted the Japanese onslaught, they believed. Also, many isolationists became even more skeptical of Roosevelt's approach to foreign policy, assuming that he had some hand in encouraging an attack upon the United States to lead us into war. Interventionists/internationalists, on the other hand, viewed the surprise attack as an object lesson in appeasement and an example of what can happen if the United States relinquished its role as a world power and refused to construct an adequate defense establishment.

In Congress the controversy provided one more issue to reinforce the partisanship already present. Democratic stalwarts, who long supported the administration's foreign and domestic policies, sought to defend those policies through adherence to the official Pearl Harbor stand. Republicans and some Democratic critics, skeptical of the New Deal and internationalism, used the Hawaii disaster vicariously as an argument against FDR's policies and programs. Through the debates over extending the statute of limitations, into the election of 1944, and ending with the congressional investigation in 1945–1946, the Republican critics used Pearl Harbor as a symbol of all the evils they associated with the Roosevelt administration. Thus, for Democrats and Republicans alike the surprise attack was more often a vehicle for dispute than an object of that dispute. Certainly many politicos earnestly wanted to know what transpired in Hawaii on December 7 and why so many American lives were spent there, but beyond that short-term interest there were many possible political benefits to be derived from the disaster. In lining up on one side or the other of the issue, congressmen and senators only helped to reinforce the divisions it generated. While the war raged and the need to find solutions to the postwar problems loomed ahead, too many political leaders spent precious time groping for partisan advantage.

The press and radio were largely responsible for defining the boundaries of the controversy. By providing fairly extensive coverage, they, too, contributed to the divisiveness over the issue. Like the politicians, many journalists and radio commentators found themselves on one side or another of the dispute. Newspapers like the *Chicago Tribune*, which challenged the official view of the disaster from the start, helped to force the administration into its defensive position.

The impact of the controversy on the public is difficult to gauge in an absolute sense, but it appears from the various surveys taken during the war that the war responsibility issue generated substantial attention, especially as an adjunct to war policy. Of course, the prosecution of the war itself was a more constant source of concern and often overshadowed the debate, which recorded many of its most dramatic moments away from the public gaze. The complexity of the war responsibility question also confused rather than enlightened the public. Lacking much of the vital information necessary to make a judicious decision, most citizens relied upon previous loyalties and political affinities in making judgments of blame. Rumors of sensational evidence proving the guilt or innocence of various parties involved in the disaster received much more attention than they would have given a better-informed public. The public reaction was, in many ways, simply a reflection of the confusion and hostility that Pearl Harbor produced.

And finally, those who had been singled out in the controversy —especially Kimmel and Short—had become "political footballs." Although the Hawaiian commanders may have been guilty of some lapses, they were forced to carry the brunt of responsibility at least until 1945, when the army and navy reports were publicized. Even after that disclosure they bore the scars of scapegoats, and they were often used by their own supporters as symbols of injustice for purposes beyond their exoneration. Individual causes were lost in the debate over the larger questions. Both Kimmel and Short died troubled men, never having had the satisfaction of receiving a truly impartial hearing from their government.

In the end, the Pearl Harbor controversy produced much heat and very little light. The many investigations gave the illusion that the Roosevelt administration and Congress had scrutinized the surprise attack in great detail and with objectivity. Instead, the results of those inquiries were used to reinforce preconceived notions of guilt or innocence. With some care the administration could have avoided the years of contention if it had employed a more straightforward approach to the question of responsibility. Roosevelt, Stimson, Knox, and others never seemed to realize that the shock of the surprise attack had not faded with the war declaration on December 8; Americans needed to be reassured that U.S. defenses were not flawed permanently. And in trying to reassure the public, disclosure of the most secret military information, like Magic, did not hang in the balance. It was likely that most citizens would have accepted the limitations imposed by "national security" if the executive had admitted that the Pearl Harbor affair was the result of correctable weaknesses in a system instead of the fault of individuals alone. Without publicly accepting blame for the disaster, Roosevelt could have made culpability an institutional instead of an individual affair and likely disarmed his critics.

By the end of the congressional investigation the political value of Pearl Harbor had finally come to an end. But the controversy initiated by the administration did not die. Long after the war, FDR's critics and faithful admirers alike continued the battle in the form of a sophisticated pamphlet war. Book after book poured from the presses speculating about Roosevelt's responsibility, and, in reply, administration supporters in the academic and journalistic communities defended the president. FDR, rather than Kimmel and Short, became the focal point of a renewed debate over the December 7 debacle. The dispute did not garner the breadth of attention it once had during the war, but it simply extended the critique of Pearl Harbor from the narrow perspective of personal guilt. "Revisionists" and "court historians" did not stray very far from a quest for the responsible parties. It was, after all, the impossibility of resolving the question of guilt on which the Pearl Harbor debate had always thrived.

The controversy, therefore, had been and continued to be a superficial debate in some important ways. The attention paid to personal culpability was disproportionate to its practical value. Loss of ships and aircraft and structural damage to the base had been quickly rectified. The more than three thousand dead and wounded Americans could not be replaced in an eternity, but the war provided a grim outlet for revenging those losses—and more. What lingered after the Hawaiian base had been assaulted was a feeling less tangible than death and destruction. It was a sense of insecurity. In a society which so highly valued its world prestige, its economic omnipotence, and its "social progress," the Pearl Harbor disaster was humiliating. Creating scapegoats appeared to be the simplest method of relieving the uneasiness brought on by the attack, and the Roosevelt administration provided the forum upon which the superficial question of personal responsibility could emerge and grow.

Ultimately, the Pearl Harbor controversy grew beyond the event, and the attention to seeking out the guilty parties indicated an intense concern about the security of the nation and the safety of its people. The days of a United States insulated geographically from a decadent Europe and a volatile Asia appeared to be over. The Japanese raid demonstrated the vulnerability of the United States to direct enemy attack; no wonder the specter of "national security" surfaced as a factor immutably tied to Pearl Harbor. One of the important legacies of the disaster was the object lesson about proper military preparedness which would continually be cited in the halls of the White House, Congress, and the Pentagon. As the Cold War mounted after World War II, the question of "national security" would be not only the focus of the policy debates, but also a veil used to obscure any issue which promised political hazards. Justifying its actions upon the premise of preserving American security in wartime, the Roosevelt administration kept the details of the Pearl Harbor affair close and stood by its criticism of Kimmel and Short. Congressional enemies of FDR demanded the "truth" about the surprise attack in the name of "national security." And journalists became fascinated with the intrigue and exotic possibilities of a high-level cover-up because it drove at the heart of the issue of "national security."

The preoccupation of Americans with a lapse in their Pacific defenses, as grave as it was, demonstrated the first real signs of uncertainty about U.S. invincibility and invulnerability. Yet admission of any sort of national weakness was set aside in the pursuit of a rather elaborate search for scapegoats. In the cry "Remember Pearl Harbor!" is a hint of something beyond revenge against Japan— there is a hint about the state of political life in the United States during the war and after.

Bibliography

Archival Materials

Hanover, N.H. Dartmouth College Library. Charles W. Tobey Papers.
Hyde Park, N.Y. Franklin D. Roosevelt Presidential Library. Democratic National Committee Papers.
————. Franklin D. Roosevelt Papers.
————. Harry Hopkins Papers.
————. Henry Morgenthau, Jr., Collection.
————. Samuel I. Rosenman Papers.
————. Stephen T. Early Papers.
————. Wayne Coy Papers.
Independence, Mo. Harry S Truman Presidential Library. Alben W. Barkley Oral History Interview, 1953.
————. Frank McNaughton Papers.
————. Harry S Truman Papers.
Laramie, Wyo. University of Wyoming Library, Division of Rare Books and Special Collections. Charles C. Hiles Collection.
————. George Morgenstern Collection.
————. Harry Elmer Barnes Collection.
————. Husband E. Kimmel Collection.
————. Pearl Harbor File (P 316-h).
New Haven, Conn. Yale University, Sterling Memorial Library, Manuscripts and Archives. Henry L. Stimson Papers (microfilm).
New York, N.Y. Columbia University, Naval History Project, 1962. Reminiscences of H. Kent Hewitt.
————. Reminiscences of Thomas C. Hart.
Princeton, N.J. Princeton University Library. James V. Forrestal Papers.
Stanford, Calif. Hoover Institution on War, Revolution and Peace. Delos C. Emmons Papers.
————. Joseph W. Ballantine Papers.
————. Robert A. Theobald Papers.
————. Stanley K. Hornbeck Collection.

————. Tracy B. Kittredge Papers.
Washington, D.C. Department of the Navy, Naval History Division. Central Security-Classified Files of the Office of the Chief of Naval Operations.
————. Harold R. Stark Papers.
————. Harry E. Yarnell Papers.
————. Thomas C. Hart Papers.
Washington, D.C. Library of Congress, Manuscript Division. Clark H. Woodward Papers.
————. Claude C. Bloch Papers.
————. Cordell Hull Papers.
————. Elmer Davis Papers.
————. Felix Frankfurter Papers.
————. Frank Knox Papers.
————. Frank R. McCoy Papers.
————. Raymond Swing Papers.
————. Robert A. Taft Papers.
————. Robert P. Patterson Papers.
————. William D. Leahy Papers.
Washington, D.C. National Archives. Record Group 80, General Records of the Department of the Navy.
————. Record Group 107, Records of the Office of the Secretary of War.
————. Record Group 125, Records of the Office of the Judge Advocate General (Navy).
————. Record Group 128, Records of the Joint Committees of Congress.
————. Record Group 165, Records of the War Department, General and Special Staffs.
————. Record Group 335, Records of the Office of the Secretary of the Army.
Williamstown, Mass. Williams College, Roper Public Opinion Research Center. Roper-Fortune Polls, 1941–1945.

Unpublished Works

Bateman, Herman E. "The Election of 1944 and Foreign Policy." Ph.D. dissertation, Stanford University, 1952.
Jacques, Raymond W. "The Pearl Harbor Investigations." M.A. thesis, University of Wyoming, 1964.
Lobdell, George H. "A Biography of Frank Knox." Ph.D. dissertation, University of Illinois, 1954.
Weinberg, Sydney S. "Wartime Propaganda in a Democracy: America's Twentieth-Century Information Agencies." Ph.D. dissertation, Columbia University, 1969.

Government Documents

Public Papers of the President of the United States: Harry S. Truman, 1945. Washington, D.C.: Government Printing Office, 1961.

U.S. Bureau of the Budget. *The United States at War: Development and Administration of the War Program by the Federal Government.* Washington, D.C.: Government Printing Office, 1946.

U.S. Congress. *Congressional Record,* 77th–79th Congs., 1941–1946, 87–91.

————. *Pearl Harbor Attack: Hearings before the Joint Committee on the Pearl Harbor Attack.* 79th Cong., 1st sess., 1946. 39 vols.

————. *Report of the Joint Committee on the Investigation of the Pearl Harbor Attack.* 79th Cong., 2d sess., 1946.

————, House of Representatives. *Hearings before the Committee on Rules.* 77th Cong., 2d sess., 1942.

————, ————, Select Committee Investigating National Defense Migration. *Fourth Interim Report.* 77th Cong., 2d sess., 1942.

————, ————, ————. *Hearings.* 77th Cong., 2d sess., 1942.

————, ————, Special Committee on Un-American Activities. *Report on Japanese Activities.* 77th Cong., 2d sess., 1942.

U.S. Department of the Army, Western Defense Command and Fourth Army. *Final Report: Japanese Evacuation from the West Coast, 1942.* Washington, D.C.: Government Printing Office, 1943.

U.S. Department of the Interior, War Relocation Authority. *WRA: A Story of Human Conservation.* Washington, D.C.: Government Printing Office, 1946.

Books and Articles

Albion, Robert G., and Robert H. Connery. *Forrestal and the Navy.* New York: Columbia University Press, 1962.

Alexander, Charles C. *Nationalism in American Thought, 1930–1945.* Chicago: Rand McNally and Co., 1969.

Allen, Robert S., and William V. Shannon. *The Truman Merry-Go-Round.* New York: The Vanguard Press, Inc., 1950.

Baker, Leonard. *Roosevelt and Pearl Harbor.* New York: The Macmillan Co., 1970.

Barkley, Alben W. *That Reminds Me—.* New York: Doubleday and Co., 1954.

Barnes, Harry Elmer, ed. *Perpetual War for Perpetual Peace.* Caldwell, Idaho: The Caxton Printers, Ltd., 1953.

Beard, Charles A. *President Roosevelt and the Coming of the War, 1941: A Study in Appearances and Realities.* New Haven: Yale University Press, 1948.

Beatty, Frank E. "Another Version of What Started War with Japan," *U.S. News* 36 (May 28, 1954): 48–50.

―――. "The Background of the Secret Report," *National Review* 18 (December 13, 1966): 1261–1265.

Bidwell, Percy W., ed. *Our Foreign Policy in War and Peace: Some Regional Views.* New York: Council on Foreign Relations, 1942.

Borg, Dorothy, and Shumpei Okamoto, eds. *Pearl Harbor as History: Japanese-American Relations, 1931–1941.* New York: Columbia University Press, 1973.

Brownlow, Donald Grey. *The Accused: The Ordeal of Rear Admiral Husband Edward Kimmel, U.S.N.* New York: Vantage Press, 1968.

Burtness, Paul S., and Warren U. Ober, "Secretary Stimson and the First Pearl Harbor Investigation," *Australian Journal of Politics and History* 14 (April, 1968): 24–36.

Cantril, Hadley, and Mildred Strunk, eds. *Public Opinion, 1935–1946.* Princeton: Princeton University Press, 1951.

Chadwin, Mark L. *The Hawks of World War II.* Chapel Hill: University of North Carolina Press, 1968.

Childs, Marquis W. *I Write from Washington.* New York: Harper and Bros., Publishers, 1942.

Clapper, Raymond. *Watching the World.* Ed. Mrs. Raymond Clapper. New York: McGraw-Hill Book Co., Inc., 1944.

Cline, Ray S. *Washington Command Post: The Operations Division.* Washington, D.C.: Department of the Army, Office of the Chief of Military History, 1951.

Cole, Wayne S. "American Entry into World War II: A Historiographical Appraisal," *Mississippi Valley Historical Review* 48 (March, 1957): 595–617.

Complete Presidential Press Conferences of Franklin D. Roosevelt. Vols. 18–25. New York: Da Capo Press, 1972.

Correspondents of *Time, Life,* and *Fortune. December 7: The First Thirty Hours.* New York: Alfred A. Knopf, 1942.

Current, Richard N. *Secretary Stimson: A Study in Statecraft.* New Brunswick, N. J.: Rutgers University Press, 1954.

Dallek, Robert, ed. *The Roosevelt Diplomacy and World War II.* New York: Holt, Rinehart and Winston, 1970.

Daniels, Jonathan. "Pearl Harbor Sunday: The End of an Era," in *The Aspirin Age, 1919–1941.* Ed. Isabel Leighton. New York: Simon and Schuster, Clarion Books, 1949.

Daniels, Roger. *Concentration Camps USA: Japanese Americans and World War II.* New York: Holt, Rinehart and Winston, 1972.

Davids, Jules. "The Bombing of Pearl Harbor," in *America and the World of Our Time: United States Diplomacy in the Twentieth Century.* New York: Random House, 1960.

Davis, Forrest, and Ernest K. Lindley. *How War Came, an American White Paper: From the Fall of France to Pearl Harbor.* New York: Simon and Schuster, 1942.

Divine, Robert A. *Foreign Policy and U.S. Presidential Elections, 1940–1948*. New York: Franklin Watts, Inc., New Viewpoints, 1974.

———. *Second Chance: The Triumph of Internationalism in America during World War II*. New York: Atheneum, 1967.

Drury, Allen. *A Senate Journal, 1943–1945*. New York: McGraw-Hill Book Co., Inc., 1963.

Dupuy, T. N. "Pearl Harbor: Who Blundered?" *American Heritage* 13 (February, 1962): 64–81.

Edwards, Jerome E. *The Foreign Policy of Col. McCormick's Tribune, 1929–1941*. Reno: University of Nevada Press, 1971.

Farago, Ladislas. *The Broken Seal: "Operation Magic" and the Secret Road to Pearl Harbor*. New York: Random House, 1967.

Feis, Herbert. *The Road to Pearl Harbor*. Princeton: Princeton University Press, 1950.

Ferrell, Robert H. "Pearl Harbor and the Revisionists," *The Historian* 17 (Spring, 1955): 215–233.

Flynn, John T. *The Final Secret of Pearl Harbor*. Privately published, 1945.

Freedman, Max, ed. *Roosevelt and Frankfurter: Their Correspondence, 1928–1945*. Boston: Little, Brown and Co., Atlantic Monthly Press Book, 1967.

Furer, Julius A. *Administration of the Navy Department in World War II*. Washington, D.C.: Department of the Navy, Naval History Division, 1959.

The Gallup Poll: Public Opinion, 1935–1971. New York: Random House, 1972.

Girdner, Audrie, and Anne Loftis, *The Great Betrayal: The Evacuation of the Japanese-Americans during World War II*. London: The Macmillan Co., 1969.

Goodman, Jack, ed. *While You Were Gone: A Report on Wartime Life in the United States*. New York: Simon and Schuster, 1946.

Grodzins, Morton. *Americans Betrayed: Politics and the Japanese Evacuation*. Chicago: University of Chicago Press, 1949.

Handlin, Oscar. *Chance or Destiny: Turning Points in American History*. Boston: Little, Brown and Co., 1954.

Heinrichs, Waldo H., Jr. *American Ambassador: Joseph C. Grew and the Development of the United States Diplomatic Tradition*. Boston: Little, Brown and Co., 1966.

Hinshaw, David. *The Home Front*. New York: G. P. Putnam's Sons, 1943.

Hoehling, Adolph A. *The Week before Pearl Harbor*. New York: W. W. Norton and Co., Inc., 1963.

Huie, William Bradford. *The Case against the Admirals: Why We Must Have a Unified Command*. New York: E. P. Dutton and Co., Inc., 1946.

Hull, Cordell. *Memoirs*. Vol. 2. New York: The Macmillan Co., 1948.

Jonas, Manfred. *Isolationism in America, 1935–1941*. New York: Cornell University Press, 1966.

Karig, Walter, and Welbourn Kelley. *Battle Report: Pearl Harbor to Coral Sea*. New York: Farrar and Rinehart, Inc., 1944.

Kendrick, Alexander. *Prime Time: The Life of Edward R. Murrow*. Boston: Little, Brown and Co., 1969.

Kimball, Warren F., ed. *Franklin D. Roosevelt and the World Crisis, 1937–1945*. Lexington, Mass.: D. C. Heath and Co., 1973.

Kimmel, Husband E. *Admiral Kimmel's Story*. Chicago: Henry Regnery Co., 1955.

King, Ernest J., and Walter Muir Whitehill. *Fleet Admiral King: A Naval Record*. New York: W. W. Norton and Co., 1952.

Langer, William L., and S. Everett Gleason. *The Undeclared War, 1940–1941*. New York: Harper and Brothers Publishers, 1953.

Lawrence, Bill. *Six Presidents, Too Many Wars*. New York: Saturday Review Press, 1972.

Lingeman, Richard R. *Don't You Know There's a War On? The Home Front, 1941–1945*. New York: G. P. Putnam's Sons, 1970.

Lord, Walter. *Day of Infamy*. New York: Henry Holt and Co., 1957.

McCoy, Donald R. "Republican Opposition during Wartime, 1941–1945," *The Historian* 17 (Spring, 1955): 215–233.

McKechney, John. "The Pearl Harbor Controversy: A Debate among Historians," *Monumenta Nipponica* 18 (1963): 45–88.

Morgenstern, George. *Pearl Harbor: The Story of the Secret War*. New York: The Devin-Adair Co., 1947.

Morison, Elting E. *Turmoil and Tradition: A Study of the Life and Times of Henry L. Stimson*. Boston: Houghton Mifflin Co., 1960.

Morison, Samuel Eliot. *The Rising Sun in the Pacific, 1931–April, 1942*. Boston: Little, Brown and Co., 1958.

Morton, Louis. "1937–1941," in *American–East Asian Relations: A Survey*. Ed. Ernest R. May and James C. Thompson Jr. Cambridge: Harvard University Press, 1972.

———. "Pearl Harbor in Perspective, A Bibliographical Survey," *U.S. Naval Institute Proceedings* 81 (April, 1955): 461–468.

———. *Strategy and Command: The First Two Years*. Washington, D.C.: Department of the Army, Office of Chief of Military History, 1962.

Ogden, August Raymond. *The Dies Committee*. Washington, D.C.: Catholic University of America Press, 1945.

Perrett, Geoffrey. *Days of Sadness, Years of Triumph: The American People, 1939–1945*. Baltimore: Penguin Books, 1973.

Phillips, Cabell. *1940s: Decade of Triumph and Trouble*. New York: The Macmillan Co., 1975.

Pogue, Forrest C. *George C. Marshall: Ordeal and Hope, 1939–1942*. New York: The Viking Press, 1965.

————. *George C. Marshall: Organizer of Victory, 1943–1945.* New York: The Viking Press, 1973.

Polenberg, Richard. *War and Society: The United States, 1941–1945.* Philadelphia: J. B. Lippincott Co., 1972.

Richardson James O. *On the Treadmill to Pearl Harbor: The Memoirs of Admiral James O. Richardson.* Washington, D.C.: Department of the Navy, Naval History Division, 1973.

Richardson, Seth W. "Why Were We Caught Napping at Pearl Harbor?" *Saturday Evening Post* 219 (May 24, 1947): 20–21, 76.

Rogow, Arnold A. *James Forrestal: A Study of Personality, Politics, and Policy.* New York: The Macmillan Co., 1963.

Roosevelt, Elliott, ed. *F.D.R., His Personal Letters.* New York: Duell, Sloan and Pearce, 1950.

Rose, Ernest D. "How the United States Heard about Pearl Harbor," *Journal of Broadcasting* 5 (Fall, 1961): 285–298.

Rosenman, Samuel I., comp. *The Public Papers and Addresses of Franklin D. Roosevelt.* Vols. 10–11. New York: Harper and Bros., 1950.

————. *Working with Roosevelt.* New York: Harper and Bros., 1952.

Schroeder, Paul W. *The Axis Alliance and Japanese-American Relations, 1941.* Ithaca, N.Y.: Cornell University Press, 1958.

Sears, Louis M. "Historical Revisionism Following the Two World Wars," in *Issues and Conflicts: Studies in Twentieth Century American Diplomacy.* Ed. George L. Anderson. Lawrence: University of Kansas Press, 1959.

Sherwood, Robert E. *Roosevelt and Hopkins: An Intimate History.* Revised edition. New York: Grosset and Dunlap, 1950.

Smith, Bradford. *Americans from Japan.* New York: J. B. Lippincott Co., 1948.

Spicer, Edward H., et al. *Impounded People: Japanese-Americans in the Relocation Centers.* Tucson: University of Arizona Press, 1969.

Standley, William H., and Arthur A. Ageton. *Admiral Ambassador to Russia.* Chicago: Henry Regnery Co., 1955.

————. "More about Pearl Harbor," *U.S. News* 36 (April 16, 1954): 40–42, 45–46.

Stimson, Henry L., and McGeorge Bundy. *On Active Service in Peace and War.* New York: Harper and Bros., 1947.

Sweeny, Charles. *Pearl Harbor.* Privately printed, 1946.

Tansill, Charles Callan. *America Goes to War.* Boston: Little, Brown and Co., 1942.

Theobald, Robert A. *The Final Secret of Pearl Harbor: The Washington Contribution to the Japanese Attack.* New York: The Devin-Adair Co., 1954.

Thomas, Dorothy Swaine, and Richard S. Nishimoto. *The Spoilage.* Berkeley and Los Angeles: University of California, 1946.

Toland, John. *But Not in Shame: The Six Months after Pearl Harbor.* New York: Random House, 1961.

Truman, Harry S. "Our Armed Forces Must Be Unified," *Collier's* 114 (August 26, 1944): 63ff.

Tully, Grace. *F.D.R., My Boss.* New York: Charles Scribner's Sons, 1949.

Waller, George M., ed. *Pearl Harbor: Roosevelt and the Coming of the War.* Rev. ed. Boston: D. C. Heath and Co., 1965.

Wallin, Homer N. *Pearl Harbor: Why, How, Fleet Salvage and Final Appraisal.* Washington, D.C.: Department of the Navy, Naval History Division, 1968.

Watson, Mark Skinner. *Chief of Staff: Prewar Plans and Preparations.* Washington, D.C.: Department of the Army, Office of the Chief of Military History, 1950.

Weinberg, Sydney. "What to Tell America: The Writers' Quarrel in the Office of War Information," *Journal of American History* 55 (June 1, 1968): 73–89.

Westerfield, H. Bradford. *Foreign Policy and Party Politics: Pearl Harbor to Korea.* New Haven: Yale University Press, 1955.

Wittner, Lawrence S. *Rebels against War: The American Peace Movement, 1941–1960.* New York: Columbia University Press, 1969.

Wohlstetter, Roberta. *Pearl Harbor: Warning and Decision.* Stanford: Stanford University Press, 1962.

Young, Roland. *Congressional Politics in the Second World War.* New York: Columbia University Press, 1956.

Newspapers and Periodicals

America
America Preferred
Army and Navy Journal
Catholic World
Chicago Tribune
Christian Century
Collier's
Commonweal
Current History
Foreign Policy Bulletin
Forum
Kiplinger Washington Letter
Life
Nation
National Review
New Republic
Newsweek
New York Times

Public Opinion Quarterly
Saturday Evening Post
Time
U.S. Naval Institute Proceedings
U.S. News
Washington Post

Index